# The Comparative Method *in the* Science *of* Law

JCL Studies in Comparative Law:
Second Series

Series Editors

Professor William E. Butler
Professor Michael Palmer

1. W. E. Butler and O. V. Kresin (eds.), *Discovering the Unexpected: Comparative Legal Studies in Eastern and Central Europe* (Clark, New Jersey, Talbot Publishing, 2021). ISBN 9781616196554

2. Simon Palmer and Zhai Xiaobo (eds.), *Bentham Around the World* (Clark, New Jersey, Talbot Publishing, 2021). ISBN 9781616196561

3. O. V. Kresin, *Comparative Law in Warsaw: 1800-1835*, transl. W. E. Butler (Clark, New Jersey, Talbot Publishing, 2021) ISBN 9781616196585.

4. W. E. Buler and O. V. Kresin (eds.) *The Comparative Method in the Science of Law* by Lev Rebet (Clark, New Jersey, Talbot Publishing, 2021) ISBN 9781616196653.

# The Comparative Method *in the* Science *of* Law


**Lev Rebet**

SOMETIME PROFESSOR OF LAW, UKRAINIAN FREE UNIVERSITY

EDITED AND TRANSLATED BY

**William E. Butler**

FOREIGN MEMBER, NATIONAL ACADEMY OF SCIENCES OF UKRAINE;
NATIONAL ACADEMY OF LEGAL SCIENCES OF UKRAINE

AND

**O. V. Kresin**

ДОКТОР ЮРИДИЧНИХ НАУК, ПРОФЕСОР
KORETSKY INSTITUTE OF STATE AND LAW,
NATIONAL ACADEMY OF SCIENCES OF UKRAINE



TALBOT PUBLISHING
Clark, New Jersey

ISBN 9781616196653



TALBOT PUBLISHING
AN IMPRINT OF
The Lawbook Exchange, Ltd.
33 Terminal Avenue
Clark, New Jersey 07066-1323

Please see our website for a selection of our other publications
and fine facsimile reprints of classic works of legal history
www.lawbookexchange.com

Library of Congress Cataloging-in-Publication Data

Names: Rebet, Lev, 1912-1957 author. | Butler, William Elliott, 1939- editor, translator. | Kresin, Oleksiĭ, 1976- editor, translator.
Title: The comparative method in the science of law / Lev Rebet ; edited and translated by William Elliott Butler, Foreign Member, National Academy of Sciences of Ukraine, National Academy of Legal Sciences of Ukraine and Oleksiy V. Kresin, Koretsky Institute of State and Law, National Academy of Sciences of Ukraine.
Other titles: Porivnal'na metoda v nau͡tsi pro pravo. English
Description: Clark : Talbot Publishing, 2022. | Series: JCL studies in comparative law: second series ; no. 4 | Translation of author's thesis (doctoral - Ukraïns'kyĭ vil'nyĭ u͡niversytet, 1948) issued under title: Porivnal'na metoda v nau͡tsi prava. | Includes bibliographical references and index. | Summary: "A study of the history and theory of comparative law"-- Provided by publisher.
Identifiers: LCCN 2022042058 | ISBN 9781616196653 (hardcover)
Classification: LCC K552 .R43 2022 | DDC 340/.2--dc23/eng/20221005
LC record available at https://lccn.loc.gov/2022042058

Printed in the United States of America on acid-free paper

TABLE OF CONTENTS

# Preface and Translation Note

Continuing our undertaking to illuminate lesser-known dimensions of Central and Eastern European contributions to the world of comparative jurisprudence,[1] we turn our attention to a treatise by a Ukrainian jurist, Lev Rebet (1912-1957). His name will be unfamiliar to western and eastern comparatists alike. A product of the Lviv University Faculty of Law which produced a remarkable generation of international and comparative lawyers during the interwar period,[2] he found himself released from three years of German captivity late in the Second World War and, once hostilities had ceased, pursued postgraduate research at the Ukrainian Free University in Munich.

Having completed a magister degree in 1938 at Lviv University, he defended his dissertation for a lower doctorate, "The Comparative Method in the Science of Law", in 1948 – a work overlapping in scope Harold Cooke Gutteridge's introductory monograph on comparative law.[3] The dissertation remained unpublished. It was, as the examiners noted, written in a non-literary style punctuated with idiomatic regional expressions. The source material was almost entirely German-language comparatist literature up to ca. 1940: four English works (Bacon, Fortescue, Gutteridge, Selden) and references to a handful of French and Italian writers. For the modern English-language reader, the evaluation of the German schools by a Ukrainian jurist is a valuable

[1] W. E. Butler, O. V. Kresin, and Iu. S. Shemshuchenko (eds.), *Foundations of Comparative Law: Methods and Typologies* (2011); W. E. Butler and O. V. Kresin (eds.), *The Interaction of Legal Systems: Post-Soviet Approaches* (2015); O. V. Kresin, Comparative Legal Studies: 1750-1835, transl. W. E. Butler (2019); W. E. Butler and O. V. Kresin (ed.), *Discovering the Unexpected: Comparative Legal Studies in Eastern and Central Europe* (2021).

[2] Philippe Sands, *East-West Street: On the Origins of 'Genocide' and 'Crimes Against Humanity'* (2016), translated into Ukrainian as Sands, Східно-Західна. Повернення до Львова, transl. Pavlo Migal (Lviv, 2017).

[3] H. C. Gutteridge, *Comparative Law* (1946; rev. ed.; 1949). Rebet cited the first edition of Gutteridge in his bibliography but made no use of the book in his dissertation text, presumably either because he had no access to the volume or his command of English was not sufficient to work with the text. It was the only contemporary English-language work cited.

perspective and interesting contribution. Nonetheless, there is no comparable work on the comparative method generally by a Belorussian, Russian, or Ukrainian jurist of that period or, for that matter, in the world. And although Rebet doubted that there could be meaningful comparison with Soviet law – a view disputed by his examiners, he had neither colleagues or intellectual adversaries at the time. His dissertation stands as a pioneering and lonely monument in the discipline of comparative jurisprudence as developing in Central and Eastern Europe immediately after the War.

Producing the present translation has been a challenging exercise for several reasons. The original dissertation is a typewritten manuscript with a handful of textual emendations by its author and reposes in the Archive of the Ukrainian Free University in Munich.[4] There it was "discovered" by Professor Dr. O. V. Kresin several years ago. He deciphered, "translated", and edited the text into modern Ukrainian legal terminology and published that version at Kyiv for the Ukrainian legal community,[5] an event noted in western comparative media.[6] For the purposes of the present text, however, Kresin prepared a Russian translation of his Ukrainian text. The present English version has been translated from the Russian translation, which itself remains unpublished.

William E. Butler

September 2022

---

[4] L. Rebet, Порівнальна метода в науці права [The Comparative Method in the Science of Law] (Munich, 1947). Dissertation for the Degree of Doctor of Laws. Archive of the Ukrainian Free University (Munich), Item 3338.

[5] L. M. Rebet, Порівнальна метода в науці права [The Comparative Method in the Science of Law], ed. O. V. Kresin and I. O. Kresina (Kyiv/Munich, 2017).

[6] O. V. Kresin, "Lev Rebet: Pioneering Ukrainian Comparatist", *Journal of Comparative Law*, XIII (2018), pp. 214-222.

# Lev Rebet: Distinguished Ukrainian Comparatist

O. V. Kresin

Lev Roman Rebet, the son of Mykhailo Rebet and Kateryna Nedokys, was born on 3 March 1912 in the town of Stryi (now a district center in Lviv region). His father worked for the postal service. From 1922 to 1930 Lev Rebet studied at the Stryi Gymnasium, was active in the boy scout movement, and in 1927 joined a Ukrainian military organization and then, automatically, the Organization of Ukrainian Nationalists (OUN).

In 1930 he enrolled at the Law Faculty of Lviv University. During his legal studies he was the commander of the Stryi district division of the OUN, was often arrested by the Polish police, and was sentenced to and served two years imprisonment. After release, he continued his legal studies, and also, from 1935 to 1939, headed the central executive committee of the OUN in the western Ukrainian territories; on several occasions he illegally crossed the border and met with the leader of the OUN, Colonel Evhen Konovalets (1891-1938). Having completed his legal studies in 1938, he was awarded the degree of magister of law. He found employment as a store clerk and at a bank in Krakow and Lviv. In March 1939 he was again sentenced to prison in Lviv and was released together with other prisoners on 20 September 1939 with the arrival of Soviet forces.

In that same year Rebet moved to Krakow and married Daria Omelianivna Tsisyk (1913-1992) in 1940, his long-time comrade and fiancée (they were engaged in the mid-1930s). He continued to take an active part in the activities of the OUN, supporting its revolutionary ("Bandera") section. In 1941, with the infantry groups of the OUN, he moved to Lviv and, after the proclamation of the restoration of Ukrainian statehood (30 June 1941), became on 5 July 1941 the Second Deputy to the Chairman of the Provisional State Board, Yaroslav Stets'ko (1912-1986) and performed the duties of Chairman after the arrest of Stets'ko. On 15 September 1941, Rebet was arrested by the German authorities and sent to Montelupich Prison in Krakow, and then confined in the Auschwitz concentration camp (Oświęcim), where he remained for more than three years.

In December 1944 he was released by the Germans and traveled to Bratislava, Vienna, Innsbruck, and Munich. He worked on the newspapers "Час" [Time], "Українська трибуна" [Ukrainian Tribune], and "Сучасна Україна" [Contemporary Ukraine], and from 1955 was the editor in chief of the newspaper (later a journal), "Український самостійник" [Ukrainian State Partisan]. From 1945 to 1946 he was a member of the Foreign Center of the OUN and chief judge of the Foreign Section of the OUN. From December 1946 he was removed from political life by the leadership of the OUN.

On 12 February 1948 Rebet defended his first doctoral dissertation (doctor of laws: The Comparative Method in the Science of Law) and in 1949 his doctor habilitation (The State and the Nation) at the Ukrainian Free University in Munich. He worked as an Assistant (1948-1949), Docent (1950-1954), and Professor (1954-1957) of State Law and the Philosophy of Law at the Ukrainian Free University. There he served as the supervisor of a dissertation written by Iu. Horak on "Sovereignty – Contemporary World Problem" in 1955-1956.

From 1952 Rebet was a member of the Foreign Representation of the Ukrainian Chief Liberation Council, and from 1952 to 1955, was the Head of the Council of Referees at the Foreign Representation of the Ukrainian Chief Liberation Council. From 1953 he was a member of the Collegium of Plenipotentiaries of the Territory Executive of the OUN(b) in Ukraine. In December 1955 at a conference of delegates he was elected Chairman of the Political Council of one of the branches of the OUN – the OUN in Exile.

Lev Rebet and his wife Daria had two children: a son Andriy (born 30 March 1942) and a daughter, Oksana (born 27 September 1951).

Lev Rebet died in Munich on 12 October 1957, at the age of 45. Five years later it became known that his death was not a natural one, but caused by poisoning and committed by an agent of the Committee of State Security of the USSR (KGB), Bohdan Mykolayovych Stashynskyi (b. 1931). According to testimony of

Stashynskyi given in a German court in 1962, Rebet was regarded in Moscow as a dangerous leading theoretician of the Ukrainian political émigré community and had been under the observation of Soviet agents. Authoritative contemporary specialists believe that this homicide was personally sanctioned by the First Secretary of the Communist Party of the Soviet Union, Nikita Sergeevich Khrushchev (1894-1971) and carried out with the assistance of a special weapon manufactured in Department Thirteen attached to the First Chief Directorate of the KGB of the USSR.[1] For the murder of Rebet and of Stepan Bandera (1909-1959), Stashynskyi was awarded the Order of the Red Banner, bearing the inscription: "For Carrying Out an Extremely Important Government Assignment".[2]

In 1962 the Federal Court in Karlsruhe, Germany deemed Stashynskyi to be only an accomplice in the crimes, and the main culprit, the Government of the USSR who had institutionalized political murder. The significant resonance of this court case led to the termination of the mass sanctioning of such murders on the part of the Politburo of the Central Committee of the CPSU and the leadership of the KGB.[3]

In recalling Rebet, Vasyl Markus (1922-2012), a leading member of the Ukrainian diaspora, wrote:

> He belonged to those who in the name of higher interests and principles preferred to take unpopular decisions. The history of the movement and ancestors with far-reaching prospects, and not our irritating passions and passing moods, will judge him and all of us for what we have done. This court will be more just than a transient court. But even for now … in one matter one cannot reproach the Deceased – for insufficient patriotism and personal honor.[4]

[1] Christopher M. Andrew and Oleg Gordievsky, *KGB: The Inside Story of its Foreign Operations from Lenin to Gorbachev* (1990), pp. 464-465. In August 1961 Stashynskyi defected to the Federal Republic Germany and confirmed the course of events with respect to Rebet to the satisfaction of western intelligence agencies, who at first did not believe him, and a German court.

[2] Ibid., p. 465.

[3] Ibid., p. 465.

[4] V. Markus, «Борець за українську державність (слово над могилию Лева Ребета, голови Політичної ради ОУН за кордоном)» [Fighter for Ukrainian Statehood (Address at the Grave of Lev Rebet, Head of the Political Council of the OUN in Exile)], Український самостійник [Ukrainian Samostiynyk], no. 3 (1957), p. 6.

## "THE COMPARATIVE METHOD IN THE SCIENCE OF LAW"

Rebet's dissertation on "The Comparative Method in the Science of Law" was completed under the supervision of the Professor of the History of Law and Philosophy of Law, Lev Okynshevych (1898-1980), and submitted to the Ukrainian Free University in 1947.[5] This work undertook a detailed consideration of the philosophical, science of science, and historical aspects of the origin of the methodology of comparative legal studies in Europe. It should be noted that the problem of the methodology of comparative jurisprudence began to be developed much earlier, but only individual aspects thereof were considered by specialists.[6] The foundations in this sphere were laid by Paul Johann Anselm Ritter von Feuerbach (1775-1833), Eduard Gans (1797-1839), Emerico Amari (1810-1870), and others, and in the second half of the nineteenth century the first general works appeared on comparative jurisprudence where brief sections were devoted to methodology; in the first half of the twentieth century a significant number of articles were published on methodological problems.

One may say that after the Second World War various aspects of comparative jurisprudence were the focus of attention on the part of scholars, evidence of which were the large-scale initiatives and discussions in UNESCO, as a result of which the International Committee for Comparative Law was created, which became the International Association of Legal Sciences. Within that process the question was raised of writing general works and textbooks on comparative jurisprudence.

[5] L. Rebet, Порівнальна метода в науці права [The Comparative Method in the Science of Law] (Munich, 1947). Dissertation for the Degree of Doctor of Laws. Archive of the Ukrainian Free University (Munich), Item 3338.

[6] The present writer has devoted two monographs to this problem. See O. V. Kresin, *Comparative Legal Studies: 1750 to 1835. Approaches to Conceptualization*, ed. & transl. W. E. Butler (2019). 2 vols.; Kresin, *Comparative Law in Warsaw: 1800-1835*, ed. & transl. W. E. Butler (2021); Kresin, Становлення теоретичних засад порівняльно-правових досліджень у другій половині XVIII – першій третині XIX століття: компаративна концептуалізація [Genesis of the Theoretical Foundations of Comparative Legal Studies in the Second Half of the XVIII and First Third of the XIX Centuries: Comparative Conceptualization] (Kyiv, 2017); Kresin, Порівняльне правознавство у XIX – XX століттях: проблеми становлення [Comparative Jurisprudence in the XIX and XX Centuries: Problems of Formation] (Kyiv, 2011); and many other works.

The monographs by Harold C. Gutteridge (1876-1953),[7] René David (1906-1990),[8] and Felipe de Solá Cañizares (1905-1965),[9] as the founding fathers of the postwar comparative legal movement, were written in the mainstream of the tasks set in those times. They became the basis for the synthesis of the General Part of comparative jurisprudence, including the systematization of its methodology. These books remained influential for several decades, were translated and republished in revised editions, and served as the basis for introducing comparative legal disciplines into the curriculum of universities and law schools.

Of these, only Gutteridge's book was published somewhat earlier than the time when Rebet submitted his dissertation. But Gutteridge's monograph is in substance a textbook. Moreover, despite its title, Gutteridge discussed not methodology, but primarily the method of undertaking comparative legal research, illuminating briefly the history thereof, subject-matter, and object (Chapters I and II), significance for the science of law as a whole and international public and private law (Chapters III-V), the techniques of teaching comparative jurisprudence (Chapter X). Thus, with some caution and not precluding the possibility of finding publications and manuscripts unknown to us, the Rebet dissertation may be considered to be the first monograph in the world devoted to the methodology of comparative jurisprudence.

The sources of Rebet's work is an important question. The general list of sources used for the dissertation numbers eighty-one publications. Of these fourteen are only mentioned in the text, but not used. These were works by European scholars, beginning with Antiquity up to the early nineteenth century. Sixty-seven publications issued between 1824 and 1942 were directly used. Virtually all were in the German language and by German authors; one was in English and one in the Italian language. The use of sources was rather unequal: about a third of them (22) the author cited only once; and another third (19), two or three times. The sources most used were an article by Friedrich Wilhelm von Rauchhaupt (1881-1989), on the consideration of comparative law

[7] H. C. Gutteridge, *Comparative Law. An Introduction to the Comparative Method of Legal Study and Research* (1946; 2d ed.; 1949).

[8] R. David, *Traité élémentaire de droit civil comparé: introduction á l'étude des droit étrangers et á la méthode comparative* (1950).

[9] F. de Solá Cañizares, *Iniciación al derecho comparado* (1954).

as a science, published in 1929 (31 times);[10] a book by Julius Binder (1870-1939), *Philosophie des Rechts*, published at Berlin in 1925 (26 citations), an article by Franz Bernhöft (1852-1933) on the purposes and means of comparative jurisprudence,[11] published in 1878 and another by Erich Hans Kaden (1898-1973) on comparative law[12] published in 1938 (25 citations each).

As can be seen from the title of his dissertation, Rebet considered comparative law to be a method. In turn, he defined "method", following other scholars, as the targeted use of a complex of means of effectuating scientific research on the basis of previously determined rules which also provide the formulation of the concepts and forming of a systemic notion about the subject-matter of the research.

In Rebet's view, comparison is not purely an inductive method; its purpose is not only the accumulation of empirical material, but the further contemplation thereof, and in and of itself it always seeks a synthesis: "In and of itself the external juxtaposition of various norms without a search for the inner mutual correlation between them is not comparison"; "comparison can never be confined to purely formal and technical limits, but will automatically touch upon sociological and philosophical questions, such as the unity of the human character, natural law, universal laws of law-creation, and so on"; "specialists attempt comparison not only to clarify analogies and differences, but also to determine which social, economic, cultural, and political factors influenced in each instance the development of law in one or in various directions"; "although the comparative method in its essence was empirical, it was at the same time often within the range of philosophical and theoretical quests in the field of law". Juxtaposition itself is characterized as the external, and "comparative-analytical consideration" ("comparative processing") – as the internal part of comparison.

The above unambiguously goes beyond the limitations of comparison proposed by Rebet himself as a "search for similarities and differences between norms of different legal systems". He

[10] F. W. von Rauchhaupt, "Die Wissenschaftliche Pflege des Rechtsvergleichung", *Archiv für Rechts und Wirtschaftsphilosophie*, XXIII (1929).

[11] F. Bernhöft, "Über Zweck und Mittel der vergleichenden Rechtswissenschaft", *Zeitschrift für vergleichende Rechtswissenschaft*, I (1878).

[12] E. H. Kaden, "Rechtsvergleichung", *Rechtsvergleichendes Handwörterbuch* (1938), VI.

also pointed to the different types of comparative-legal studies (dogmatic, historical, genetic, ethnological comparison), the methods of which differ, and therefore he suggested the possibility of the use of the term "comparative science of law" for the characterization of comparative methodology.

Comparison, in Rebet's view, as a method and as a "technique of research", depends upon particular subject-matter (and they are all distributed among existing legal scientific disciplines) and therefore in and of itself cannot create a separate system of autonomous concepts "which classify, elicit, and order the historically determined content of law" – and this makes science a science. By using "ordering principles" created by legal science, the comparison of law leads to several distinctive replies to the same questions, but these replies are not absolute (being based on the material of changeable positive law) and therefore cannot be a separate science. We note that in this discussion Rebet makes a logical error: part of the whole in principle is not the whole, and the question of the scientific status of the comparison of law cannot be considered in juxtaposition with legal science, if it is considered as a single science, and not a complex of sciences.

It is important to stress that the sociology of law, legal ethnology, and the philosophy of law Rebet also calls "sectors of the science of law" (adjacent and connected with the comparison of law), which indicates his understanding of legal science as a single whole and therefore makes less logical the juxtaposition and contrast of the comparison of law and legal science as a whole. At the same time, he points to the possibility of understanding the sociology of law, legal ethnology, and the philosophy of law as sciences and notes that their spheres to a significant degree overlap with the comparison of law, and deems the "ethnological comparison of law" to be an autonomous "sector" of legal science.

Despite the unequivocal denial by Rebet of the scientific status of comparison of law, it clearly corresponds to the task declared by him of any of the legal sciences: "the critical elucidation and general description of legal phenomena". As Rebet noted, "the degree of unreliability of research in the comparison of law is no greater than in the other sciences". The requirements of Rebet for science to create a "system of obligatory concepts" and "to explain the legal phenomena comprehensively" are applicable only to legal science as an integral or complex of legal sciences as a whole. At the same time, Rebet asserts that the comparison of law, just as the philosophy of law, "aspires to create by its own means generally obligatory concepts". Rebet also noted that "in abstracting from purely philosophical speculations, comparison provides a deep view into the essence of legal phenomena and enables one to see the unchangeable and perpetual through the changeable forms of positive law".

Rebet assumes the existence of a separate mission, the object of the comparison of law (receiving knowledge about foreign law, the universalization of legal science, the promoting of international economic ties, the avoidance of legal isolationism, the rapprochement of legal systems, the interpretation of law). But this, in his view, does not transform the comparison of law into a separate science, for a new quality (universality) of legal science as a whole is the object.

In Rebet's view, comparison may not be regarded as a self-sufficient path to the cognition of law, for the measure of its evaluation should be outside the sphere of the valid/existing, in the realm of the ideal, or at least the ideal should have a negative character, separating law from non-law. The last comprehends the philosophy of law. Ultimately, he asserts that the question of absolute cognition is beyond the scope of legal science, but legal concepts and categories may be created with the assistance of dogmatic comparison.

At the same time, Rebet noted that the purpose of comparison is the determination not only of similarities, but of differences, for it is not only an auxiliary means in connection with the search or confirmation of an ideal of homogeneity of legal phenomena. He pointed out that the knowledge of foreign law does not always have a practical purpose, and comparison in this event may be considered an autonomous study. Even after this, Rebet insists all the same that the significance of comparison lies in promoting the coming together of legal orders.

Many times in the text, when characterizing comparison in law only as a method, Rebet actually considers it as a science and sets requirements for it as though it were a science (for example, the combination of the inductive and deductive approaches, although he also points to the existence of primarily inductive sciences). Comparative law is defined also as a specialized sphere ("sector", "territory") of research, and he indicates the lengthy existence in the nineteenth and twentieth centuries of a comparative school, or comparative orientation, in legal studies. Rebet points to the "theoreticians of the comparison of law", the "theoreticians of the comparative method", "researches in the domain of comparative law", and "researchers of comparative law" as a specialization in scientific research.

Ultimately, Rebet calls it a science ("the comparison of law, just as each inductive science", "the comparative method is using deduction in significant measure, although in principle being an inductive science", and so on). But, in his view, at the end of the nineteenth century the "practical aspect receives primacy with respect to the theoretical, and comparison is either limited to the accumulation of materials and confirmation of differences or similarities without deriving conclusions, or limits its purpose to the determination of the most progressive and perfected law". The "great synthesis of comparative law" or "the great system of the comparative science of law" remains, in his view, an ideal which will hardly ever be achieved.

Quite different discourses about the character of the comparison of law are contained in an inset in the text (pp. 26a, 26b). Here Rebet refutes the impossibility in principle postulated by him of the scientific status of comparative law: it may become a separate scientific discipline in the future, outgrow from being a method into being a science, just as comparative linguistics, comparative religion, comparative anatomy, if comparative legal studies "achieve a sufficient degree of autonomy, having established a separate range of speciality", propose "a more profound vision of phenomena", and elicit the essence of phenomena.

The probable reasons for the comparison of law not yet becoming a science, Rebet considers to be the later emergence of comparative-legal studies, and also the special character of law – the lack of material differences between national legal orders. Here Rebet points to the system of comparative law proposed by "early pioneers", or comparative science of law, but noted that later comparative legal studies concentrated on minor issues, the reasons for which he considers to be positivism, the complexity of the synthesis of positive experience of all legal orders, the deflection to resolving urgent practical tasks and the related dominance of out-of-context dogmatic comparison. But the task of the comparison of law is not only analysis, but also synthesis, the forming of an integral system of knowledge, programs, and prospects for further research. Rebet suggests the possibility of an autonomous scientific mission or role for the comparison of law, but the determination thereof should be considered a complex problem because it should not be overlap the roles of other sciences: "This is a basic question of the comparative science of law, on the resolution of which its autonomous existence depends".

Outside the insets, in the text, these reflections to a certain extent correspond to cautious statements concerning the fact that "the large system of comparative science ... may be effectuated rather in the far future after the performance of a significant preparatory work", "the tendency to treat comparative studies as something more than a method is very strong", and also that the future comparative science of law will study the natural laws and reasons for the development of legal phenomena on a universal scale, and its conclusions will be the basis of the sociology of law (for the moment the comparison of law is a part thereof). Ultimately, Rebet stresses that the science of comparative law is not yet "finally established", but movement is occurring in the respective direction, and there is a need to form a comparative history of law "along the model of comparative linguistics".

The historical development of comparison Rebet summarized as the movement from fact (from ancient times) to scientific method (early nineteenth century) and to a "system of research", "conscious, systematic comparison" transcending the limits of the occasional and purely practical purpose. The apogee of this evolution he calls the relatively recent (especially since the emergence of the sociological positivist orientation in the second half of the nineteenth century) forming of the theory of comparison (or the theory of the comparative method), the acquisition by it of theoretical scientific significance which, to be sure, as of the mid-twentieth century is considered to have been lost, but the theory of comparison is still topical.

The changes of legal reality and legal outlook were, in Rebet's view, the major historical prerequisites for completion of the forming of the comparative method: overcoming the legal universalism of the Middle Ages (including the hegemony of Roman law) and the origin of national legal orders, historicism, positivist legal thought as opposed to the traditional speculative natural-law (which assumed the emergence of the need to seek sense in the multiplicity of legal orders) and the influence of the evolution of comparative methodology in other sciences (especially in comparative linguistics). One prerequisite of the assertion of comparison in legal science Rebet considered to be historicism in the form of the idea of evolution proposed by G. W. F. Hegel (1770-1831).

The consideration of legal phenomena against the materials of a multiplicity of legal orders (and in the sociology of law, legal ethnology, and the philosophy of law), recognition of the inevitability of the pluralism of legal development, the simultaneous and mutually-linked existence of similarities and differences between legal orders with concentration on the reasons and character of the differences, and the spatial dimension of law Rebet considers to be the peculiarities of the comparison of law. The spatial dimension, as a cross-section of law, and the discovery of movement and links of legal phenomena in space Rebet considered equal with historical, as a lengthwise temporal section. Only the combination of both dimensions or approaches, in his view, is capable of representing the complex picture of legal development.

The theory of comparison being "processed and tested" encompassed, among others, the principles and criteria for the effectuation of comparison (for example, the existence of the general grounds of comparable legal phenomena, inadmissibility of replacing an empirical study with speculative conclusions, the comparison of legal orders in groups, the need to take into account the contexts of the development of law), and others. Thanks to this, comparison is becoming the foundation of the contemporary philosophy of law.

Rebet also considered the prospects for the development of the comparison of law. He was quite skeptical in assessing the rationalist universalist approaches. Progressivism in its Hegelian variant, in his view, was not sufficiently substantiated: "Concealing a metaphysical presumption of a non-scientific character which accepts without objective grounds that development proceeds constantly and obligatorily from the bottom upward and that later phenomena are more perfected". In his view, this a variant of evolutionism does not facilitate comparison, but replaces it. On the contrary, Rebet stressed concrete historical links of legal orders and the inadmissibility of neglecting differences in law to the advantage of a mechanical universalism.

The rational and abstract orientation of contemporary dogmatic comparison, in Rebet's view, is directed in essence at the mechanical unification of law on a world scale and counteracts the development of the theory of comparability. Without denying the process of such unification as a fact (but not an absolute one), Rebet did not believe this to be the purpose of comparative legal studies.

Rebet recognized the potential of a culture-centered approach to the comparison of law, but he emphasized that the measure of the evaluation of law proposed by this approach transcends law, carries over to the philosophy of culture, and this problem has no solution.

Rebet also believed that the development of comparison in law leads to the affirmation of a new school of natural law. The last is not connected with the classical school, is not metaphysical, does not suggest eternal legal ideals, but perceives discovered universal similarities as elements of a natural, correct law and forms an image of universal history and the contemporary world of law and substantiates the theory of comparability.

In Rebet's view the comparative method also correlates, harmonizes, and partially synthesizes the basic approaches to law (jusnaturalism, historical school, and legal positivism), find a place and limits for each, their points of contact in legal science, "participating in the effectuation of the ideal of philosophy – formalization of an integral comprehensive scientific world outlook" – and this is its greatest achievement.

After successfully passing the doctoral examinations at the end of 1947, Rebet was allowed to defend a dissertation. The defense occurred on 12 February 1948; the Commission was chaired by Professor Okynshevych, and the members were docents M. Stakhiv and Iu. Studynskyĭ.

In his review, Okynshevych noted that Rebet raised a broad problem of philosophical-legal and theoretical-legal character, and that it was "far from fully elicited in science, and only the first, basic lines of development of the main principles and propositions of the comparative study of law were noted before". Unlike Rebet, Okynshevych used the term "comparative jurisprudence" – rather in the sense of a science than a method. Assessing the dissertation as a whole positively, he pointed out that a topic so broad did not enable the author to deeply investigate some of its components, and also to confining the sources of the dissertation only to German literature. Stakhiv, in his review of the Rebet dissertation, also evaluated it positively, but pointed to the inaccurate definition of science as such by Rebet and the illogicality of the refusal to impart to the comparison of law a scientific status. The reviews also pointed to linguistic and stylistic imperfections of the dissertation.

So far as we know, Rebet had no other works devoted to the methodology of comparative legal research. But an article published in 1956 on rights and interests in German and Austrian administrative law should be mentioned.[13] Important too is a characterization of his 1949 unpublished habilitation dissertation, "The State and Nation" by Markus:

The work of Rebet on the State and nation is comparative; the methods and treatment of the problem are peculiar to interdisciplinary studies of history, sociology, law, and the theory of culture. The author based himself on European historical experience and did not take into account those new elements which introduce into the process of nation-building the new peoples and nationalisms of the Third World. Also his sources and theories are rather classical and primarily by German authors. However, he commented on them considerably and submitted a weighed synthesis of the theory and thoughts about these questions as of the end of the 1940s. Greater use of French and Anglo-Saxon literature might have imparted to this fundamental work of Rebet a fuller and, for us, a new scale.[14]

## CONCLUSION

On the whole, it should be noted that Rebet's work on comparative jurisprudence is exceedingly interesting and occupies a unique place in the history of the development of comparative jurisprudence and the philosophy of law (teaching on the methodology of law). It might have materially influenced the development of Ukrainian scientific studies, and not only them. Regrettably, its fate was otherwise than the works by Gutteridge, David, and de Solá Cañizares – it remained in the Archive of the Ukrainian Free University; the title was mentioned several times in

[13] L. Rebet, «Права та інтереси в німецькому й австрійському адміністраційному праві» [Rights and Interests in German and Austrian Administrative Law], Науковий збірник Українського Вільного Університету [Scientific Collection of the Ukrainian Free University] (Munich, 1956), VI, p. 219-234.

[14] V. Markus, «Лев Ребет – політик, публіцист, науковець і людина» [Lev Rebet – Politician, Publicist, Scholar, and Person], Сучасність [Modernity], no. 12 (1977), p. 43.

essays about Rebet and in a book published in 2003, where it was briefly annotated.[15] This study was not recognized; happily, this injustice has begun to be rectified.[16]

[15] O. Panchenko, *Лев Ребет: нація і держава, демократія і право* [Lev Rebet: Nation and State, Democracy and Law] (Hadiach, 2003), pp. 144-145.

[16] Rebet's work on comparative jurisprudence was published in Ukrainian thanks to the assistance of Andriy and Ivanna Rebet and Academician W. E. Butler. See L. M. Rebet, Порівнальна метода в науці права [The Comparative Method in the Science of Law], ed. O. V. Kresin and I. O. Kresina (Kyiv/Munich, 2017). My thanks for access to the archival materials to Professor Maria Pryshliak, the Rector of the Ukrainian Free University (Munich) and Magister Ivanna Rebet, Director of the Library and Archive of the Ukrainian Free University.

# Chapter I. General Definitions

1. Method, 2. Comparison as Phenomenon of Psychology and Logic. 3. Induction and Deduction in Comparison. 4. Concept of Law as Limit of Comparison of Law. 5. Conceptual Identity as Prerequisite of Comparison

## 1. METHOD

The comparison of law is a method, and this means a planned action in which human thought is used to achieve purposes in scholarly research, because we understood by method the wholeness of rules which determine the means of investigating a particular subject-matter.[1] A method strives to create generally-obligatory concepts and to link that achieved with the assistance of research to material in a unified systematic whole.[2]

## 2. COMPARISON AS PHENOMENON OF PSYCHOLOGY AND LOGIC

The comparative method uses comparison in order to achieve a set purpose. From the standpoint of psychology, comparison is the location and confirmation of similarities and differences by means of the connected experience in consciousness (apperception) of two or more objects. Comparison requires a certain mental set directed towards the determination in phenomena of the desired purpose of comparison.[3] It is a narrower concept than a mutual relation and emerges when the experience is transformed in the consciousness in individual categories belonging to the same class of mental experiences – unlike single experiences which one

[1] Giorgio del Vecchio, *Lehrbuch der Rechtsphilosophie* (1937), p. 16.

[2] Rudolf Eisler, *Wörterbuch der philosophischen Begriffe* (4th ed.; 1930), II, pp. 140-141.

[3] Ibid., III, p. 391.

may encounter without comparing them between themselves.[4] From the standpoint of logic, comparison is the linkage of the similar and the exclusion of the contradictory. The comparative method consists of comparative studies (that is, the finding of homogeneous phenomena and gradations of heterogeneity, depending of the degree of their difference) being used to obtain general conclusions.[5]

## 3. INDUCTION AND DEDUCTION IN COMPARISON

The comparison of law comes to its conclusions gradually, analyzing and comparing first individual phenomena of law and then synthetizing the results into a certain whole. This movement during comparison imparts to it the character of the inductive method because a comparative study, according to the grounds of induction, first compares individual phenomena and only gradually comes to general conclusions.

The definition of the comparative method as inductive, however, is not precise insofar as the delimitation of science in general according to the criteria of induction and deduction is relative – the science uses both methods simultaneously. The inductive sector of science from the beginning, having accumulated empirical material, sought general truths and at a moment when empirical conclusions were interpreted as fundamental for further studies, was transformed into deductive.[6] And this is how we move forward when comparing the law.

In addition, the comparison of law, just as every inductive science, rests on certain deductive prerequisites which during the research and observation are accepted as a whole. For example, comparison uses the concept of causality in studies. Although it is the foundation of every science, it is not derived from experience; it is an innate organizing category of reason. Experience affirms only this *a priori* truth, demonstrating in each instance that a certain

[4] Wilhelm Wundt, *Grundriss der Psychologie* (1896), p. 304.

[5] Wundt, *Logik: eine Üntersuchung der Principien der Erkenntnisslehre* (1880-1883), II, p. 280; Eisler, note 2 above, III, p. 392.

[6] del Vecchio, note 1 above, p. 17.

phenomenon has its cause.[7] Moreover, when comparing law, all deductions and speculations are used relating to the determination of legal concepts: the essence of law, the limits of the concept of law, the idea of law, and so on. Changeable, empirical, positive law is organized and evaluated with the assistance of a priori and, consequently, deductive principles because only by this means can one come to general results, to a synthesis of phenomena.

## 4. CONCEPT OF LAW AS LIMIT OF COMPARISON OF LAW

The comparison of law especially proceeds within confines determined by the concept of law in general. In the broadest understanding, the comparison of law is engaged with all typically legal phenomena, irrespective of their type. It encompasses in the broadest understanding all rules which members of a particular community adhere to under threat of the use of public force or permitted self-help – for the purpose of preserving the existence of the community, its further development, and ensuring domestic order. This definition of law encompasses not only written and customary law, but also all that in beliefs, customs and morality has a legal character.[8] This most extensive definition of the concept of law enables comparative studies to embrace all phenomena having the character of law without looking back to what form the existed or exist.

## 5. CONCEPTUAL IDENTITY AS PREREQUISITE OF COMPARISON

This does not prevent interpreting law as an empirical phenomenon linked with other contemporary phenomena and enables legal phenomena to be evaluated variously – but in each instances reference is being made to law. Although, as noted, the definition of law is the result of pure speculation and transcends the framework of empirical studies engaged in concrete legal facts, and is not an investigation of their logical form, it is essential for empirical studies, and thereby for comparison.

[7] Ibid., p. 19.

[8] Hermann Trimborn, "Die Methode der ethnologischen Rechtsforschung", *Zeitschrift für vergleichende Rechtswissenschaft*, XLIII (1928), p. 419.

Indeed, it is only possible under the direction and on the basis of a conceptual scheme organizing and classifying phenomena. Thus is preserved the unanimity of the research studies having all law as their subject-matter, despite the differences of legal phenomena. Therefore, comparison also is possible in the broadest understanding: it makes sense only when it relates to something identical by its nature and therefore in essence comparable. This element of identity, this conceptual identify of law, is a prerequisite and a limit of any legal study such that it actually is found in all legal phenomena, but is specially formalized and has changeable content, and simultaneously encompasses all possible instances of a legal character and therefore crosses the limits of all individual empirical phenomena. And so experience is a source of knowledge of the content of law which over history crystallized changeably at various times and among various peoples, whereas the very definition of law is a logical speculation which is determined by means of abstraction from any concrete formalizations in which it finds adaptation and actual embodiment.[9]

The comparative method is thus used to a significant degree by deduction, although in principle it relates to the science of induction. The collection, comparison, and extraction of conclusions from historical material of positive law are basically inductive and empirical actions which are merely auxiliary and use a deductive concept for control.

On the whole, its general features the comparative method of the investigation of law is a planned operation in the study of legal phenomena with distinctive rules of analysis and synthesis. These rules will be the subject-matter of analysis in the present work.

[9] Del Vecchio, "Die Idee einer vergleichenden universalen Rechtswissenschaft", *Archiv für Rechts und Wirtschaftsphilosophie,* VII (1913), p. 232.

# Chapter II. History of Comparison



## 1. MOST ANCIENT TRACES OF COMPARISON

The comparison of law did not crystallize at once as we know it now. For a long time it was a fact before being formalized into a scientific method and crystallized into a certain system of research. The theory of comparison is of recent origin, although its history goes far back into history.

The earliest traces of the comparison of law may be determined by finding imitation or reception of law, because it may be asserted that this was preceded by comparison. When and under what circumstances such relations arose in ancient times it is difficult to prove today. History is silent on this, and the similarities noted which generate occasion for various hypotheses are not persuasive evidence.[10] For this reason, the complex question remains open: whether and to what extent it is possible to assume the influence of Near Eastern law on the law of the Greeks and the Romans, especially whether one can ascribe the assumed influence to conscious systematic comparison.[11]

The earliest instances of taking law (one may assume that comparison preceded this) we find in ancient Greece. The beginning of the comparison of law in Greece arrives at a time when it became

[10] Paul Koschaker, "Forschungen und Egenisse in der keilschriftlichen Rechtsquellen", *Zeitschrift der Savigny-Stiftung für Rechtsgeschichte: Romanistische Abteilung*, XLIX (1929), p. 195.

[11] Ibid., p. 192; Julius Lautner, "Die Methoden einer antik-rechtsgeschichtlichen Forschung", *Zeitschrift für vergleichende Rechtswissenschaft*, XLVII (1933), p. 30; Egon Weiss, *Die Rechtsvergleichung in der Rechtswissenschaft und Gesetzgebung* (1934), p. 6.

clear to the Greeks that not only native, local law was valuable, but also the legal institutions of other cities have an inner value. After mutual respect was affirmed in the mutual relations between Greek city-States for the "foreign" customs and laws and Greeks began to contrast them in aggregate with Barbarian orders, this automatically led to a comparison of the laws of Greek cities, and thereafter to the coming together and likening of law. Thus, the preliminary mutual coming together of ethnically and culturally kindred Greek cities created an atmosphere in which one city was capable of interpreting the legal norm of another as a better form of its own law and took it as a better and more perfected resolution of the issue. The earliest traces of such taking of law are achieved in the seventh century BC and demonstrated their vital practical nature.[12]

## 2. COMPARISON OF LAW IN ANCIENT GREECE

The beginning of comparative studies of law in ancient Greece represented not so much the theoretical legal interests of philosophers as an urgent need affected by inter-city and inter-State conditions of that time. This led to the comparison of law in the proper understanding during the fourth century BC. An indicator of topicality is all the comparative-legal works of that period which have been preserved. First and foremost, the *Nomoi* [Laws] of Plato. They are in essence a model of Greek law because they compare norms of Greek cities or arose as a result of such comparison. Plato was not satisfied by the contrasting of laws, but he processed them all together, adapting them to his idea of the ideal State.[13] Similarly, in his *Politica,* Aristotle took up the most important forms of State structure of the Greek cities.

The said works by Plato and Aristotle are based, as noted, primarily on positive law of that time, and the authors derive from it, by way of a comparison, the material for autonomous processing. During this processing, however, they depart from the positive base and follow their own universal-philosophical interests, using facts primarily for abstract speculations. The

[12] Weiss, *Greichisches Privatrecht auf rechtsvergleichender Grundlage* (1923), I, p. 7.

[13] Erich H. Kaden, review of Walter G. Becker, *Platons Gesetz und das griechische Familienrecht, eine rechtsvergleichende Untersuchung* (1932), in *Deutsche Literaturzeitung für Kritik der internationalen Wissenschaft,* no. 38 (1933), p. 1811.

subsequent comparative developments of ancient Greece which have come down to us are more juridical in character.[14] The law in force is processed with the assistance of the comparative method and only in passing with philosophical reflections intertwined within purely legal studies. Of such works known from the third century, Theophrastus [371-287 BC], Heraclides Pontico [c. 390-310 BC], and Demetrios of Phaleron [c. 350-280 BC], only fragments of the Theophrastus "Laws" have been preserved. It gives an impression of the value of this kind of research, and it may be asserted that by method they were an early systematic processing of a particular German or Swiss civil law. The generally-accepted foundations were developed there basically, and then the distinguishing norms of individual States were presented.

## 3. COMPARISON OF LAW IN ANCIENT ROME

The Roman period of history did not further the comparison of law. The practical intellect of the Romans and their conservatism were satisfied by the very high level of their law, and although, as studies showed, Roman law had absorbed something from the Mediterranean institutions of various peoples, this occurred spontaneously, without contemplative work in this direction by Roman jurists. The facilitating political and psychological conditions as had existed in Greece were not ultimately present for this process. Rome dominated the cultural world, having conquered province after province, and no political or moral impetus could inspire the proud victors to view foreign institutions other than with arrogance and contempt. This was so embedded that even when educated Roman circles came to respect Greek culture in general, Greek law was an exception. The legal norms of a subjugated people can never be pleasing to the conqueror. For this reason even Cicero, who was influenced by Greek culture, neglected Greek law. Other leading Roman jurists shared the same view, and it is no surprise that whereas foreign law was mentioned in their works only in passing and rarely, there could be no comparative studies of foreign law.[15]

[14] Kaden, "Rechtsvergleichung", in *Rechtsvergleichendes Handwörterbuch* (1938), VI, p. 20.

[15] Bernhardt Kübler, "Griechische Tatbestände in den Werken der kasuistischen Literatur", *Zeitschrift der Savigny-Stiftung für Rechtsgeschichte: Romanistische Abteilung,* XXVIII (1928), p. 174; Leopold Wenger, "Römisches Recht und

Nor is it surprising that in all there was only one work of a comparative character: *Collatio Mosaicarum et Romanorum Legum*. The author, probably a Jew, attempted to show the concordance and equal value of Roman and Hebraic law. This religious-political inclination of the work deprives it of scholarly value, principally because Hebraic law is incorrectly presented.

## 4. COMPARISON OF LAW IN THE MIDDLE AGES

The Middle Ages also were not favorable for the development of the comparison of law despite the plethora of legal systems that arose on the ruins of the ancient Roman Empire. There were various reasons for this. First and foremost, together with the decline of all Roman civilization, the science of law also declined, and this automatically excluded the possibility of any comparative studies.[16] When later there was a certain rise of legal science (the Langobard School in Pavia), there was insufficient knowledge of Roman law to undertake comparison. Ultimately, the unstable political conditions of that time could not facilitate the development of comparative inquiries. Later, in connection with the aspiration of the Church to take possession of the world in the legacy of Rome, Roman and Canon law so ascended that there was no inclination to seriously consider individual national laws of separate peoples so underdeveloped in comparison ultimately with Roman and Canon law. The universalist inclinations of the Church, on one hand, and of the Empire, on the other, whose struggle endured for centuries deadened interest in peoples and their laws liberated from the Roman imperial system. Scholars, theologians, and jurists of that time recognized only the authority of Roman and Canon law and devoted attention solely to them. The universalism of the Middle Ages which existed in the political domain as an aspiration to create one center of authority over the entire Christian world, and in the spiritual domain as the desire to preserve the Latin and developing Christian-Romanist culture with new customs and morality – the general well-being of the progressive estates of all peoples – this universalism ignored and opposed the disparate

Rechtsvergleichung", *Archiv für Rechts und Wirtschaftsphilosophie*, I (1920/1921), p. 106; Ernst Schönbauer, "Studien zum Personalitätsprinzip im antiken Rechte", *Zeitschrift der Savigny-Stiftung für Rechtsgeschichte: Romanistische Abteilung*, XLIX (1929), p. 383.

16 Kaden, note 14 above, VI, p. 21.

laws of peoples. It did not seem paradoxical that internationalism, in this case Christian, did not promote national development nor create the basis for the development of the comparison of law.

Nonetheless, however, the comparison of law occurred during the Middle Ages. Peoples matured in the shadow of the Church and Empire, and their territorial laws had to be respected to some extent. World law, which knew only the individual, increasingly conceded the principle of the territoriality of law. The growth of the significance of particular law created in passing the conditions for the comparison of law. It found application obviously within modest limits and was confined to the comparison of particular laws of the motherland between themselves and with respect to Roman law. Such comparison led to the coordination of law in individual States and a single general law grew from fractionated local laws. Internal comparative studies emerged at first in England during the tenth century and later on the continent. They acquire special significance in France during the thirteenth century, confined to local French laws. The Glossators in Germany during the fourteenth century attempted to coordinate the Saxon collections of law with Roman and Canon law.[17]

To the inter-State comparison of law proper one may point to two works of the fifteenth century by Sir John Fortescue (1394-1479).[18] In both works the author compared for the first time in history English law with continental law, especially French, and attempted to show the superiority of English law. Although these works were not an objective analysis of comparable laws, they had influence in France even before the time of Montesquieu.[19]

Thus, with the development of national cultures the science of law became more profound, the comparative method being applied incidentally and not systematically, solely for practical purposes. The epoch of humanism intensified this process, although it did not bring material changes in the consideration of law.

[17] Richard Schröder, *Lehrbuch der deutschen Rechtsgeschichte* (6th ed.; 1922), p. 724.

[18] John Fortescue, *De laudibus Angliae* (1442); Fortescue, *The Governance of England: Otherwise Called the Difference between an Absolute and a Limited Monarchy*, ed. C. Plummer (1885).

[19] William Searle Holdsworth, *A History of English Law* (1903-1909), I, p. 569.

## 5. EPOCH OF HUMANISM

The fifteenth, sixteenth, and seventeenth centuries brought a more critical attitude towards the authority of faith of the Middle Ages. The developed knowledge of the ancient world and the discovery of new sources of law created the idea of the history of law. Roman law was interpreted more as a product of many centuries of development, and not as the law of Justinian. An awareness of this advanced local laws more strongly forward and, as Roman law lost a monopoly position, national systems acquired autonomous significance. The intensified formation of national States facilitated this decisively, having during the preceding epoch crystallized an integral law from individual particular laws and put an end to the universalism of the Middle Ages. All the political and cultural barriers which in the Middle Ages had precluded the comparison of law disappeared. Therefore, in the epoch of humanism a noticeable increase of the comparison of law happens in many countries. Especially in Germany the acceptance of Roman law gave special impetus to the comparative notions of the law in force. An urgent need existed to have textbooks containing information about the law in force. Therefore, a number of works appeared devoted basically to the law of the country and contrasting it at the same time with Roman and Canon law.[20] Comparative works of this period, having a practical purpose, rarely had a purely scientific character. The comparative method was used thus in other countries of Western Europe: Netherlands, England, Scotland, Italy, Spain. Everywhere national law was compared with Roman, and sometimes with Canon law as well. Such works were few in number, however, in comparison with Germany, where Roman law was encountered directly and there was a natural interest in a comparison of the laws in force in that country. Matters were completely opposite in France, where the dominant school of monarchomaques completely terminated the comparison of law.

On the whole, the epoch of humanism brought the development of the comparison of law. It did not, however, go beyond the bounds of practical needs and only in exceptional instances were laws compared not binding within one country. Comparative works did not consciously engage with foreign law

[20] Kaden, note 14 above, VI, p. 22.

with a view to deepening legal knowledge and clearly formalizing legal concepts. The few works in this sphere arose without being linked to one another, without mutual influence, and without an understanding of the methodological value of comparison. During the epoch of humanism, one cannot speak of the systematic use of the comparative method in law.

## 6. EPOCH OF LAW OF NATURE

The epoch of the law of nature became a turning point in this matter, despite the fact that it, being speculative and *a priori*, was a theoretically negative structure opposed to all empiricism, and therefore also opposed to the comparison of law.

The law of nature became from the time of Hugo Grotius up to the second third of the nineteenth century the dominant world outlook in the science of law. It proclaimed the existence of a law which, independently of positive law and often in agreement with it but even more often not in agreement, should be an ideal, just law. The task of the natural law school was to find and substantiate natural law by way of intellectual speculations, by logical derivation, by deductions from the highest philosophical foundations.[21]

For this reason only the leading minds assessed the value of the comparative method and used it significantly in their works, although it served them only as an additional argument to prove their *a priori* assertions. Ultimately, the brilliant flowering of the national science of law in individual countries which ensued after the complete liberation of legal thought from under the hegemony of Roman law – temporarily weakened interest in other systems, being directed primarily to the legal life and problems of the homeland. For all these reasons the comparative method was not sufficiently recognized and adapted, although leading authors used it, and others acknowledged its value, even theoretical. Sir Francis Bacon (1561-1626) required that a jurist liberate himself from the influence of his national law if he wants to evaluate the value of this law.[22] The object of evaluation cannot simultaneously

[21] Fritz Berolzheimer, *Die Kulturstufen der Rechts- und Wirtschaftsphilosophie* (1905), p. 13.

[22] Francis Bacon, *De dignitate et augmentis scientiarum (1623);* Max Salomon, *Grundlegung zur Rechtsphilosophie* (1919), §10, p. iii.

be the measure of evaluation.[23] Therefore, one should cognize foreign law and compare it with domestic law. Bacon thus acknowledged the value of the comparison of law for a critique of law. Gottfried Wilhelm Leibniz (1646-1716) was interested in the comparison of law from a universalist point of view. In his *Nova methodus discendae docendoeque jurisprudentiae* (1667) he suggested a plan to comparatively present the law of all peoples, all countries, and all times.

Although no one brought to fruition the ideas and plans of these philosophers, the intuition of the scholars of that period was characteristic, for they plainly saw the fruitfulness of the comparative method in legal studies long before its conscious application in the science of law.

Jurists of that time actually used the comparative method in practice. In England, John Selden (1584-1654),[24] a contemporary of Bacon. Such theoreticians of the law of nature as Grotius and Pufendorf used the comparative method in order to prove the truth of their science on natural law.[25] Vico attempted to demonstrate with the assistance of comparison that natural law arose autonomously in every people.[26] Montesquieu proved with the assistance of the comparative method that the development of legal institutions depends on national, social, political, and religious conditions. Ultimately, the value of the comparative method for legal education was underscored. Johann Stephan Pütter (1725-1807) advised in his draft legal encyclopedia to study the ancient cultural laws of Egypt, Greece, and the Jews.[27] August Friedrich Schott (1744-1792) suggested in his draft legal encyclopedia that students study the law of neighboring peoples in order to improve their knowledge of German law.[28] But these

[23] Kaden, note 14 above, VI, p. 23.

[24] John Selden, *Titles of Honour* (1614); Selden, *The Historie of Tithes: That is, the Practice of the Payment of Them. The Positive Laws Made for Them. The Opinions Touching the Right of Them. A Review of it is also Annext, which Both Confirmes it and Directs in Use of It* (1618).

[25] Ernst Landsberg, *Geschichte der deutschen Rechtswissenschaft* (1910), III, p. 12.

[26] Giovanni Battista Vico, *Principi di una scienza nuova intorno alla natura delle nazioni per la quale si ritruovano i principi di altro sistema* (1725).

[27] Johann Stephan Pütter, *Neuer Versuch einer juristischen Enzyklopädie und Methodologie* (1757; 2d ed.; 1767).

[28] August Friedrich Schott, *Entwurf einer Juristischen Enzyklopädie und Methodologie,*

authors themselves did not go beyond these remarks or apply the improvements which they assigned.

It is evident from the above that at the time of the natural law school the comparative method was valued and used even though it lacked a full theoretical and practical substantiation. The method itself had not yet been elaborated and applied, being, as noted, supplementary and unscientific for underpinning *a priori* assertions. This is clearly seen, for example, in Montesquieu's *L'Esprit des lois*. There the laws of various peoples and various times are contrasted without system and plan, and non-comparable laws are compared between themselves.

How the old natural law school interpreted empirical material unscientifically is shown by the fact that it assumed the real existence of natural law in the earliest period of history and interpreted this law as an ideal for all subsequent legal development. Early researchers cited as evidence of the existence of the law of nature the pre-historical state which for the most part they thought up along with their theories. Despite all deductive constructions, they turned additionally to arguments for empirical material with whose assistance they sought to demonstrate the example of ideal law by referring to an imagined legal state. The theoreticians of the law of nature attempted to substantiate through intellectual speculations the old science of theology that a perfected law was given sometime in Paradise and was lost through sinfulness. Because the idea of an eternal law has roots in the notion that man is a perfected work and has a predestination to remain in a state of immutable perfection.[29] Thus arose the mythology characteristic for the natural law school of an ideal state of the past which was interpreted as a source of truth having timeless value. For it, the re-creation of a lost past and a return to what had passed – which for theoreticians was imagined to be a model for all possible law, as the ideal natural law, was a development.

The theories of the social contract may be an example of such proof of natural law, being substantiated in various variants of a kind of artificial historical dialectic. In all these theories the significance of a norm for the modern day was ascribed to the past.

---

*zum Gebrauch akademischer Vorlesungen* (1772).

[29] Josef Kohler, "Rechtsphilosophie und Universalrechtsgeschichite", in Franz von Holzendorff (ed.), *Enzyklopädie der Rechtswissenschaft in systematischer Bearbeitung* (7th ed.; 1915), p. 3.

Only a law to which one might refer to in the last became an ideal. Moreover, it was analyzed according to theoretical grounds which must be proven, changing historical reality by a distortion of the facts or the construction of assumptions.[30]

It is obvious that such an approach to historical material did not create a reliable foundation for the scientific nature of comparative conclusions, and comparison had no serious significance in spite of all the references to empirical material.

Nonetheless, in this epoch the comparative method was so understood that three great codifications at the turn of the eighteenth and nineteenth centuries were prepared by comparative studies: the 1794 Prussian Allgemeines Landrecht on the basis of the Royal directive of 14 April 178[...];[31] the 1804 Code Napoleon, during the compilation of which the Prussian Allgemeines Landrecht was used and was translated for this purpose;[32] and the Austrian Civil Code.[33]

## 7. HISTORICAL SCHOOL

The Historical School, which was a denial of the science on natural law, created the foundations for the further development of the science of law, and especially charted the path for consistent comparison. Proceeding, however, from the correct foundations, it pursued an incorrect direction. The Historical School actually upheld the view that law is a work of the spirit of a people which operates in everything actively,[34] and emphasizing the national character of law, rejects the excessive dominance of Roman law but did not go beyond the traditional limits of the science of law at the time.[35] Savigny himself recognized German law beside Roman law and rejected the study of other laws. In the similar understanding of Puchta, Roman law is a medium of communion between

[30] Del Vecchio, note 6 above, p. 469.

[31] Franz Förster, *Preussisches Privatrecht* (4th ed.; 1889), I, p. 7.

[32] Kohler, "Über die Methode der Rechtsvergleichung", *Grünhuts Zeitschrift,* XXVIII, no. 1 (1901), p. vii.

[33] Weiss, note 11 above, p. 8.

[34] Friedrich Carl von Savigny, *System des heutigen Römischen Rechts* (1840), I, p. 14.

[35] Kaden, note 14 above, VI, p. 24.

peoples and a general law for civilized peoples.[36] The Historical School thus adhered to narrow limits of national systems. This was ultimately a time which in general did not further the comparison of law. The great modern codifications that emerged drew all the attention of scholars, and there was no place for the comparison of different systems of law. These circumstances explain why during the first half of the nineteenth century the comparison of law was little practiced.

However, by a total denial of the science of natural law, the Historical School created the prerequisites among which the idea of the comparison of law might subsequently develop. First and foremost, the Historical School decisively denied the existence of law outside positive law. The foundations were created by this emphasis on positive and historical material for the further development of legal science, which later made it easy to acknowledge the full theoretical and practical value of the comparative method. Obviously, this did not happen rapidly. Even the rejection of the law of nature proceeded slowly and gradually.

At this time, Schelling's assertion became crucial that the task of the science of law is the expression in legal norms of the highest idea once again with the assistance of historical reflections. In his words, the science of law should create a synthesis of historical material with ideas so that facts became an expression of ideas. Schelling thus gave to the science of law the task of cognizing law in development, and this, on one hand, destroyed the view presented by the natural law school and, on the other, creates the foundations for a new school of the science of law, later called the Historical School.[37]

The theory of the Historical School elaborated under the influence of Schelling specially pursued the generation and origin of positive law. The assertions of the founders of the Historical School – Hugo, Savigny, and Puchta – became the basis of the understanding of law and binding to a great extent on later theoreticians of the comparison of law who to a greater or lesser degree recognized the national conditionality of law.

The "legal consciousness of a people" is the central concept of the Historical School of law. It was taken from the philosophical

[36] Georg F. Puchta, *Kursus der Institutionen* (1853), I, p. 106.

[37] Berolzheimer, note 21 above, p. 229.

historicism of Schelling and Hegel and adapted to the sphere of law. According to the Historical School, every people has its own spirit manifested in a series of phenomena such as morals, law, art, and language.[38] These phenomena are not a closed perfection, but merely a work of the spontaneity of a particular people. They are combined into a single integral whole by the general conviction of a people, a feeling of inner need excluding any thought of incidental and arbitrary origin. Law is in an organic link with the character of the people and in its development is part of the development of the people. It matures together with the people and in the people, is formed with it and in it , and dies away together with the death of the people. This law arises as customary and only later is developed by the science of law. The inner spontaneous forces of a people are so decisive, and not the arbitrariness of the legislator.[39]

In its genesis and function law demonstrates many similarities especially with language. Just as language arises and develops by itself, without the involvement of experts in grammar who merely in passing on the basis of linguistic material already existing determine the rules of grammar, so law is not the work of the legislator but merely a spontaneous creature of the spirit of a people which actually exists for centuries and only later becomes the subject-matter of the conscious processing by jurists – the technicians of law. Legislation later rests on the works of jurists, by its nature being based on ancient customary law. Laws thus have secondary significance; they should crystallize the grounds created spontaneously by the legal consciousness of a people. Customary law, as the real and initial source of law, changes over time; legislation called upon to systematically formalize it may prove to be harmful. Having consolidated a certain state of spontaneous customary law, laws stabilize it and make it immutable. The path is thus closed to the further natural development of law. For these reasons, the old historical school opposed legislation, and the more so, codification.[40]

In Savigny's view, all human life in time and space is a constituent part of a higher whole and subordinate thereto. Man cannot be imagined abstractly and in isolation. He is necessarily a member of a people and a State. So too every epoch of a nation is an

[38] Del Vecchio, note 6 above, p. 143.

[39] Berolzheimer, note 21 above, p. 231.

[40] Del Vecchio, note 6 above, p. 144.

evolutionary continuation of the past. Because of this organic link of the present with the past, every epoch must recognize something as given: values inherited by generations. They are imposed by the determinism of social life into which man is born, grows, and displays himself – and at the same time they are a free, voluntary, and natural choice of organically linked elements. Inherited values link unconditionally because they are not dependent on the arbitrariness of the present. They simultaneously are free manifestations of the culture of a nation as a whole in the state of development.

For these reasons Savigny opposed the forcible acceleration and artificial forming of natural law by political revolutions and by legislation. Law is not an arbitrary work, but only conditioned by the entire past of the nation – and so the science of law should confine itself to the review and preservation of the vitality of inner determinism by the history of actual legal material.

Therefore, only after the study of natural law has matured over history may it be systematized in a codification. Different laws within Germany may be understood if they are reduced to their common root because all historical law of individual regions has a natural interest for the entire nation. In that indirect but well-founded in a certain sense evolutionary way, Savigny thought to approach codification, built on the firm foundations of the legal tradition of an entire nation.[41]

These were ideas that undoubtedly enlarged the horizon and deepened the understanding of legal phenomena. Thereafter, however, the Historical School did not follow the path of idealistic romanticism of its founders. A narrow positivism came in its place which carried historical studies of law away from the programmed purpose set solely to the collection and ordering of legal antiquities. This imparted to the Historical School an antiquarian character, although it, in drawing attention to the consciousness of the people and its historical works and consequently to the historical and positive aspect of law, was a progressive factor in comparison with natural law. However, in excessively emphasizing and juxtaposing positive law to natural law, the Historical School went to another extreme.

[41] Julius Binder, *Philosophie des Rechts* (1925), p. 1059.

The Historical School had other delusions. It fostered a cult of transplanting past positive legal forms and by this uncritical deification of the old law denied any progress possible only with a critical attitude towards phenomena. The exclusive interest in old positive law and the idealization thereof in practice excluded a quest for the ideal of law. The mixture of reality with the ideal is the major delusion of the Historical School, analogous to that of the natural law school to which it was juxtaposed. If the natural law school reduced the idea of law to the level of empirical significance, then the Historical School – on the contrary – took a historically created law to the heights of an absolute ideal, mixing positive and ideal law. In those times the observation of reality which the Historical School set as the exclusive task for itself, could not provide knowledge of the theoretical and abstract foundations of law. And the concept of law, some ideal measure of its value, is inevitable when gathering and ordering monuments of antiquity, albeit to distinguish law from morality, religion, and mythology.[42]

Another error of the old historical orientation is the over-evaluation of customary law as a source of law, which led to its being juxtaposed to the newest law. In fact, having accepted that from the outset law was developed by way of custom, one must see that over time legislation replaced customary lawmaking, initially only confirming and formalizing customary aw but over time becoming an autonomous source of law which, thanks to a critical approach to legal material, is a higher degree of legal consciousness of people. The improvement of law by the free and conscious discussion thereof by specialists cannot be denied and instead took as a model the beginning stages of law.[43]

Another delusion of the Historical School is the romantic reference to the spirit of a people, which creates law mystically. In reality, the consciousness of a people does not exist outside the consciousness and will of individuals, between whom there is no idyllic unity in the understanding of law. Being linked by objective ties of a joint tradition and culture and a feeling of belonging to one community, they do not unequivocally and automatically recognize some single law as an ideal. Positive law is the result of various views and intersecting interests which impart to it an

[42] Del Vecchio, note 6 above, p. 144.

[43] Ibid., p. 143.

appearance of being dependent on the predominant trends of a particular time.

And even the basic thesis, that is, the assertion that every people has its own separate spirit and as result its own separate law, the Historical School has not tried to prove. Adherents of the Historical School were Romanists and, wallowing in the consideration of Roman law, considered it to be a prototype of all laws. Because of this contradiction between the proclaimed theory and practice, the Historical School did not become the engine of historical research that might have been expected. Only the ethnological-comparative school undertook this, actually setting for itself the task of explaining the law of all peoples.

As noted, however, the principal assertions of the Historical School, namely the assertion about the historicity and conditionality of law, have been retained down to the present and are the predominant scientific view.[44] It was merely necessary to rework the extreme positivist orientation in which the Historical School developed for a long period, contrary to its basic ideas.

Over time, it collected sources of law and investigated the development of legal institutions and their interdependence solely in Roman and German law. But even there the Historical School could not determine national distinctive features which, according to its theory, should have been reflected in national law. With his "The Spirit of Roman Law", Rudolf Jhering had no noticeable impact on the Historical School of law and it, turning to the positive and concrete, did not seek answers to questions about the meaning and history of law.[45]

In addition to the lack of profound contemplation of historical material, the researchers of the past had, as noted, narrow interests. German jurists were long occupied almost exclusively with Roman and German law, which for them were of direct interest. Even these two laws were not analyzed separately, but within a body of "customary law" (*gemeines Recht*) – the subject-matter of scientific studies, and German legal science rarely had been seen in its full distinctiveness. The laws of other States of the Middle Ages had for German jurists only the significance of a cultural phenomenon. The science of law proper did not interest them. Nor

[44] Ibid., p. 146.

[45] Binder, note 41 above, p. 1026.

were contemporary foreign laws of interest at the time to German jurists because they saw no scientific value in investigating them.

This standoffish partiality in studies only of the law in force in Germany provided certain results. Roman law, to which most attention was devoted, was pursued in all directions as a system, as a whole, and as individual institutions. Thus, the externally accepted Roman law was organically appropriated by German legal thought.[46]

Such partiality, however, could not be preserved in the long term. The more that studies developed on the law in force in Germany, the more it became evident that the practical narrowness of historical research with all its useful consequences could not facilitate a cognition of law beyond a certain point. The early controversial issues already centuries old found no convincing resolution within the narrow studies only of Roman and German law. Despite new useful ideas, the gaps in Roman sources could not be filled. The insufficient sources promoted the emergence of fantastic hypotheses to address questions put by the science of law. Worst of all was the state of the philosophy of law. Because of the lack of comprehensive studies of sources, philosophical reflections on law were undertaken still under the sign of nature by philosophers who knew nothing at all about law. It is evident that their systems, lacking firm foundations, could not claim to be of legal value.

For these reasons an aspiration emerged to expand the empirical base of the science of law. By the first half of the nineteenth century attention was devoted to studies of ancient Greek trials. Later scholars began to use Scandinavian law in order to understand German and early Germanic law, and even ancient Indian collections of laws became the subject-matter of legal studies. Finally, interest arose in the contemporary institutions of foreign peoples.[47]

Thus did the idea of studying and comparing foreign law gradually emerge. It found ideological support in the theory of the Historical School, despite its delusions and partiality and despite the fact that it did not determine an attitude towards comparison.

[46] Franz Bernhöft, "Über Zweck und Mittel der vergleichenden Rechtswissenschaft", *Zeitschrift für vergleichende Rechtswissenschaft*, I (1878), p. 1.

[47] Ibid., p. 2.

First, the contrasting of law with language and a reference of the Historical School to the natural development of law had a direct impact on the development of the comparative method. The successes of comparative linguistics over time led directly to the idea of using the comparative method in legal studies. Once again the reference to the natural development of law provided a basis for universal constructions of the development of law which, referring to the natural origin of all law in human nature, established a link with modern theories of natural law. At that time, when the Historical School, in combatting the old natural law, built a path for studies and comparisons of foreign law by virtue of the fact, the theoretical ideas about the comparison of law also had begun to develop, despite the positivism of the Historical School.

Of these, there should be noted: the philosophical quests of Feuerbach, the critical works of Thibault, and the universalist studies of Gans. Feuerbach, an adherent of Immanuel Kant, asserts that the science of law as an empirical science may lead to the cognition of legal phenomena only by comparison of the laws of all peoples and times. Philosophical speculations in and of themselves can never lead, and without comparison the science of law is inconceivable. He came to these ideas by 1810 and set them out later in a work on the idea and necessity of a universal science of law.[48] But he did not undertake to realize his assertions in practice, and only later did Giorgio del Vecchio (1878-1970) begin to propagandize his thoughts anew.

Thibault clearly put a question similar to Feuerbach's. In his words, the history of law is not real and vital whose view is directed only towards the history of one people. In order to be true and pragmatic, it should encompass the legislation of all other ancient and modern peoples. These thoughts Gans inscribed as an epigraph to his work on the law of inheritance.

## 8. THREE ROOTS OF CONTEMPORARY COMPARISON

Gans separately substantiated the need for the comparison of law in the spirit of Hegel and therefore it is believed that it established roots in his philosophy. In his day, Gans spoke out resolutely

[48] Johann Anselm von Feuerbach, "Die Idee und Notwendigkeit einer Universal-jurisprudenz", *Biographischer Nachlass* (1853), p. 408.

against the Historical School which, embedded in individual issues of an antiquarian past, lost its initial idea: to determine the spirit of a people in law. Therefore, Gans contrasted historical positivism to a historico-philosophical program in the Hegelian style: to seek out ideas in historical reality.[49] Investigating the law of inheritance, where he compares Indian, Chinese, Jewish, and Islamic law, Gans speaks out against Savigny with the assertion that law is the result of a reasonable, independent will of a legislator and not dependent on historical laws of development.[50] Every people creates its own laws by its own vital efforts and desire irrespective of the past.[51] These views led him to the comparison of law. It connected in his universalist method with Montesquieu, who he considered to be the creator of the universalist understanding of the science of law.[52] Gans simultaneously opposed the antiquarian nature of the science of law, insisting that the history of law included the totality of the concept of law in time and it also is essential from a universalist position.[53] The real historical science of law is the total development of the concept of law, of universal history, in which every people should be considered as a stage of development. The Historical School, in confining itself to studies only of Roman and German law, did not even seek the principal vectors of the development of leading ideas therein. History was considered to be the investigation of the past as though history was exhausted by this. However, it should pursue the idea that one step followed another in the gradual development of concepts, and in this chain of development the contemporary world also has the right to form a legal life. Therefore, the law of the present should not be treated in the sense of positivism as a concrete separated fact of existence, but merely as a stage of development, as a state of history.[54]

In the polemic of the Historical School against positivism, Gans drew attention from facts of the past to the idea of history. Thus was advanced the first idea of the comparative history of

[49] Eduard Gans, *Erbrecht in weltgeschichtlicher Entwicklung* (1824), I, p. xxxix.

[50] Ibid., I, p. xi.

[51] Ibid., I, p. x.

[52] Ibid., I, p. xviii.

[53] Ibid., I, p. xxxi.

[54] Binder, note 41 above, p. 944.

law. Although in practice Gans had no great influence[55] and few followed his thoughts, these ideas had been contributed and it was merely a question of time as to when they would be fully accepted.

Theoretical and philosophical reflections ultimately developed in the same direction, as did the requirements of legal policy. They led the Heidelberg criminologist, Carl Joseph Anton Mittermaier (1787-1867) to the idea of comparing law for practical purposes. In his comparative studies he did not have recourse either to law of the past or to the law of primitive peoples, confining himself to searches for the most progressive law among contemporary cultured peoples. He was of the opinion that the science of law should be launched from the clouds of the concepts of the pure, and this means non-existent law, as well as discarding pre-historical studies: it should return to firm reality.[56]

In addition to authors who engaged with the theory of comparative research, there were others who used it for practical purposes. As well as Mittermaier in Germany, there were a number of scholars in France and England.[57]

How material at the time was theoretical and practical interest in comparison is demonstrated by the fact that in 1832 a Chair of Comparative Law was created at Paris, and in 1848 a similar chair for the comparison of criminal law. Despite the fact, however, that the scientific value of the comparative method was recognized, it did not achieve general recognition in the science of law. Positivism did not facilitate this once again, for having reigned in the mid-nineteenth century, it merely faced practical cognition.[58] Comparative-legal studies froze after the deaths of the pioneers, and the journals published in France (*Revue étrangere de législation*, 1834-1850) and in Germany (*Zeitschrift für Rechtswissenschaft und Gesetzgebung des Auslandes* (Heidelberg, 1829-1856) ceased to appear.

A new revival of comparative studies in law occurred from a completely different side. Neither philosophical nor critical works in the domain of law reversed the trend. It came from completely

[55] Landsberg, note 25 above, III, p. 361, 433, and 723.

[56] Binder, note 41 above, p. 945.

[57] Kaden, note 14 above, p. 25.

[58] Landsberg, note 25 above, III, pp. 732, 834.

outside the law. At a time when jurists lose interest in comparison, the comparative method achieved great success in ethnology, developing as an autonomous science, and linguistics, which thanks to the comparative method, explained many linguistic phenomena. A journal on comparative linguistics was founded in 1851. These facts decisively influenced the introduction of the comparative method into research on law. Initially, interest turned to the Indo-European peoples, and then in connection with Biblical studies, to early Jewish law and then to Islamic, Egyptian, and others.[59]

Johann Jakob Bachofen (1815-1887) from Basel had a decisive impact in this direction in his work on the "mother law".[60] He is considered to be the founder of ethnological jurisprudence.[61] Bachofen set out the theoretical and developed the practical task of studying this idea in the development of law fully with the assistance of the comparative method. He collected and contrasted from mythology and legends, from ancient beliefs, from old monuments, from ancient Greek dramas, and from ancient sources all characteristic data which proves that the ancient cultured peoples had before the patronat; that is, a system where the father is the central figure in the family, religion, law, and State – a system of mother law in which the mother held a central place in religion and law.

As noted, Bachofen's works are considered revolutionary for the comparative method. Whereas prior to this comparison was used fragmentarily in order to obtain practical one-off results, Bachofen used comparison for deeply scientific studies resting on sources. He thus proved the value full-scale of the comparative method for scientific studies of law.

Albert Hermann Post (1839-1895) was the second pioneer of this method – the author of numerous ethnological works and the creator of the name "ethnological jurisprudence". These works demonstrated, together with Hegelianism, the influence of French positivism and naturalism, which came from Isidore Marie Auguste François Xavier Comte (1798-1857) and signified

[59] Albert Hermann Post, *Grundriss des ethnologischen Jurisprudenz* (1894), I, p. 3.

[60] Johann Jakob Bachofen, *Das Mutterrecht: eine Untersuchung über die Gynaikokratie der alten Welt nach ihrer religiösen und rechtlichen Natur* (1861).

[61] Josef Kohler, "Nachruf an J. J. Bachofen", *Zeitschrift für vergleichende Rechtswissenschaft*, VIII (1889), p. 148.

a sociological orientation. Post's comparative works were under the dual influence of French sociologism and Hegelianism. He combined these two, supposedly completely separate and even in contradiction with one another. Post changed (just as Karl Marx in his historical materialism) Hegel's theory that history is the logical development of the spirit in reality – a naturally conditioned process in which individual periods have a significance similar as that of epochs in the history of the Earth. The titles of Post's works are themselves expressive: "The Natural Law [*lex*] of Law [*jus*]"; "Introduction to the Nature-Descriptive Science of Law"; "The Fundamental Principles of Law and Survey of the History of its Development on a Sociological Basis". Post set out his principal idea in these works: that identical consequences follow from identical conditions under the influence of identical causes.[62]

Post's works combine two roots of contemporary comparison – the Hegelian and the natural approach. They leave their trace on all later theories of the comparison of law and in the eyes of some they disqualify the comparative method as a means of scientific research.[63] The practical needs of legislation and legal policy are considered to be the third root of comparison.[64] Although the origins of the comparison of law should be sought in historical, philosophical, and idealist interests,[65] in later times practical moments were added to them. They are considered to be the third impetus for comparative studies which over time became actually the first and increasingly imparts tone to the comparison of law.[66]

Post's works also reveal his theoretical interests. He processed the material as a natural scientist, using the comparative method. Despite this, his works are not finished mature works because of the inadequacies of preparatory studies. Post regarded the law of various peoples fragmentarily and by way of illustration. Particular legal phenomena in various peoples for him were a basis for final assertions. Therefore, instead of an image of the laws of individual

[62] Binder, note 41 above, p. 946.

[63] Felix Holldack, *Grenzen der Erkenntnis ausländischen Rechts* (1919), p. 71.

[64] Binder, note 41 above, pp. 943-947.

[65] Leonhard Adam, "Franz Bernhöft zum 75. Geburtstage", *Zeitschrift für vergleichende Rechtswissenschaft*, XLIII (1928), p. 9.

[66] Ibid., p. 10.

peoples he created a mosaic.[67] Notwithstanding this, Post's works had great influence on the development of the comparison of law, not from his processing, but rather the very fact of their appearance. They provided an impetus to further work.

## 9. TRIUMPH OF COMPARATIVE METHOD

Josef Kohler (1849-1919) was the first jurist who perceived the scientific value of Post's approach and followed the same road. In researching law ethnologically, however, he raised special issues, believing synthetic works to be premature.[68] Kohler set the task of tracing the law of individual peoples and ordering the material according to legal concepts. Kohler's synthetic works which one may consider to be the result of preparatory studies, namely the respective book on modern-day culture and in the Holtzendorff encyclopedia, should be regarded as an introduction to a final processing of the subject-matter.[69] Kohler, however, is considered to be a positivist despite his universalist-historical orientation.[70]

The entire comparative school proceeded further in the direction indicated by Kohler. Comparative studies occupied themselves increasingly with positive law instead of immersion in theory and philosophy. The practical aspect prevailed over the theoretical, and comparison either confined itself to the collection of materials and assertion of differences and similarities without drawing conclusions or limited its purpose to a determination of the most progressive and improved law.

The comparison of law acquires greater recognition and increased success. The *Zeitschrift für vergleichende Rechtswissenschaft*, founded in 1878, was taken over in 1881 by Kohler, the master of ethnographic studies. The comparison of the laws of cultural peoples commenced to develop simultaneously.[71] The Société française de legislation comparée, founded in 1869, set as its task

[67] Adam, "Josef Kohler und die vergleichende Rechtswissenschaft", *Zeitschrift für vergleichende Rechtswissenschaft*, XXXVII (1919), p. 26.

[68] Ibid., p. 27.

[69] Ibid., p. 28.

[70] Binder, note 41 above, p. 497.

[71] Kaden, note 14 above, p. 26.

to improve legislation by means of the comparison of foreign laws.[72] Lorenz von Stein (1815-1890) declared in his *Die Gegenwart und Zükunft der Rechts- und Staatswissenschaft* (1879) that the comparison of law is an essential foundation of the historical and dogmatic elaboration of law.

Thus was the idea gradually established that the comparative method should be used not only in ethnological studies of law, but should be expanded also to other spheres of law, to the history of law, and to dogmatics.

The great value of the comparison of law began to be recognized simultaneously in various countries for various reasons. Initially not historical or philosophical interests were advanced, as in former times, but only practical needs. The general turn towards the use of the comparative method in law led in many countries to associations, institutions, and journals being founded whose declared purpose was the comparative studies of law. In 1900 the first International Congress of Comparative Law was held at Paris under the leadership of Raymond Saleilles (1855-1912) and Edouard Lambert (1866-1947).[73]

After the First World War, comparative studies developed on a new scale. Germany, which until then had been under the influence of Kohler and his ethnological studies, now embarked upon the path of the dogmatic comparison of foreign law. Dogmatic and historical comparison distinctly disengaged from ethnological comparison. A manifestation of this was the change in the title of the Journal of the comparative science of law, which from volume 38 (1920) added the words "including the ethnological study of law and society". Comparative law institutes were established in France and Italy, and the International Academy of Comparative Law was founded in 1924 at Geneva, and in 1932 a second international congress was held at the Hague.[74] Between 1870 and 1928 about 4,000 books and works appeared in Western Europe

[72] [Added in the margins: "In England the Society of Comparative Legislation also appeared which published the *Journal of the Society of Comparative Legislation*. At this time the German journal was principally occupied with ethnographic and ... law, and the French with foreign law in force, and the English [journal] devoted principal attention to the law of its Empire and in addition also to other foreign law" – web/ok].

[73] [Written in the margins: "The Congress was ...basically by French scholars" – web/ok].

[74] [Written in the margins: "and in 1937 the third" – web/ok].

and America only on civil and commercial law where various laws were compared. This number speaks to the development and significance of the comparative method in the most recent law. It is now under the sign of the comparative method.[75]

[75] Kaden, note 14 above, p. 27. [Written in the margins: "Report on the 1932 Congress in Acta Academiae Berlin. German abstracts in Sonderheft der Ztscht. f. ausl. Recht VI (1932)" – web/ok; The Report and resolutions of the 1937 Congress were published in the *Acta Academiae and in the Bulletin de la Société de Législation Comparée.* The German abstracts were published in the *Sonderheft der Zeitschrift für auslandisches Recht*, XI (1939) – web/ok].

# Chapter III. Concept of Comparison

1. Searches for Differences and Similarities. 2. Negative Description. 3. Comparison within Systems and between Systems

## 1. SEARCHES FOR DIFFERENCES AND SIMILARITIES

Throughout its historical development, the comparative method was defined and its theory elaborated. The New and Newest times especially provided decisive confirmation. The determination of the concept and essence of comparison of law was the early supports of confirmation of the theory of comparison by which one should be engaged.

The special distinctiveness of the rules of the comparative method is imparted by comparison. Concisely formulated, the comparison of law aspired, as it name suggests, to compare a large quantity of legal phenomena among themselves.[76] It contrasts the laws of different systems and studies their correlation.[77] Comparison encompasses basically those legal norms of different legal systems which affect identical issues or, more accurately, offer decisions for identical problems within their legal orders. We refer not to the contrasting of individual sciences or norms as such, but only to determination of their correlation: on finding similarities and differences.[78]

Through the determination of similarities and differences, the comparison of law goes beyond the fundamental base of the community of legal phenomena, beyond the idea of law, which imparts a conceptual trace of homogeneity to the most unique

[76] Friedrich Wilhelm von Rauchhaupt, "Die wissenschaftliche Pflege des Rechtsvergleichung", *Archiv für Rechts und Wirtschaftphilosophie*, XXIII (1929), p. 149.

[77] Ernst Rabel, "Aufgabe und Notwendigkeit der Rechtsvergleichung", *Rheinische Zeitschrift für Zivil- und Prozessrecht des In- und Auslandes*, XIII (1925), p. 280.

[78] Kaden, note 14 above, p. 9.

legal works and, permeating all phenomena which we ascribe to the sphere of law, binds them into one sociological and logical whole.[79] Within the confines of this homogeneous sphere of social life, the comparison of law links similar legal forms of different systems and derives contradictory ones, grouping them according to distinctions. The comparison of law in the most expansive and basic definition is engaged in the determination of similarities and differences in the objects being compared.

## 2. NEGATIVE DESCRIPTION

According to the above, the external contrasting in and of itself of various norms without a search for the inner correlations between them is not comparison. Such contrasting may be very valuable for the comparison of law to such a degree that it provides a solid survey of various laws according to an identically conceived plan exhausting theory and practice to an equal extent. Such contrasting, however, is not comparison because that essential for comparison is not present: the internal linkage of the similar and contrasting of the distinctive norms.[80] It is evident, moreover, that studies of foreign law, although necessary for comparison, are not comparison in and of themselves. Therefore, researchers in the field of comparative law study in the preparatory phase and publish foreign legal material for further comparative processing.[81] Franz Alwin Friedrich August Bernhöft (1852-1933) had already drawn attention to this, pointing out that in order to understand well the ideas of other peoples, one should understand their law, just as this had been achieved with respect to Roman and Germanic law. Therefore, all studies within individual systems are important from the standpoint of the comparative method. They lay the path for the comparative science of law by the collection of material and expansion of the field of vision.[82]

The number of objects to be compared has in and of itself no significance when comparing. To be sure, the value of comparison may be greater when we compare simultaneously more foreign

[79] Karl Petraschek, "Rechtsverglelichung", *Staatslexikon* (1931), IV, p. 669.

[80] Kaden, note 14 above, p. 10.

[81] Rauchhaupt, note 76 above, p. 151.

[82] Bernhöft, note 46 above, I, p. 37.

norms, but the narrower comparison of two objects is sufficient to relegate it to the comparison of law. Also, the laws to be compared need not necessarily be of one time. Norms which were or are in force at different times may be compared, some in force and others of historical significance, or only earlier and current between themselves. It is immaterial for comparison whether the systems to be compared are within a single State or they are the systems of different States. Finally, the laws to be compared need not necessarily be analogous and comparable by their nature, although comparison in a group of kindred systems is fruitful and, as a rule, advisable, whereas the comparison of laws with different foundations is useless. For these reasons, European laws are basically the objects of comparison, although comparison between European and Eastern systems may have significance and be interesting.[83]

In order to define the comparison of law it is not essential to set out some special purpose of comparison which would transcend the limits of the grammatical interpretation of the concept of comparison. The comparison of law exists when during the contrasting of law we seek an inner link or difference between the objects being compared. To determine some special purpose for the comparison of law would be to narrow its tasks to certain possibilities whereas it might serve different tasks. The comparison of law begins when in addition to external contrasting we investigate the correlation of objects we compare; that is, we undertake comparative-analytical consideration.[84] For the same reasons, one should not elevate any individual possible task of comparison above others. And so, the definition of comparison is exhausted by the assertion that it is a search for similarities and differences between norms of different legal systems.[85]

[83] Kaden, note 14 above, p. 10.

[84] Ernst Immanuel Bekker, "Aus den Grenzmarken der geschichtlichen Rechtswissenschaft", *Zeitschrift für Savigny-Stiftung für Rechtsgeschichte: Romanistische Abteilung*, VI (1885), p. 90.

[85] Kaden, note 14 above, p. 9.

## 3. COMPARISON WITHIN SYSTEMS AND BETWEEN SYSTEMS

Comparison is possible when there are at a minimum two different objects of comparison. They should show similarity and differences because only then can comparison give positive results. If there are no differences, there is no interest in comparison; when there are no similarities – comparison is impossible. All distinctions may be seen precisely on the basis of something common and all non-similiarity may be asserted only on the basis of comparison.[86]

Accordingly, objects of comparison must be, on one hand, sufficiently analogous and, on the other, sufficiently different. As noted, the first most general prerequisite for the comparison of law is the fact that the object of comparison is everything that falls under the concept of law. Comparison, however, should within this general concept find more precise points of contiguity which, while preserving basic identity, offer sufficiently different and at the same time analogous material relating to the problems and decisions in order to study the legal phenomena to be compared more precisely.

Comparison within a single legal system might be such. It occurs within a narrower range of similarities created over history by one people under identical political and social conditions. This gives a similarity to legal norms while retaining spheres of difference at the same time which might be the subject-matter of successful comparison.

The comparison of domestic particular law was over the centuries an important factor in the development of law. By means of the comparison of particular laws German private law was created just as at one time French or Swiss. The comparison of local laws paved the road to the unification of national laws in those States.[87] It is no surprise that the German Civil Code in the commentary refers primarily to the results of the comparison of particular German laws.[88]

[86] Petraschek, note 79 above, IV, p. 669.

[87] Kaden, note 14 above, p. 16.

[88] F. Schlegelberger (ed.), *Rechtsvergleichendes Handwörterbuch für Zivil- und Handelsrecht des In- und Audandes* (1929), I, Introduction, p. iii.

Beyond this, however, when not referring to the comparison of particular laws, comparison within a single legal system is rarely used. Comparison assumes the presence of different objects. But the comparative investigation of the norms of a single legal order does not rely on objects sufficiently different in their problems and decisions to speak of comparison in the full sense of this word. Each system is unified to a great degree and integral, so that there is not enough analogous material for comparison with respect to questions and at the same time different with regard to answers. For this reason, some authors do not enumerate comparative studies of a single system to the comparison of law, even if different branches of law are compared within one system[89] or different institutions,[90] despite the fact that the method of research is the same. Comparison does not have significance when it does not indirectly further the coming together of law. And this in principle is excluded and inconceivable when reference is made to different institutions of one system which has individual institutions taking into account the specific functional purpose of each of them. For this same reason comparison of different branches of law of one system has limited and basically theoretical value.

The principal field of activity for the comparison of law remains the comparative investigation of different systems. This makes possible a comparison of the decision by various orders of the same vital questions and legal problems that provides greater equilibrium between an individual difference (in decisions) and typical similarity (in problems) than is possible when comparing within a single system. Entire legal systems may be compared, or individual branches or institutions thereof which are identical or similar. Excluded from comparison by its very nature is law which is itself the result of comparison.[91]

89 Kaden, note 14 above, p. 10.

90 Rauchhaupt, note 76 above, p. 150.

91 Petraschek, note 79 above, IV, p. 669.

# Chapter IV. Essence of Comparison

1. Comparison is Not Separate Science. 2. Term "Comparative Science of Law". 3. Comparative Method does Not Impart to Studies the Character of Autonomous Science. 4. Autonomous Purpose of Comparison of Law. 5. Comparison is Auxiliary Means: a) for the Philosophy of Law; b) for Critique, Policy, and Legislation

## 1. COMPARISON IS NOT SEPARATE SCIENCE

The comparison of law in and of itself is not a science. It is merely a method and, as a technique of research, depends on the firmament of research, and this means may not create a separate system of autonomous concepts. The character of a separate science is imparted to the science of law because it uses autonomous ordering principles, concepts inherent in law by which the science of law encompasses changeable and conditional legal phenomena. Specific forms of legal thought are such ordering categories of any possible content of law at any time which classify, elicit, and order the historically conditioned content of law.[92] The comparison of law, using these ordering principles, develops by its own means that certain material of positive law which relatively-generally is found in all systems, giving to identical questions in general similar but, in details, different answers. But by means of comparison and generalization of changeable positive law, one never comes to absolutely important ideas which along might provide to reflections the character of a separate science.[93] There are two possible different tasks of science: the critical eliciting and the general description of legal phenomena.[94] The comparison of law does not perform either of these tasks. In and of itself it does not create from the comparison of legal norms a new system of

[92] Rudolf Stammler, *Lehrbuch der Rechtsphilosophie* (1923), p. 6.

[93] Ibid., p. 12.

[94] Ibid., p. 12, note 7.

obligatory concepts and does not externally elicit legal phenomena exhaustively. Therefore, the comparison of law is not a separate science: it does not have the indicia which determine the character of the concept of a science.[95]

The view that the comparison of law is not a separate science does not mean that it cannot be developed into a separate discipline in the future. Although to date comparative studies of law cannot be equated to comparative linguistics or to the comparative science of religion, it is not to be excluded that sometime they will achieve a sufficient degree of autonomy, having established a separate range of its specialty just as comparative linguistics did.

The earlier incomplete development of comparative studies may be ascribed, in addition to the delayed interest in comparison in the science of law, to the fact that it is much easier in law to ascertain phenomena than in other sciences, which must with difficulty determine the facts in and of themselves in their field. This possibly was a reason why the science of law engaged primarily in developing positive material which would be superfluous at a time when, for example, linguistics was forced to painstakingly work on establishing the phenomena, achieve a more profound view of phenomena, which in turn was made possible from advanced comparative research. This may also explain the fact that until now the comparative studies of law could not be equated to comparative linguistics.[96]

Possibly an obstacle to the development of comparison in law into an autonomous discipline also was the lack of a sufficient quantity of variants in legal phenomena which (unlike language, has as many possible distinctions as there are sounds) are different only within the narrow limits of individual and social indicia of man, identical in his nature.[97] Such a limitation in differences of legal phenomena which also, as typical works are repeated in all countries and all times, to a certain degree leads to the comparative method not being developed into an autonomous science.

[95] Binder, note 41 above, p. 838; Carl August Emge, *Vorschule der Rechtsphilosophie* (1925), p.121; Kaden, note 14 above, p. 22.

[96] Mario Rotondi, "Dogmatik und Rechtsvergleichung", *Zeitschrift für vergleichende Rechtswissenschaft*, XLVII (1933), p. 23.

[97] Bernhard Rehfeldt, *Grenzen der vergleichenden Methode in der rechtsfeschichlichen Forschung* (1942), p. 6.

It remains to discuss the question why positivism did not play a decisive role here. It seems that comparison in law, although it opposed in its day the antiquarianism of the Historical School, itself was submerged with the passage of time into a detailed processing of positive law, occupied itself with positivist prescriptions after, as became understood, grandiose at first glance systems of comparative law of the pioneers did not provide sufficient grounds for a comparative science of law. On one hand, the thorny path of preparatory work necessary for a large synthesis grounded the former high flight of comparative studies, and on the other – practical vital needs which gradually came to the forefront turned their gaze by the power of their everyday weight from ideal tasks to concrete issues. It is not surprising that Julius Binder (1870-1939) in his time evaluated the comparative science of law as a research technique which did not aspire to build something new from the laws to be compared, but collects materials which are not used.[98]

The comparison of law, however, just as any research, cannot in the long term be satisfied only by analysis. Accumulated observations require ordering, combining, and systematics which would provide a survey and an image of the whole and a perspective on the past and future. Therefore, it is not surprising that a voice was raised from time to time drawing attention to the need for a synthesis of the results of comparison[99] and representing a program thereof.[100]

It is another matter that when one refers to the great task of comparison in law it is difficult to determine an individual autonomous range of studies without ascribing to comparison a role which an autonomous science already performs. This is a basic question of the comparative science of law, on whose resolution its autonomous existence depends.

In any event, until all the possibilities of comparison were absolutely exhausted, it would be premature to make a final judgment in this matter given that in other sciences, for example, comparative anatomy or comparative linguistics, the comparative method has attained for itself an autonomous place as a science.

[98] Binder, note 41 above, p. 947.

[99] Ernst Heymann, "Auslandsrecht", *Handwörterbuch der Rechtswissenschaft* (1926), I, p. 425.

[100] Rotondi, note 96 above, p. 21.

Therefore, although the comparison of law cannot yet be considered a science in equal degree with comparative linguistics and the comparative science of religion, one may be assured, following Ernst Rabel (1874-1955), that it has a future. Perhaps his words will sometime be justified, and "a sufficiently developed comparison of law will become the basis of the entire science of law and the culmination thereof together with philosophy".[101]

## 2. THE TERM "COMPARATIVE SCIENCE OF LAW"

In asserting that the comparison of law is not a separate science, it should be acknowledged that the name "comparative science of law" is not completely precise and at a minimum premature. This was suggested long ago by the pioneers of the comparative method and to this day is used by some. The term "comparative jurisprudence", introduced at one time by Post, entered the science of law by analogy with comparative linguistics, which was one impetus for the use of the comparative method in legal studies, but it was never specially substantiated because the assertion in general about a special calling for the comparison of law was not critically substantiated. It is not surprising that one of the early authors, a contemporary of the modern development of comparison of law, in calling the comparison of law a science at the same time is asserting that the science of law is receiving a new method in the person of comparative science which may perform in this science a role which comparative studies had in philology.[102] This identification of the comparative science of law with method clearly characterizes the imprecise use of this concept.

Recent researchers not only actually interpret the comparison of law as a method, as did Rabel,[103] but in principle evaluate it as a method and consistently call it a method;[104] this term is increasingly squeezing out the somewhat imprecise old term "comparative science of law".

[101] Rabel, note 77 above, p. 281.

[102] Berolzheimer, note 21 above, p. 403.

[103] Rabel, note 77 above.

[104] Rauchhaupt, note 76 above, p. 153; Julius Lautner, "Die Methoden einer antik-rechtsgeschichtlicher Forschung", *Zeitschrift für vergleichende Rechtswissenschaft*, XLVII (1933), pp. 65-66; Koschaker, note 10 above, p. 97, note 1.

At the same time, the view is held that although the comparative method is used in various branches of law for various tasks, the term "comparative science of law" should be retained as a general designation for all types of the comparison of law. Individual types of comparison develop their own somewhat specific method of comparison; for them the old definition should be a collective name: comparative science of law. It indeed should be understood as a methodological concept, despite the fact that it generates the impression of a separate subject-matter and not a method. This factual limitation of the concept of the comparative science of law would be analogous to a limitation of the concept of ethnology, which, despite the verbatim meaning of the word ethnology, we understand as the science which investigates uncultured peoples of a non-European group.[105]

In reality, although the term comparative science of law is now used for one reason or another, it should be considered a designation not for a separate science, but only as an individual method of research.

## 3. COMPARATIVE METHOD DOES NOT IMPART TO STUDIES THE CHARACTER OF AUTONOMOUS SCIENCE

Notwithstanding this, some authors place special tasks on the comparative method which they hope to resolve by individual means and thereby create the impression that the comparison of law is a separate discipline. In his day Kohler suggested a program for the universal history of law which he identified with the comparative science of law.[106] Del Vecchio supported the same idea with enthusiasm, arguing it comprehensibly and convincingly.[107] Mario Rotondi (1900-1984) advanced a similar view, suggesting that a general science of law be created by constructing a comparative history of law analogous to comparative linguistics.[108] This goal

[105] Adam, "Bemerkungen zu der Abhandlung", *Zeitschrift für vergleichende Rechtswissenschaft*, XLVII (1933), p. 25.

[106] Kohler, note 29 above.

[107] Del Vecchio, note 9 above.

[108] Rotondi, note 96 above.

ultimately attracted the interest of Ernst Heymann (1870-1946)[109] and Friedrich Wilhelm von Rauchhaupt (1881-1989).[110] Other authors, such as Saleilles and Lambert, gave to the comparison of law the task of inventing universal principles for legislation and a system of universally binding law.[111]

In all these instances the character of a separate science is ascribed clearly or implicitly to the comparison of law which it already has or will have in the future. Such a setting of the matter is contrary to the aforesaid understanding of the question of whether comparison is a separate science. This view may be explained only by the fact that the tasks which individual researchers have set or are setting for the comparison of law dominate in their studies so strongly that they leave their own trace on comparison. Especially the early authors identify the method with the subject-matter of research. Kohler refers to the comparative science of law in the understanding of a universal history of law, evidently confusing the method with the subject-matter. Saleilles similarly, in proving the scientific character of comparison, assumes those tasks which he places on comparison, but not comparison itself. It was in this way that early authors interpreted the comparison of law as a science: it was a consequence of identifying it with the science, which the comparison of law should substantiate. More recent authors, such as Reiman, Rotondi, and Rabel, more cautiously than their predecessors and placing of the comparison of law the performance of a special scientific task, expect their hopes from future confirmation. In Rabel's words, only a sufficiently developed comparison of law will become the foundation of the entire science of law.[112]

Understanding the aspiration for a synthesis by which every researcher would want to complete his works, one should regard positively the constant reference of authors of comparative studies to the idea of a large synthesis of comparative law as the ultimate goal of comparison. But for the moment such a system is an

[109] Heymann, note 99 above.

[110] Rauchhaupt, note 76 above.

[111] Raymond Saleilles, "Conception et objet de la science du droit comparé", *Congres international de droit comparé, Procès-verbaux des séances et documents* (1905), I; E. Lambert, *La fonction du droit civil comparé: Les conceptions étroites ou unilatérales* (1903).

[112] Rabel, note 77 above, p. 231...

ideal which will not be rapidly achieved. Therefore, at present identification of the subject-matter of research with the method is permissible only when the subject-matter of comparative study has the character of a separate science, but in and of itself the comparative method cannot impart to these studies the character of a separate science. For example, a general science of law built on the comparative method will be a science not thanks to comparison, but only thanks to its inner characteristics. If for any reason the science of law is denied the character of a separate discipline, one cannot prove the opposite, referring to the comparative method which in this instance is the basic of research. The question of the comparative science of law will be possible to resolve positively only when in combination with the use of the comparative method it will be possible to ascertain an autonomous sphere of research in which the comparative method will be especially useful, on one hand, and on the other, this sphere will not be covered by any existing discipline.

To date the tasks noted by individual researchers, and also such general concepts, orientators for legislation, system of universal law, history of the development of law, and the like themselves, appertain to the philosophy of law, history of law, or politics of law. Basing studies of the said specific problems of law on the comparative method therefore can change nothing. Even if these studies are distinctive in method from other philosophical, historical, or political reflections, they do not acquire because of this enough autonomy to ascribe to them the character of a separate science.

For these reasons, the comparative method not only cannot impart to studies the character of a science, but in general cannot be linked with one possible purpose, because it can serve and serves all possible purposes if one succeeds in using it in studies.

## 4. AUTONOMOUS PURPOSE OF COMPARISON OF LAW

The comparative method is used in investigating law in order to achieve various tasks. Although, as has been said, the purpose of comparison does not determine the concept and essence of the comparison of law, it is not a goal in itself. Comparison has meaning when it serves a determined purpose. It imparts to scientific work the value of its results.[113]

First and foremost, the comparison of law can expand knowledge of law outside the range of the native system and provide a survey of legal relations in contemporary States. Practical reasons encourage this: international links generate the need for a knowledge of foreign law in order to resolve private-law and basically commercial matters, and at the same time inter-State relations create many problems relating to the law of nations and various treaties and conventions. One may cope with this requirements of life only when necessary foreign laws are sufficiently well-known, and this knowledge may be acquired primarily by way of comparative studies. This also concerns a knowledge of foreign systematics and foreign legal terminology. This kind of knowledge is essential in order to orient oneself in foreign legal systems.[114]

A knowledge of law is a common method of the comparison of law not connected with any other reasons. In this understanding, comparison is an autonomous study bringing respective material of different legal systems both for practice and for theory. It thus serves to help create a great synthesis of the science of law. Comparative studies of law preserve national law from partiality and stagnation, on one hand, and on the other – facilitate an easing of international relations. In this function, thereafter the comparison of law is for various legislative systems the basis for their coming together, with whose assistance the moderation of differences occurs, the mutual likening and merger of national legal systems into a universal, world legal system. In any event, this role was ascribed to the erstwhile universal Roman law by its extoller, Jhering, who expected and wished that the comparison of law would eliminate the dispersion of legislation, overcome national particularities, and in another form would lead to the universality of a legal system that Roman law created at one time, having been in force in the greater part of Europe.[115]

[113] Adam, note 67 above, p. 1; Kaden, note 14 above, p. 11.

[114] Heymann, note 99 above, p. 425.

[115] Rudolf Jhering, *Geist des römischen Rechts auf den verschiedenen Stufen seiner Entwicklung* (2d ed.; 1866), I, . 14.

And indeed, as theoretical speculation the comparison of law ascended above all systems and serves all possible purposes, and especially the universality of the science of law. Bernhöft advanced the theoretical value of the comparison of law to the forefront, asserting that the comparison of law seeks the idea of law in legal systems.[116]

## 5. COMPARISON IS AUXILIARY MEANS

Besides these general tasks, the comparison of law also has special tasks which without it would be unattainable or difficult to realize. Although for all purposes comparison has a supplementary, auxiliary character, some of them are set out as an autonomous task of comparison. The auxiliary character of the comparison of law serves only to deepen legal studies of a certain subject-matter and is subordinate to this purpose.[117] The science of law uses comparison to elicit past or present legal questions from various branches and in various aspects: for the philosophy, critique and politics of law, legislation. In this understanding, the comparison of law is an auxiliary means for further research and therefore cannot be an autonomous science.[118]

In the broad sense, the philosophy of law uses the results of the comparison of law, as do legal critique and legal politics, which derive material from the comparison of law for their own purposes. Finally, having elicited certain legal problems or pointing to the delusions, gaps, or injustice in a legal system, theory influences also this diagnostic work towards a future science of law and legislation. Therefore, one may recognize as a further indirect purpose of the comparison of law an influence on the critique and politics of law which ultimately is only an eventual motive, but never an end in itself.[119]

a) *Comparison is auxiliary means for the philosophy of law.* The value of comparison for the philosophy of law is the most complex and most controversial question. Comparison was linked with

[116] Bernhöft, note 46 above, I, p. 36; Rauchhaupt, note 76 above, p. 154.

[117] Weiss, note 11 above, p. 9.

[118] Kaden, note 14 above, p. 11.

[119] Rauchhaupt, note 76 above, p. 154.

the philosophy of law, and the early pioneers of the comparative method moved it to the forefront in their studies. Ultimately, the comparative method is indebted to the philosophical attraction for its beginning and development and from that time the comparison of law continued to be linked with the philosophy of law.

Bernhöft emphasized that the comparison of law provided the foundation for the scientific philosophy of law[120] because it seeks the idea of law in legal systems.[121] During the dominance of the school of natural law and of the Historical School, studies were confined to Roman and German law and therefore there were no grounds for the philosophical construction of law, just as linguistics does not emerge from the studies of two languages. Only the comparison of law will provide, in the author's view, materials for philosophical conclusions.[122]

For Kohler, the philosophy of law, the universal history of law, and the comparative science of law are closely intertwined. In his view, only the universal history of law, which he identified with the comparative science of law, can show what influence law has on culture, how it conditions the existence of a people, and how it further cultural development. Only on this basis can the philosophy of law indicate what role law has played in the theological development of the world, what significance it has in various cultural conditions, and how law is one of the factors of the realization of the purpose of mankind. Without a universal history of law, in Kohler's opinion, there is no philosophy of law.[123]

Attracted by the comparative method, Post went farther. Pursuant to this nature-descriptive approach, he believed the role of philosophical speculation in general to be completed in the face of results of the comparative science of law, which should assume the previous role of the philosophy of law.[124]

Fritz Berolzheimer (1869-1920) assessed the role of the comparison of law for the philosophy of law with greater skepticism. He asserted that although the comparative science

[120] Bernhöft, note 46 above, p. 3.

[121] Ibid., p. 36.

[122] Ibid., p. 2.

[123] Kohler, note 29 above, p. 14.

[124] Post, *Über die Aufgaben einer allgemeinen Rechtswissenschaft* (1891), p. 2.

of law in ethnological studies was merely an auxiliary science, individual researchers such as Post and Kohler had processed material achieved by the comparative method also philosophically. The scientific comparison of law was not directed (in any event, in priority) towards practical conclusions from comparison, but merely sought theoretical cognition and conceptual scope for the basic concepts of law. For these reasons, the comparison of law has been developed increasingly systematically and universally, and therefore has been coming closer to the philosophy of law. In the comparison of law, philosophy and the history of law received a new method of research, but one cannot expect from it the resolution of all the basic problems. For example, such major questions as the origin of State and law cannot be studied by means of the comparison of law, because it accepts as the existing law and State as given and compares them as finished objects.[125]

No doubt the comparison of law may deepen the investigation of the essence of legal institutions, but it is useless to expect all the success of the philosophy of law from the comparative science of law.[126]

Analogously to these observations, Del Vecchio did not link the philosophy of law so closely with the comparison of law. In his view, the comparative science of law, having extracted empirical material, rests on certain philosophical grounds. The comparison of law creates a bridge between the science of law and the philosophy of law: on one hand – derives basic principles and concepts from philosophy; and on the other – provide the philosophy of law with its conclusions for the verification of its criteria. The idea of law, which following Del Vecchio can be extracted from pure reason, does not replace and does not exclude knowledge of empirical legal phenomena that may be obtained by a comparison of legal provisions from all times and peoples. Both approaches to research seek the same thing and complement one another. The comparative-universal science of law reconstructs the idea of law on the basis of empirical, historical material, and this idea comes as a closed whole from pure reason.[127]

[125] Berolzheimer, note 21 above, p. 403.

[126] Ibid., p. 20.

[127] Del Vecchio, note 9 above, pp. 406-408.

Assessing the comparative methods from the standpoint of Kant's theory of cognition, Felix Holldack (1880-1944) rejects in general its capacity to cognize the essence of legal phenomena. In fact, the comparative method, in Holldack's view, in accepting as a whole the basic unity of legal phenomena which human nature or reason creates analogously in all times and all peoples, comes in its metaphysics closer to philosophy; however, it therefore provides hypotheses instead of truth. The abstractions of comparison are only true when they are confirmed in real law. Outside this, norms of law may be cognized only having determined their relation to a scheme of values, and this is not part of the program of comparison.[128]

Binder also does not see the significance of the comparison of law for philosophy. Together with positive law, in Binder's opinion, it is subordinate to the idea of law and should identify the relation to it of the laws to be compared.[129]

Rabel cautiously ascribed to the comparison of law a certain role in the philosophy of law. He singled out in the comparison of law a separate type of general-legal comparison which is adjacent to the philosophy of law. To this he relegated all that is juridical in the philosophy of law.[130] He fully recognizes the auxiliary significance of comparison for theory. The comparison of law in his view enlivens the consideration by impulses and by the enrichment of problems. It eliminates gossip and clarifies concepts. The comparison of law insists on objective thought.[131] It teaches to search for the basic idea outside definition and a more advisable formalization along with the existing form of an institution. Comparison also by means of research of possible changes, transformations, and linkages creates an appreciation of subtleties and nuances.[132]

Heymann is among the recent authors to more boldly evaluate the role of the comparison of law for the philosophy of law. He is persuaded that only from comparative studies of law can one

128 Felix Holldack, *Grenzen der Erkenntnis ausländischen Rechts* (1919), pp. 68-69.

129 Binder, note 41 above, p. 962.

130 Rabel, note 77 above, p. 281.

131 Ibid., p. 285.

132 Ibid., p. 286.

obtain grounds for philosophical conclusions. Generally-binding assertions can be suggested only when an empirical unity becomes evident and at the same time the differentiation of legal phenomena in the world. The relative analogousness of different systems truly offers grounds for philosophical analysis when investigating unique or a few legal orders; however, philosophical works are not satisfied by these approximately true results and will seek an expansion of the base of their cognition. In any event, comparison of law will strengthen the understanding of the essence of legal phenomena.[133]

Karl Otto Petraschek (1876-1950) evaluated the relation of comparison to the idea of law similarly as Binder. In Petraschek's view, the similarities affirmed by comparison do not prove that the objects being compared are just. This may be judged by a verification made not from the standpoint of limited purposes, but only by proceeding from the higher position of the idea of law.[134] The idea of law based on a concept of morality and security is pursued variously among different peoples at different times, and positive law changes and develops as social relations change. The idea of law, however, as before remains the leading purpose and criterion for evaluation in order to direct the comparison of law.[135]

As is evident from the foregoing, an evaluation of the value of the comparison of law for philosophy varies from the complete identification thereof (Post) to complete denial (Holldack) of the capacity of comparison to provide objective absolute cognition. Between these two extremes views are divided and will be for a long time. All the differences of views in philosophy from materialism and positivism to idealism with all the branch Hegelian and Kantian schools are reflected in the evaluation of the value of the comparison of law for the philosophy of law. It is evident that contradictory views on the cognitive value of the comparative method will exist so long as the differences of ideas quoted are not reconciled within the philosophy itself.

The faith of the pioneers of comparison such as Post and Kohler in its ability to give philosophical results was typical. This is how the yearning for a synthesis of phenomena manifested itself in

[133] Heymann, note 99 above, p. 425.

[134] Petraschek, note 79 above, p. 672.

[135] Petraschek, *System der Rechtsphilosophie* (1932), pp. 315-316.

the epoch of the antiquarian morass of details of the Historical School. The disappointment with regard to the results of a science built on analysis led researchers to seek greater syntheses, to construct integral syntheses which would elucidate the essence of phenomena. Therefore, in the broad surveys of the universal history of law built with the assistance of the comparative method they saw a path on which the essence of legal phenomena might be cognized.

But their contemporaries evaluated this faith with skepticism, believing that they overestimated the value of the comparative method for the philosophy of law.[136] The more so, because it relied on examples of the nature-descriptive method. Researchers attempted to identify the essence of law, comparing positive laws by analogy to that which a naturalist designated as the essence of a mammal or a tree: by the comparison of indicia and the determination of differences.[137]

This purely naturalist approach researchers later cast aside. They began to be more careful in ascribing the significance of comparison for philosophy, asserting merely the value on the whole for the material itself which the comparison of law gives to the philosophy of law. Indeed, abstracted from purely philosophical speculations, comparison offers a deep view into the essence of legal phenomena and enables the immutable and the eternal to be seen through changeable forms of positive law.

b) *Comparison as auxiliary means for critique, policy, and legislation.* Unlike the evaluation of the philosophical value of the comparison of law, the evaluation of its value for critique and for the politics of law is unequivocally positive. The comparison of law leads from nature to critique and to the politics of law. In order to evaluate law, one must contrast it with other possible variants of decisions and then the Hegelian view – all that exists is reasonable – will be seen in its true light. Comparison elicits how much is obsolete, arbitrary, premature, and erroneous concealed by the centuries through all legislation.[138] The comparison of law also increases the number of possible solutions of problems for the politics of law. Existing decisions beckon towards an imitation of foreign law. Often it is

[136] Berolzheimer, note 21 above, p. 20.

[137] Ibid., p. 27.

[138] Rabel, note 77 above, p. 286.

not thought out and occurs spontaneously and accidentally. Only the scientific comparison of law ensures a reasonable reception which is not allowed as a result of the fact that all contemporary legislation is built on models and investigation of the old world.[139]

Contemporary authors evaluate the role of comparison for legislation in this way. But Bernhöft understood that the comparison of law should play a large role in a question then topical in Germany of the codification of law. The comparative method then faced the task of the final demise of Roman and German law and, drawing upon models of other foreign law, providing ideas for the planned code.[140]

Those authors who decisively reject the capacity of the comparative method to achieve absolute cognition even emphasize the prominent auxiliary role of comparison for legislation. Holldack recognizes the auxiliary role of comparison in the search for a better law. The comparative method, in his view, already justifies itself in determining to what extent the laws to be compared are consistent with generally-recognized values of culture. Legal prescriptions must be created consistently with these values as a means of preserving and protecting ideals, and from this standpoint law may be the subject-matter of comparison usefully. The comparison of law also may elicit that identical social motives and international links that facilitate the emergence of identical or similar prescriptions in different legal systems find advisable decisions in rare instances. The affirmation of analogy and differences on its own is an indicator how legal provisions in comparable laws are correct with respect to the ideals of culture.[141]

Binder evaluates the role of comparison for legislation positively as well. In his view, the comparison of law should – together with consideration of the relation of the laws to be compared to the ideas of law – consider their relation to empirical goals which law should undertake with the assistance of its institutions, having regard to typical conditions of peoples manifesting their individuality in law. The comparison of law thus becomes a complex process in which the empirical task of an individual legal institution should be identified. In comparing, for example, the German and the

[139] Ibid., p. 287.

[140] Bernhöft, note 46 above, p. 3.

[141] Holldack, note 128 above, p. 73.

French law of mortgage, one may from the standpoint of security given under one or the other place the German higher. One cannot conclude from this, however, that the German provisions should be introduced everywhere. Mortgage registers may be kept only where cadaster registers have been fully introduced, and where, for example, in the Balkan countries these do not exist, having regard to the conditions, one may consider to be advisable only an imperfect mortgage law with lower security. The same is so for the comparison of different criminal laws. In comparative studies one can never confine oneself to the question of whether legal prescriptions correspond to the idea of law and whether they perform an abstract purpose of the criminal law; it is necessary to investigate whether a concrete people has matured in its state of culture and morality to determined positions or not.[142]

With this reservation, a useful and important task of the comparison of law is to influence legislation, to orient how individual peoples and States have resolved analogous legal questions and what practical experience they have with these decisions. By way of comparison one may verify whether a certain decision in a foreign system corresponds to the conditions and requirements of one's own people, or whether own provisions perform their role better than foreign models. Therefore, it would be mistaken to adhere in legislation blindly to trends of development and equate to "types of development" when law should be a regulator of vital relations of a people cultivated throughout history – and not the application of abstract benchmarks identical for all countries and moralities. One should take from foreign provisions only those which can be harmonized with the native legal system and will be responsive to the actual vital requirements better than traditional institutions. The task of comparative science to make possible by its studies the proper choice and organic mastery of objectively justified foreign models.[143]

The publishers and authors of the large and solid Dictionary of Comparative Law[144] understood the role of the comparison of law in this way. In the Introduction, they formulate as the task of a comparative-legal dictionary: to influence the development of the science of law and practical legislative improvements. Similarly,

[142] Binder, note 41 above, p. 962.

[143] Ibid., p. 963.

[144] Schlegelberger, note 88 above.

just as at one time comparative studies of German particular law removed it from isolation and connected with the world development of science, so too in the present period of closed codifications the comparison of law may eliminate the danger of the ossification of law, which is an undesirable consequence of great systems with their cult of written law. The comparison of law looks forward, expanding the horizon, and preserves fresh a consciousness of the tasks inherent in law.

The comparison of law probably conceals certain dangers: unhealthy unification, premature erosion of national distinctiveness, inappropriate acceleration of changes which should mature slowly and organically. With, however, the cautious application of the comparative method, one may avoid these dangers. In any event, the benefit which the comparison of law may bring to the development of legislation enables one to proceed even given the said possible dangers.[145]

Besides the impact on legislation, the comparison of law greatly assists historical studies.[146] It has been especially successful in the reconstruction of the survivals of old law which have come down to us.[147] The comparison of law also has significance for interpretation within systems which, such as the Italian, enable the general conclusions of science to be used in the absence of a positive prescription.[148]

In evaluating as a whole the tasks which the comparative method faces, it should be emphasized that practical moments basically impart the tone at present to comparative studies. One may note the leap forward of interest in our day in the historical, philosophical, and theoretical spheres which were models in earlier comparison with vital practical issues.[149] In tandem with those, attempts were abandoned to create a large system of the comparative science of law, and even if someone advanced this idea, he was aware that it might be realized in the far future after undertaking great preparatory work. The significance of

145 Ibid., I, pp. iii-iv.

146 Lautner, note 11 above, p. 65.

147 Del Vecchio, note 9 above, p. 231; Del Vecchio, note 6 above, p. 24.

148 Rotondi, note 96 above, p. 18.

149 Adam, note 65 above, pp. 9-10.

the comparison of law, however, for the theory and philosophy of law is preserved, to be sure, within more modest limits than previously. It is, instead, built on more critical grounds. For all this, the significance of comparative studies for theory and practice is growing and one may suppose that the tasks of the comparative method in law are far from exhausted.

# Chapter V. Demarcation of Comparison of Law

1. Demarcation from Sociology; 2. Demarcation from Ethnology; 3. Demarcation from Philosophy

As noted above, the comparative method is engaged in the comparative processing of a large number of laws. The comparison of law, however, is not the sole branch of the science of law which is engaged with a large number of legal orders. Sociology, ethnology, and philosophy also consider legal phenomena on the basis of a multiplicity of legal systems of different peoples and times and rest their assertions on the results of these studies. Therefore, one must determine the limits distinguishing the comparison of law from the said branches.

## 1. DEMARCATION FROM SOCIOLOGY

The comparison of law and the sociology of law clearly differ if the definition of the comparison of law set out in the preceding chapters is accepted.

The sociology of law is interested in the living aspect of law; it attempts to determine the significance and the purpose of law in life. Sociology seeks the beginning of law and the reasons for and societal laws of its development. The comparison of law has as its task to compare the norms of different systems and this, speaking concisely, exhausts its role. It determines whether and to what extent the objects to be compared are similar, close, or different, from time to time attempting to create a synthesis on the basis of the results of these comparisons. Basically, these differences separate both branches, and although even sociology uses the comparative method of research, it is not capable of resolving its tasks with the assistance only of the comparison of law. As a social phenomenon, law depends of many types of factors (political, economic, psychological, and so on) which are not determined with the assistance of the comparison of law.[150]

On the other hand, comparison does not want to be satisfied only with comparing, and this means the collection of comparative material, but often researchers aspire, using the comparative method, to a synthesis of the results of comparison. They more than once have determined tasks in comparison which distinctly transcended the strict frameworks of comparison in the understanding of a method. Often it was emphasized that comparison is a perfect means for the cognition of the essence of legal phenomena, the principles and changes thereof, their linkage with the life as a whole and the tasks thereof. There was a time, as noted above, when the interests of this kind belonged to sociology. It is clear that, in fact, there are serious overlaps between sociology and comparison.

Taking this fact into account, however, the predominant opinion considers comparison and sociology to be concepts which do not cover one another, although views differ as to their correlation. Some authors believe the comparison of law to be an auxiliary science of the sociology of law. Others, on the contrary, consider sociology to be an auxiliary science for the comparison of law. This controversial issue is not resolved in the broader dimension of the relation of sociology to the science of law in general.[151]

A certain number of authors, despite the views cited, go farther in the direction of eroding the distinctions between sociology and comparison and identify sociology with the comparison of law, leaving to comparison the task of explaining the beginning, reasons for changes, and borrowing of legal norms and, consequently, specifying the role of comparison of legal norms consistently with the tasks of sociology.

The sociological trends of comparison become understandable if one takes into account that the sociological orientation of research became in its day an impetus for the emergence of the comparative method of investigating law. The works of Post were influenced by the French sociological school of Comte.[152] Kohler also planned

[150] Kaden, note 14 above, p. 13.

[151] Emge, note 95 above, p. 49.

[152] Binder, note 41 above, p. 946.

to construct a universal history of law with the assistance of the comparative method using an extensive sociological foundation.[153]

Ultimately, each attempt to represent a universal system of law with the assistance of the comparative method cut across the domain of sociology. The comparative analysis of legal phenomena could not be abstracted from an investigation of the reasons for their emergence and their link with other social facts.

As noted, however, some considered the science of law specially empowered to engage in sociological investigations of legal phenomena. Del Vecchio believed that the fact that investigations of law on a universal basis had not been developed in the science of law was a consequence but also a reason for such studies not being planned by the science of law, but only sociology. In his view, sociology engages in the collection of facts which should belong to the comparative science of law, but which were taken from the science of law because of a narrow understanding of the limits of law. The institutions and phenomena of social life which elicit the undoubted indicia of law remained outside the official limits of the science of law only because they belong to primitive systems of tribes or peoples of little or different culture. Sociology, which in the absence of systematics chaotically accumulates facts, engaged in such studies.[154]

Petraschek pointed to the close link between comparison and sociology. Comparative studies are conditioned by the properties of the laws to be compared which emanate from social circumstances. They investigate various forms and changes of legal phenomena in the aspect of space, seeking differences in various internal and external conditions of that time. For this reason, the comparison of law is orientated towards sociology, actually performing its tasks in the field of law.[155]

Rotondi clearly ascribed sociological tasks to the comparison of law. In his view, law should be investigated not only by the systematic processing of norms as regulators in human relations, but also as a natural phenomenon of social life. Just as a normative idea of law, the existence of law as a social phenomenon may

[153] Kohler, note 29 above.

[154] Del Vecchio, note 9 above, p. 229.

[155] Petraschek, note 79 above, p. 671.

be traced.[156] It follows that laws should be traced which guide the development of law. The method of investigating these laws has the same relation to dogmatic as comparative linguistics to grammar, and consequently, should be simultaneously a historical and comparative science.[157]

Bernhöft defined and justified the tasks of comparison similarly. In his view, the comparative science of law may perform its task only when it finds, just as linguistics, general laws of the development of law which apply to the history of individual nations. Before the emergence of the comparative school of law, the development and significance of individual institutions were investigated only within a single system.[158] The comparative science of law set for itself the task of extending these studies to systems of various peoples and to seeking among them analogies and transfers of legal thought. Such an expansion of legal studies, in his view, promised a useful result – because jurisprudence was ready to perform such tasks. Earlier studies of law within national limits led to the complete command not only of national legal systems and, in general, legal problematic, but also created a method of research, the grounds of which might be models when expanding studies to different national laws.[159]

As we see, the tasks now being put to comparison do not differ from the formulations of its pioneers, and they will not differ from this standpoint so long as we refer to the comparison of law, and not to the comparative method. As noted above, the expressive or actual identification of comparison with sociology begins when comparison acquires the significance of a separate science similar to comparative linguistics. Then, naturally, its role is not exhausted only by the ascertainment of differences and similarities. In an attempt to find the laws of societal development and causality, researchers undertake studies of the living aspect of law, and comparison becomes a sociological study in the field of law.

Therefore, one must accept that the comparison of law is within the competence of sociology, from which it has no clear boundaries so long as the future comparative science of law does not become

156 Rotondi, note 96 above, p. 14.

157 Ibid., p. 15.

158 Bernhöft, note 46 above, p. 4.

159 Ibid., p. 5.

a separate discipline. Then one might determine the boundaries so that sociology would use the general results of comparative law for its purposes, for in its own sphere legal material in its universal aspect is autonomously processed.

Until then, practice will continue to mix all approaches, seeking by all means to come to a comprehensive cognition of phenomena. This approach characterizes, for example, the works of Karl Alois Haff (1879-1955), who clearly bases his studies on comparison in parallel with sociological quests. In his view, comparative law, which shows the divergence and similarity of legal norms, should not be satisfied merely with the discovery of similarities and differences, but should together with psychology and sociology identify the typical and formulate generally-binding laws for the creation of law. It is thus possible to avoid the tedious repetitions of similarities so often encountered in comparative, dogmatic, and historical works. The great similarities of sources of law of peoples geographically and in time remote from one another cannot be understood from simple comparison, but must be reduced to profound grounds, such as the laws of societal development of the mental and legal attitude towards identical or similar conditions.[160] Pursuant to these considerations, one should accept that comparison can never be confined to purely formal and methods limits, but will automatically touch upon sociological and philosophical issues such as the unity of the human character, natural law, general laws of the creation of law, and so on.

## 2. DEMARCATION FROM ETHNOLOGY

The difficulties similar to those encountered in demarcating the comparison of law from sociology we also find in demarcating it from ethnological studies. Just as in demarcating the comparative method from sociology, there is no complexity when we have in view that comparison is a method of research. Then the tasks of comparison are exhausted by finding differences and similarities in the phenomena of law being studied, in this case the legal phenomena appertaining to ethnology. On the other hand, a comparative study of ethnological law obviously is within – if reference is made to the bedrock of research – the domain of

[160] Karl Haff, *Institutionen des Deutschen Privatrechts auf vergleichender und soziologischer Grundlage, zugleich Einführung ins Bürgerliche Recht* (1927), I, p. 4.

ethnology, which is engaged with the study of all manifestations of the life of a people outside European culture.[161] Thus, the question arises first and foremost as to whether comparative research of ethnological law belongs to the field of ethnology or to the science of law.

Researchers of the past had put the question of whether comparative studies should encompass only legal phenomena or to expand them to customs which had not developed into legal institutions. Bernhöft in his programmatic article in the *Zeitschrift fur vergleichende Rechtswissenschaft* had excluded customs from consideration by the comparative method.[162] Kohler, who had become the editor of the said *Zeitschrift*, introduced studies of the customary law of primitive peoples despite Bernhöft's position. Thus, the subject-matter of the ethnological study of law which uses the comparative method became in equal degree the living phenomena of primitive or ancient peoples and legal norms which organize these phenomena.[163] The ethnological studies of law thus penetrate deeply into ethnology and therefore might be called legal ethnology from the standpoint of ethnology. Giuseppe Mazzarella (1868-1958) expressly called his works on ancient Hindu law studies in legal ethnology.[164] On the other hand, the view which considers the ethnological comparison of law to be part of the science of law which only extracts material from ethnology for research should be considered to be correct.[165] The science of law gave to ethnological law its scientific [...], and first and foremost legal concepts and terminology. For these reasons, jurists thereafter would be the pioneers of the ethnological study of law.[166] However, as Kohler constantly pointed out, ethnological studies of law should be linked to changes of culture and especially take religion into account.[167]

161 Max Schmidt, "Die Bedeutung der vergleichenden Rechtswissenschaft für die Ethnologie", *Zeitschrift für vergleichende Rechtswissenschaft*, XXXVII (1920), p. 359.

162 Bernhöft, note 46 above, p. 37.

163 Schmidt, note 161 above, p. 360.

164 Giuseppe Mazzarella, *Studi di Etnologia Giuridica: Teoria etnologica del matrimonio ambiliano* (1903), p. 437.

165 Adam, note 67 above, p. 19.

166 Ibid., p. 20.

167 Ibid., p. 21.

Ethnological studies of law penetrate deeply into the domain of sociology. This is understandable if one takes into account that ethnological jurisprudence, especially as developed by Post, draws upon, on one hand, the Comte sociological school and, on the other, on the historiosophical ideas of Hegel. The roots of ethnological-comparative studies of law affect their sociological orientation, and it is not surprising that Post determined for them the task of tracing the ethnic and social causes of legal phenomena.[168] Given that ethnological-comparative studies penetrate so deeply into sociology, all the reflections relating to establishing limits between the comparison of law and sociology become topical. The ethnological comparison of law contains, in particular, all the ambiguities concerning the limits between the comparison of law and the sociology of law.

The fact that ethnological jurisprudence uses the comparative method in a unilateral direction, against the nature of the comparison of law, which cannot be reduced to a single task, does not clarify the situation. Ethnological jurisprudence of a particular type has devoted its attention not exclusively to primitive peoples, but it compared their legal relations chiefly because the researchers believed that in this comparison they have a new source for cognition of the ancient, pre-historical past, which may be reconstructed only indirectly, with the assistance of such comparison, because of large gaps in the sources of law of times long past.[169]

In this understanding, ethnological studies of law would have been in fact merely part of the history of law, only the subject-matter of the studies being distinct. The difference between them would be that ethnological studies of law engaged with ethnological material especially, that is, the law of primitive peoples, whereas the history of law is concerned with the entire development of law. In either instance, in fact, comparison is used equally as a method of research not capable in and of itself to provide a separate character to any part of science and to separate one part from the other. In our case as well, the comparative method cannot impart autonomy to ethnological law.

[168] Post, note 59 above, I, p. 7.

[169] Post, *Bausteine für eine allgemeine Rechtswissenschaft auf vergleichend-ethnologischer Basis* (1880), p. 13; Post, *Einleitung in das Studium der ethnologischen Jurisprudenz* (1886), p. 14.

Therefore, Post's view should be considered to be mistaken, for he contrasted the comparative method of the ethnological science of law to the Historical School, believing that it imparts to ethnological studies a separate trace, so that one may use comparison in ethnological studies even where historical phenomena are not interconnected, whereas historical studies are confined by the assertion of historical mutual relations of phenomena.[170] Newer views understand ethnological studies of law as a part of the history of law, and at the same time as part of the general history of culture. Ethnological law differs from them not by a separate method of research, but only by the designated bedrock of research,[171] because the comparative method is also used in other spheres of the research of law, notably in historical studies.[172]

It is evident from the foregoing that there is no difficulty in determining the differences between the comparison of law and ethnology if comparison is understood as a method. Difficulties arise if a separate role is ascribed to comparison as an autonomous science. One should take into account all the views concerning the question and acknowledge once again that the tendency to understand comparative studies as something more than a method is very strong. Even Erich-Hans Kaden (1898-1973) has surrendered to it, who in principle took the view that comparison is a method. He believed it to be correct, however, to remove comparative-ethnographic studies of law from the comparison of law, referring (from other views, completely correctly) to the fact that it relates to the history of law, especially to ethnology, and by its extensive embrace is a link in the universal history of culture.[173]

In this understanding of the issue, he committed an obvious error. The undisputed fact that ethnological-comparative studies of law are historical research of the most ancient period of mankind cannot obscure another fact that they use primarily the comparative method. Comparative-ethnological studies are undoubtedly the comparison of law. They are not so only if the comparison of law is understood as a separate science. In this

170 Post, note 169 above (1886), p. 2.

171 Trimborn, note 8 above, p. 420.

172 Lautner, note 11 above, p. 65.

173 Kaden, note 14 above, p. 19.

event it would indeed be necessary for ethnological law to be excluded from such a science because it has too many indicia of the history of law and ethnology. In view of the fact, however, that the comparison of law is not considered to be an autonomous science, but merely a method, there is no need to exclude ethnological law from the operation of the comparative method, the more so because it has justified itself in the ethnological studies of law. The fact that Kaden committed this kind of mistake should be ascribed, as already noted, to the suggestion that the comparison of law is a separate discipline, to which he surrendered for a minute or to an ordinary error in terminology.

No material moments determine the differences between the comparison of law and ethnological-comparative studies, for there are no material contiguous lines between them: comparison is a method, ethnological law is part of science. Therefore, the argument does not work as a distinguishing moment that the object of research of both are different, for the comparison of law is engaged with legal norms, whereas the ethnological science of law is engaged with peoples whose customs have not crystallized into legal forms,[174] or customs are researched which were merely parts of the religion and culture of tribes. That is a distinctive argument ... only when the concept of law is defined very narrowly, and this is wrong when reference is made to primitive peoples in whom legal phenomena should be sought in customs, morality, rites, and beliefs.[175]

Nor can distinguishing evidence be sought between both concepts in the fact that there are many gaps in the law of primitive peoples; it is fragmentary, and therefore cannot be the subject-matter of scientific analysis or construction.[176] The history of Roman legislation is contrary to such an assertion, which until the time of Justinian was also fragmentary. Ultimately, both contemporary German or French law have gaps; however, they all can be the object of scientific studies and comparison may be used in all of them as a method of research.[177]

174 Bernhöft, note 46 above, p. 37.

175 Kohler, *Lehrbuch der Rechtsphilosophie* (1909), p. 87; Schmidt, note 161 above, pp. 359-360; Trimborn, note 8 above, p. 417.

176 Rotondi, note 96 above, p. 6.

177 Heinrich Stoll, review of M. Rotondi, *Studi di diritto privato italiano e straniero, in Archiv für die civilistische Praxis,* XIV (1931), p. 367; Kaden, note 14 above, p. 14.

## 3. DEMARCATION FROM PHILOSOPHY

All the reflections of principle relating to the demarcation of comparison of law from sociology and ethnology are found ... if one engages in the demarcation of the comparison of law from philosophy. The precise boundary which separates comparison as a method from philosophy as a separate discipline is eroded, as in the case of sociology and ethnology, at once if one ascribes to comparison a separate philosophical task.

Both concepts are readily distinguished by the definition of each. The philosophy of law has as it purpose the investigation of the concept of law and the idea of law. The comparison of law has the task to compare the legal norms of different systems. In practice, however, the direct delimitation according to these definitions is impossible because all spheres in practice have points of juncture which erode and make a clear boundary doubtful.

The philosophy of law especially depends, entirely naturally, in its philosophical abstractions on positive systems of law because it derives the bedrock for its concepts and deductions in them; to a greater extent, for methodological reasons, the comparison of law also depends upon legal systems in which objects for comparison are sought. At present, the comparison of law is directed more towards positive law, whereas the philosophy of law is distinctly drawn towards the sphere of abstraction. However, how should clear boundaries be determined for abstraction in the comparison of law, when it aspires to create generally-binding concepts by its own means? For these reasons, the boundary between the philosophy of law and the comparison of law remains unclear.[178] The sole benchmark between the comparison of law and philosophy would be that comparison by its nature is connected more with the concrete bedrock of its research, whereas the philosophy of law may be to a greater degree abstracted from any positive norms of law.[179]

The question of the value of generally-binding concepts which the comparison of law attempts to ascertain on the basis of the results of the comparison of legal orders complicates the matter even more. The question is as follows: insofar as the legal reality

[178] Rabel, "Das Problem der Qualifikation", *Zeitschrift für ausländischen und internationales Privatrecht*, V (1931), p. 256.

[179] Rauchhaupt, note 76 above, p. 155.

investigated with the assistance of the comparative method is built on generally-binding concepts, which of these should comparison apprehend and process? Because the comparison of law affirms something on the basis of the comparison of processed material of positive law, and the philosophy of law operates on the basis of its own peculiar methods. In this connection, one cannot equalize between the comparison and the philosophy of law even when comparison undertakes to resolve philosophical questions.[180]

In both instances the value of empirical material is doubtful for philosophical research. Numerous authors have pointed to this, but on the other hand others, no less numerous, have contrasted this who adhere to the opposite view. In principle, the question of calling the comparison of law to resolve philosophical questions depends upon the position of the theory of cognition and in principle cannot be resolved by the theory of comparison. Leaving aside the basic question of the competence of comparison in philosophical studies, which may be practically resolved by the finally created science of comparative law first and foremost by its positive comprehension of this bedrock, it is appropriate to assert than at the moment the matter of the mutual relation between the comparison of law and the philosophy of law is not resolved.

In general it does not exist if the comparison of law is understood as a method of research which has no autonomy in the science of law, is merely an auxiliary means for research. In this aspect, comparison compares, and philosophy draws conclusions.

[180] Kaden, note 14 above, p. 15.

# Chapter VI. Types of Comparison of Law

1. Comparison within One System and between Different Systems. 2. Ethnological and Dogmatic Comparison. 3. Genetic and Historical Comparison

## 1. COMPARISON WITHIN ONE SYSTEM AND BETWEEN DIFFERENT SYSTEMS

Several special types of comparison have been developed during the use of the comparative method. In addition, one may divide comparison into various groups, depending upon the criteria for division. First and foremost, the comparison is possible of the legal norms of one State and the norms of completely different States.

Within a single State norms are contrasted for their inherent divergences. These might be compared: from the historical standpoint – previously applied and presently applied law; from the territorial standpoint – law of the country and colonial law; from the material standpoint: public and private or general individual branches – constitutional and administrative, or trade and civil law; finally, from the formal standpoint – written and unwritten, proclaimed and customary, and so on. In such contrasting differences may be more indicated than similarities found.

Proceeding initially from the indication of similarities in legal institutions such as representation in parliament and in agencies of self-government, or mortgage and land credit, or, for example, a bill of exchange and a cheque, one might also indicate divergences and differences more clearly. Comparison of this type gives a good view of the essence of individual institutions and cognition of their separate structure and functions.

However, comparison within a legal system has both theoretical significance and practical value, especially when one speaks about a synthesis of particular laws. Bernhöft pointed to this back in 1878 and consequently at a time when the issue of the codification of law was topical in Germany, which was to finalize the merger of Roman and German law. Because the external and internal reception of Roman law in Germany did not occur at the same time. The organic adaptation of Roman law to German relations, the introduction therein of German concepts, and the mixing in general of both laws began after the formal reception of Roman law in Germany. The science of law in Germany brought both systems closer and over time adapted Roman law to German concepts and customs, introducing the German mentality through the interpretation of Roman sources. In the process of adaptation, certain unsuitable Roman institutes were cast aside, some gaps were filled by practice, but the process of unification was not completed; the law which operated in Germany did not become a unified product.

The codification of law planned in Germany was at the time of the rise of the comparative school to finally combine both laws. Therefore, comparative studies of all possible legal systems were very topical then in Germany. The verification especially of similarities and differences between German and Roman law, and the review of other foreign law in order to take useful legal provisions and avoid foreign mistakes might and did offer a wealth of ideas for the planned undertaking.[181]

Various States pursued the internal comparison of particular or regional laws. After the First World War, Polish jurists, among others, sought to unify regional law through comparison. Indeed, in the Poland created by the Versailles system three individual legal orders were compared which Poland received as a legacy; but within Poland the were understood as regional law. Although the simultaneous existence inn all branches of various laws in individual regions of a single State was from the standpoint of the unity of the legal order unbearable, codification proceeded slowly by means of comparison with the struggle of jurists of all three systems for the norms to which they were accustomed. Only comparison which showed the similarities and differences of the three systems could lead to a certain synthesis and compromise and gradually to the unification of law.

[181] Bernhöft, note 46 above, pp. 3-4.

As is evident from the foregoing, comparison within the State may sometimes have great significance and be interpreted to great benefit. However, the special assignment is to study comparatively identical or analogous subject-matter of different foreign legal systems in various branches of law.

In practice, among all the laws which are foreign for one another the object of comparison is especially the law of States having political and economic influence on a world scale. In the real mutual relations between modern States comparative lawyers discover in the view of some (Del Vecchio, Rauchhaupt) a certain trend towards mutual adaptation, an ideal of which could be the codification of the most important branches of law following the example of the Napoleonic codifications.[182] Only English law and the law which owes its origin thereto is not surrendering to this trend. But for it, to the States whose law shows an inclination to universal likening are the European States, in America the Romanic members of the Pan American Union, and in Africa and Asia individual sovereign States which are members of the community of nations. Australia, being a member of the British Commonwealth of Nations, is among the isolationist Anglo-Saxon group.

Despite the large number of States, the universal trend in law, in Rauchhaupt's view, is facilitated by the fact that the law which regulates relations in the world emanates from a few sources approximate to one another. The majority of legal systems reflect the hue of the law of European States or States, such as in North and South America, or the Near and Far East, and draw upon its culture, including legal principles, to a greater or lesser degree also from Europe. Although one may receive with skepticism the assertions of the process of mutual likening of different legal systems, it is beyond doubt that contemporary comparison is engaged with the law of States of European culture which, as written or customary law, has recognized binding force and by its content and formalization is constantly demonstrating its stability. Comparative studies of these laws have advanced to the forefront.[183]

[182] Rauchhaupt, note 76 above, p. 150.

[183] Ibid., p. 151.

## 2. ETHNOLOGICAL AND DOGMATIC COMPARISON

This occurs, *inter alia,* because codified material law is the most accessible material for comparison. The comparison of this law is called dogmatic or systematic. Juxtaposed to it is ethnological comparison of law or, more accurately, the comparison of ethnological law.

This was the most venerable and early of all developed comparison. Sometimes it is even understood as a type of comparison in general. But in reality the comparative method now has more comprehensive application. From the historical standpoint, ethnological comparison of law actually gave impetus to the emergence of the "comparative science of law" in general. Thus, the beginning of contemporary comparative law is linked with the emergence of an ethnological-comparative work by Johann Bachofen, *Das Mütterrecht* (1861).

Ethnological comparison of may be considered to be pra-model comparison in general, although in the contemporary understanding it is merely one type of comparison of law. It is engaged with the legal relations of primitive, uncultured tribes or other ancient moribund and insignificant peoples on the basis of materials collected by ethnology. In addition to notions and contrasts of old customs and morality relating to the pra-beginning of law, ethnological comparison also is engaged with identifying the basic questions of the pra-history of law: for example, the emergence of law in general, the relation of law to religion, the primacy of the maternal or paternal law in primeval society, the emergence of the law of ownership of tribes, the development of private ownership, and so on.

By this orientation to the most ancient past, ethnological comparison differs from contemporary, which is concerned solely with recent law and is under dogmatism and systematics. The difference between dogmatic and ethnological comparisons is most characterized by the development of the comparative method.

Unlike ethnological comparison, dogmatic comparison compares the law of different States which, although sometimes not autonomous and sovereign, have a contemporary civilized law. Moreover, ethnological research of law encompasses only customs described by ethnology, often of subjected peoples who are very backward compared with the law of the States by which they are ruled.[184]

It is evident that such primitive laws of uncultured or dying out tribes or peoples and the contemporary cultured laws of States which arose on their territories cannot be contrasted and compared. They do not have any common foundations, which the theory of comparison requires for the conducting of comparison. Ethnological and contemporary laws are not united by either common origin, or by the unilateral reception of any legal system by one of them, or by the similarity of cultural or economic conditions, and consequently by none of the moments which the theory of comparison considers to be essential for carrying out comparison (see Chapter VII below).

Ultimately, methods of the contemporary comparison of law and the ethnological comparison of law are absolutely opposite in their orientations. The dogmatic comparison of law is concerned with firmly established, primarily proclaimed laws, codified laws. Ethnological comparison of law is engaged with law which must be reconstructed in its initial form on the basis of discovered survivals of institutions.

For these reasons, ethnological comparison has no shared features with contemporary dogmatic comparison. The ethnological law of one tribe may only be the object of comparison in juxtaposition with the ethnological law of another tribe or people, or contrasted with the analogous pre-historical law of contemporary States. In this understanding, ethnological comparison is an autonomous type of comparison. In any event the identical method does not equate dogmatic and ethnological comparison. The indicia thereof are determined by the bedrock of research, and the comparative method, which somewhat even differs in dogmatic and ethnological comparison, is adapted thereto.[185]

As noted, dogmatic comparison is considered to be the opposite of ethnological comparison. Its task is to compare contemporary positive law, construing it dogmatically at the same time, especially conceptually formalizing it and systematically

[184] Ibid., p. 156.

[185] Ibid., p. 157.

studying it.[186] The dogmatic study of material relegates dogmatic comparison to the positive science of law. It considers the content of the legal systems to be compared as actually represented in living legal customs, binding laws, actual science, and existing practice. Dogmatic comparison investigates what problems arise in individual systems and what are the answers in each instance. From this it attempts to determine the mutual relations between the objects being compared and to ascertain analogies and differences. An evaluation of the laws being compared does not relate to systematic comparison. Comparison only provides data for the critique performing this task.[187]

Systematic comparison usually concerns contemporary operating legal orders of cultured peoples irrespective of whether they operate alongside one another within a single State or exist in different States. For this reason dogmatic comparison is concerned only exceptionally with systems belonging to the past. This is for two reasons. The very division of these spheres sets for dogmatics the task of engaging with law in force, and historians with the law of the past. The purpose of the study differs in both spheres. Law in force is studied and compared so as to cognize its content, and this cognition is deepened by comparison. The comparison of past law has the purpose of deepening knowledge of past development: ordering legal principles by time as they were born, developed, and died out, and by way of comparison to reconstruct gaps in historical memories.

The value of dogmatic comparison is now generally acknowledged. It facilitates the critical consideration of individual systems and problems by methodically contrasting various solutions of identical legal issues. It cleanses concepts, frees them from bias, and offers fresh impetus to the legislator. Systematic comparison identifies which new issues arose, how they were resolved in individual systems, what the results were from these different decisions. In certain legal systems this may have significance for interpretation. Finally, it has value for studies of law themselves, for comparison offers a living and plastic image of contemporary law and guards against the one-sidedness of tradition.

186 Binder, note 41 above, p. 936.

187 Rabel, note 77 above, p. 280.

## 3. GENETIC AND HISTORICAL COMPARISON

The bridge between ethnological and dogmatic comparison of law is created by extreme chronological limits of the material of the compared law (one is occupied with a pre-historical period, and the second, with the most contemporary) – they constitute genetic and historical comparison. They both are interested in ancient periods of law; however, the genetic only insofar and inasmuch as the objects compared still have value for the modern day. Genetic comparison is primary when the material law has been codified. By its orientation towards the law in force, genetic comparison is linked more with dogmatic comparison, whereas the historical comparison, digging into the past without a glance into its actual significance, is linked with ethnological comparison.[188]

Genetic comparison usually is a preliminary operation for dogmatic comparison. Its task is to trace the formal aspect in the objects to be compared, most importantly to ascertain the sources of law.

Every comparison should be engaged not only with comparable objects, but also embrace the frameworks of legal systems and spheres to which they belong. This principle is sometimes essential in general for the possibility of comparison. When studying trade unions, for example, in various laws it is necessary to take into account the correlation between trade law and civil law, for one system places trade at the forefront, and another, civil law. For these reasons a prerequisite of any comparison is to trace the mutual relations of entire systems and groups thereof.

In this kind of comparison one speaks above all of ascertaining the sources of law in force of the systems to be compared as having actual significance. As the experience of Spanish and English law shows, norms from ancient times may remain in force in legal systems either because law is uncodified as in England or because there are gaps in codification, as in Spain. For these instances it is essential to trace the genesis of the law in force as an introduction to comparison itself.

In this case the entire development of law of a particular legal system should be traced, commencing from the fractionalization into particular complexes; attention should then be given to the

[188] Petraschek, note 86 above, p. 670.

aspiration for unification of law and the creation of a single national law in general, and also by means of the reception of foreign law; then one should trace the gathering of the entire national law into collections and ultimately codification. The laws of the earlier periods which are still binding should be determined in this material and their practical significance against the background of the entire system. Next the existing influences of other law of this country or foreign law on the legal system should be traced, for example the influence of Germanic law on Romanic peoples should be assessed, or of Roman law on Germanic. The influence of foreign law within the country also is possible; for example, of Jewish or autochthonic law in colonies. In addition, it is necessary to trace the state of codifications of important branches of law in contemporary systems of law. Finally, in the case of the fractionalization of law into territorial or provincial laws, the presence of necessary conflicts norms should be considered.[189]

After performing such an analysis, one may set about determining the general features which unite or divide the legal objects to be compared. Attention should be drawn once more to the actual genetic links or alienation from them. This analysis may show basic similarities or differences of principle. They should be investigated more precisely.

When the genesis of the legal systems to be compared is pursued, initially each separately, and then the genetic relations between them – then the unknown is discovered which would otherwise burden the comparison of law uselessly.

On the scale of the entire system, the ordered material may seem different when it is distributed according to the branches to which it belongs. The affiliation of objects of comparison to the same branches and the comparability of the branches makes possible the comparison of the individual objects of comparison. And *vice versa*, the affiliation of the bedrock to be compared to different branches probably excludes comparison.

When comparing individual branches, it may seem that even when entire systems display similarities of development, individual parts are akin to one another only in exceptional instances. This is possible in particular when one refers to branches which are not closely linked with the entire system of law because economic or

[189] Rauchhaupt, note 76 above, p. 158.

other requirements necessitate special legal regulation outside the framework of the entire system, but with the legal regulation in other States where similar requirements led to similar solutions.[190]

Genetic comparison is not essential when we speak of a new completely objective law not genetically related, such as English laws on liability, transoceanic transport, and maritime security, and similar laws of other States. Nonetheless, these instances should be investigated for the unseen influence of national law which may disappear only in the case of a general likening of law[191]. However, in principle immediately after the basis analysis of the material to be compared within the framework of entire systems, and also within the framework of branches, it may be reduced to a common denominator and may be the subject-matter of dogmatic comparison and provide a correct positive or negative result.

This is the method of genetic comparison. It is clear from the foregoing that it is the next preparatory operation which orders material for dogmatic comparison. Other formal comparisons are useful; for example, comparative studies of legislative technique, especially the technique of civil codifications. Also questions of lawmaking, their language, terminology, and the mathematization of laws. All these questions are important for further conclusions when comparing and by their nature and task are introductory studies of sources, only after which comparison proper occurs.[192]

Historical comparison is more autonomous than genetic. It differs noticeably from genetic comparison basically in that it penetrates deeply into the past without looking into its topicality for the present. It is engaged with the law of the past or epochs long since passed and may be undertaken even before ethnological or pre-historical studies. Hans Adolf Fehr (1874-1961) compared the Hammurabi and the law of Wales, presuming a community of spiritual and social life and a law of societal development of a natural law inherent to all people. Objects may be compared, one of which emanates from an epoch historically past and the other is in the developmental stage. Thus, Kohler took up the Jewish *chazakah* and the contemporary institution of acquisitive prescription

[190] Ibid., p. 160.

[191] Ibid., p. 174.

[192] Kaden, note 14 above, VI, p. 16.

(*usucaptio*), and Victor J. Guevara (1885-1961), the customary law of the Peruvian Indians and its adaptation to contemporary law.[193]

As is evident from these examples, historico-comparative studies aspire to order the laws to be compared according to certain principles. Bernhöft sets for the comparative method the task of investigating the historical relations of different systems. "The comparative science of law" should, in his words, trace how the peoples of one origin autonomously develop common inherited concepts of law; further, how one people takes institutions of another people and respectively reformulates its own views and, finally, how without any linkage the systems of individual nations develop according to general laws of development.[194]

As we see, the tasks set by the pioneers of the theory of comparison have a historical character and, just as historical and theoretical interests as a whole, were an impetus for the use of the new method. Although now comparative studies to a large degree have a practical orientation, the interest of the comparative method in history because of this is not weakened but, on the contrary, has expanded and became more precise. The task on the whole, however, is the same as Bernhöft determined. Historical comparison should trace historical relations in legal orders, in the light of which one may assert similarities which can possibly reduced to a common origin, reception, or autonomously but in parallel operative factors.[195]

The tasks so extensively set for historical comparison create the impression that historical comparison is performing the tasks of the history of law. This even inspired Kohler in his day to identify the "comparative science of law", as he called historico-comparative studies, with the universal history of law.[196]

It is obvious that mixing comparison with history is a mistake. Historical comparison is a method,[197] and a method by its nature cannot be a material branch of science. But even if this

[193] Victor Guevara, "Das Gewohnheitsrecht der Indianer von Peru", *Zeitschrift für vergleichende Rechtswissenschaft*, XLIV (1928); Rauchhaupt, note 76 above, p. 159.

[194] Bernhöft, note 46 above, pp. 36-37.

[195] Rabel, note 77 above, p. 281; Kaden, note 14 above, VI, p. 18.

[196] Kohler, note 29 above, p. 16.

[197] Rabel, note 77 above, p. 281.

methodological reproach is omitted (which ultimately is sufficient to refute the contrary assertion) and the material character of historical comparison is acknowledged, the equalization of the two concepts is not correct. The comparison of law looks primarily into space and offers a transverse segment at a time when the history of law gave attention primarily to the temporal legacy of laws and offered a lengthwise view of the development of law.[198] For these reasons, the temporal grouping of legal systems should be relegated to the history of law, and not to the comparison of law. Otherwise the reception of Roman law in Germany might be carried over from the history of law to the comparison of law. The confusion of the two concepts leads to such paradoxical consequences.[199]

For all this, the comparative method has great significance for historical studies. The comparison of law links some phenomena of the legal past with similar phenomena of other systems. Researchers attempt with the assistance of comparison not only to ascertain analogies and differences, but also to identify which social, economic, cultural, and political factors influenced in each instance the development of law in one direction or another. Comparison performs a separate role, reconstructing, with the assistance of its method, past law from the remnants preserved.[200]

In this understanding, as a method of research, the comparison of law also serves a universal history of law, especially of a general history of ancient law and a comparative history of ancient law.[201] One may say that it is very useful as an auxiliary method for any historical studies of law in general.[202]

Historical comparison, as we see, which at one time in the form of ethnological-comparative studies introduced the comparative method to the investigation of law, still adheres to dogmatic comparison, which has assumed a leading role in comparative works. Then ethnological comparison, long the pioneer of comparison, moved to the back and was erroneously not included

[198] Lautner, note 11 above, p. 40.

[199] Bekker, note 84 above, pp. 78, 90.

[200] Rabel, note 77 above, p. 281; Del Vecchio, note 9 above, pp. 230-231.

[201] Lautner, note 11 above, pp. 48, 54, 65.

[202] Kaden, note 14 above, p. 19.

by some authors in the science of law. Together with these three types of comparison there exists genetic comparison, which performs a modest auxiliary role in dogmatic comparison.

In evaluating the aforesaid types of comparison in a hierarchy as it now exists, it is appropriate to assert once more that dogmatic comparison has developed strongly in the twentieth century. Two other types are developing in its shadow: historical, which has great possibilities, and ethnological, in which after a brilliant appearance at the commencement of the comparative method interest has weakened. Despite, however, the present differentiation of comparative studies, none of the types of comparison have exhausted their possibilities, and a vast field lies before researchers for all types of work.

# Chapter VII. Comparability

1. Concept and Types. 2. Natural Comparability: a) Similarity of Indo-European Law; b) Ethnic Groups of Law; c) Historical Movements of Limits of Ethnic Laws; d) Universal Similarity of Law; e) Natural Comparability and Universality. 3. Artificial Comparability: a) Forced Implantation of Foreign Law; b) Reception of Foreign Law: Mechanical and Organic. 4. Incidental Comparability: a) Parallelism of Law in Antiquity and at Present; b) Relation between Parallel Development and Natural and Artificial Comparability. 5. Comparability of Non-Comparable Systems and Certain Spheres.

## 1. CONCEPT AND TYPES

Any comparison proceeds, as noted in Chapter I, within the framework of a concept of law. It is an element of identity which, providing legal phenomena a trace of homogeneous categories, makes them in principle – in the broadest sense of the word – comparable. Within these basic limits of comparability, however, the theory of the comparative method determined narrower limits within which comparison is coexisting by a greater probability of a useful result, taking into account the mutual relations of individual groups of legal systems. It is understandable that within the limits of for some reason kindred systems the common denominator of the comparison of laws is so significant that one can convincingly establish analogies and thereby easily perceive differences. On the contrary, one may accept that between systems with respect to which it is known in general that they have no common kinship or similarity, a comparison cannot be made because given the lack of analogies even in basic legal constructions this would be unsuccessful. Therefore, by comparability one should understand the possibility of comparison without anticipating the result.

Bernhöft was the first to develop a theory of the comparability of laws in an introductory article to the first volume of the *Zeitschrift für vergleichende Rechtswissenschaft*. He reduced it to analogies which should basically combine comparable systems for comparison to be successful, there being three: common origin, transfer, and similar conditions of life.[203] These three types of comparability suggested by Bernhöft, which can also be called natural, artificial, and incidental, were accepted in the theory of the comparative method[204] and are the basis of the division into narrower groups of laws within whose confines comparison is, in principle, possible. The systems of peoples of common ethnic origin create the natural group of laws, and this fact provides a natural comparability. Artificial comparability is a consequence of the acceptance or imposition of foreign law, which automatically provides numerous analogies between the accepted law and the law of the country from which it came. Finally, incidental comparison has no internal or external direct cause, but is the result of the operation of the same conditions independent from one another that led to the origin of similar legal institutions or to similar solutions of separate vital questions in law.

## 2. NATURAL COMPARABILITY

Natural comparability is substantial in scope because the internal common ethnic affiliation of peoples in which the laws to be compared operate provides an extensive base for analogy. In turn, it is understood broadly and narrowly, depending on the degree of ethnic kinship which is taken into account.

a) *Similarity of Indo-European Law.* Bernhöft understood natural comparability most broadly. He proceeded from the proposition that one may find between Roman and German law identical or similar legal provisions or views, and this fact cannot be explained either by the acceptance or mutual influences of the legal systems. These similarities are so great that given the heterogeneity of the culture of both tribes they cannot be explained by incidental impacts of identical conditions. Even more worthy of attention is the fact that these analogies also can be found with other Indo-European peoples: the Scandinavians, ancient Greeks, Slavs, and even the Hindus. This universality of similarities among such heterogeneous peoples over such vast expanses excludes the possibility of the institutions being taken from one source. There

[203] Bernhöft, note 46 above, pp. 36-37.

[204] Rabel, note 77 above, p. 281; Rauchhaupt, note 76 above, p. 152; Petraschek, note 79 above, p. 670.

remains, in Bernhöft's view, one explanation: that common ideas were originate in a common Indo-European origin. Individual offshoots and peoples, sprouting from a common stump, accepted commonly inherited views which, despite later autonomous development, retained the traces of a common origin in slightly different forms.

One may assume that ancient Indo-European law did not know State sanctions; not being precisely formalized, it did not know judges, judicial procedure, or, in general, had no social means of self-assertion. The realization of law was possible only by means of mutual assistance and, besides the interested persons, no one had the moral or legal duty to participate in the assertion of law. So it seemed to Homer in his day in Greece and so it was described much later in the Nordic sagas.[205]

This similarity of Indo-European law gave occasion to Bernhöft to accept as an extensive base the natural analogousness of the laws of peoples who only later developed autonomous legal orders, especially with the assistance of autonomous lawmaking.[206] Other authors establish comparability on a narrower foundation of kinship. Following Bernhöft, Rauchhaupt spoke first generally, that a common origin shows all institutions of mutual assistance typical of primitive communities. Mutual assistance was known to the Hindus, manifested itself later as a weak trace in the procedural forms of the Romans and as a serious struggle was decisive in disputes among the Germanic peoples. Rauchhaupt acknowledged at the same time that the traces of such an ancient common origin are now difficult to find.[207] For this reason he actually defined thereafter the limits of kinship more narrowly than Bernhöft, namely by groups of Indo-European tribes.

This seems more justified because the institution of mutual assistance, which Bernhöft considered to be characteristic of Indo-Europeans, was in reality inherent in all primitive communities and, as can be judged by various details, was present in all ancient state-political organizations as the basic means of asserting an individual right. Ancient social organizations applied public sanctions only against crimes directed expressly against the

205 Bernhöft, note 46 above, pp. 5-6.

206 Ibid., p. 27.

207 Rauchhaupt, note 76 above, p. 152.

existence and foundations of the system of the community. All personal interests were defended by the interested persons with the consent of and certain assistance of society, basically by the common forces of the clan to which each individual belonged.

For this reason the grounds are not sufficient to consider Indo-European law as a group of kinship which provides a special basis for comparability within the confines thereof. On one hand, the common origin of law is difficult to prove and, on the other, if it is confined to such a large grouping of laws, outside the Indo-European systems remain an insignificant part of more or less developed law, such as Islamic and Far Eastern, and in addition the law of primitive tribes.

b) *Ethnic Groups of Law.* Therefore, Rauchhaupt, being engaged in detail with the comparability of systems based on a general ethnographical affiliation, drew attention to the principal ethnic groups of European laws.

The pre-historical unity of Indo-European law has been reconstructed to a certain degree in Antiquity by Roman law, which ensured in its own way the unity of the world then, but on the whole did not finally retain it. Universal Roman law left merely a stable trace in the law of the Romanic peoples who, in the tradition of Roman law, received a strong and fresher foundation of community. Other groups in addition to the Romanic group of laws advanced into the arena of history. The French Revolution inspired the national consciousness of various peoples, which led *inter alia* to the creation of individual codifications along the French model within some States. They formally replaced the old law; but in fact much of it passed into the new codifications in unchanged or in modernized form. Among the individual national systems there emerged groupings of large complexes of legal systems on the ethnic principle. By their formal and material state they became equal with the Germanic group.[208]

European laws can be divided into three main ethnic groups: Romanic, Germanic, and Slavic laws. These laws find their reflection on other continents, principally in America, because the European laws of the Romanic and Germanic groups were accepted there as a consequence of colonization.

[208] Rauchhaupt, "Zustand und Fortschritte der Rechtsangleichung in Amerika und Europe", *Archiv für Rechts- und Wirtschaftsphilosophie,* XXV, no 3 (1932), p. 333.

For this reason the Romanic and Germanic are the most influential groups. Their area of influence is largest because, in addition to western and central Europe, it encompasses America, Australia, and Africa. The majority of newly-civilized States of the Near and Far East introduced law oriented towards the western European models. Slavic laws are the principal ones for Eastern Europe, and for the Near East and consequently for Asia Minor and northern Africa, the group of Islamic law is characteristic. Far Eastern law has a separate genesis and structure; it has individual significance although Japan and China have borrowed the law of influential European States under the influence of mutual relations with them.[209]

Therefore, the comparison of contemporary law is confined principally to the most important laws of Europe and the laws emanating therefrom, taking into account that these laws belong to States which determine the tone of world relations. To such laws are relegated, as noted, the Germanic and Romanic with mention of the Slavic. The last had less influence outside their territories because the Slavic States had no colonies beyond the oceans nor great political or economic influence. This situation has persisted despite the contemporary undisputed Great Power status of the Soviet Union because it by its doctrinaire legislation has isolated itself from all systems to such an extent that a general comparison of it with western European systems has become impossible. For these reasons, the comparison of law is limited primarily to the law of Germanic and Romanic origin.[210]

c) *Historical Movements of Limits of Ethnic Laws.* Although the division of laws into groups according to the ethnic principle has a basis, this does not provide an absolutely precise model of the kinship of individual laws. Often they were formed not only under the influence of incidental, autonomous impetuses, but also under the simultaneous operation of historical events. Therefore Ernst Heymann, when grouping legal systems just as Rauchhaupt according to the ethnic principle, interprets them as an outcome of the historical process.

He singled out, together with the Germanic, central European, and Anglo-Saxon groups of law, also the Romanic, Slavic, and

[209] Ibid., p. 334.

[210] Rauchhaupt, note 76 above, p. 162.

Eastern groups, and in addition as a separate category the laws of primitive peoples. To the Central European group were allocated German law, Austrian, and the law of States which arose on the site of Austro-Hungary, and then Hungarian, Swiss, Danish, Norwegian, Swedish, and Finnish. The influence of this group extended even eastward: to Greece, Russia, Bulgaria, and other Slavic States, and then to Japan. England, Ireland, somewhat Romanized Scotland, the United States, the English dominions, as well as India, where local laws still operated, were relegated to the Anglo-American group. This group also influenced Chinese law.

The Romanic group encompassed primarily French and Belgian law, which had the greatest importance in this group, together with the Italian, Dutch (partially under the influence of Central European law), and then the Spanish and Portuguese, as well as all South American law. French law influenced Russia, Romania, Serbia, Bulgaria, Greece in part, and Turkey. The Slavic group is structured on its own principles (basically we refer to family law and the law of inheritance), which were influenced by French and Central European systems. Eastern laws discover eastern influences. Turkey and derivative States structure their systems on Arab law, augmented by French influences. China superficially has Americanized its old legal traditions, and Japan has received German models in private law. Africa is a space of colonial law, except for the Union of South Africa, where the Roman law of the former Dutch colonists operates in part.[211]

From the foregoing it is evident that the ethnic link of laws over time has relocated somewhat. The separation by Heymann of German law into the Anglo-Saxon group, which as customary law comprises a separate whole with an autonomous developmental process, and into the Central European group, which basically thanks to the former Austrian monarchy encompassed non-Germanic peoples, attracts attention. Numerous cross-influences override in general a stereotyped division into tribal groups and require certain adjustments and additions to be made.

Natural comparability considered concisely seems to be thus. It is to some extent an opposite understanding of Indo-European law as a homogeneous foundation of community.

[211] Heymann, note 99 above, I, p. 426.

d) *Universal Similarity of Law*. It should be recalled, however, that certain researchers suggest broader limits for natural similarity than the Indo-European community. They see a natural community of legal thought in general in the unity of the human character on a universal scale which crosses all ethnic boundaries. Therefore, they do not link natural comparability directly with ethnic kinship. Del Vecchio may be considered a representative of this view.

In his opinion, the unity of human nature is affirmed in the universal development of human law. The most diverse peoples discover in reality not always a simultaneous but always a logical homogeneity in the development of law. This testifies to the homogeneity of the human character which through time and space, often without contact and bypassing local national distinctive features, created basically identical legal provisions. The analogous nature of the national laws of various peoples has gone so far that they not only are statically similar to one another in basic features, but express a similarity of development in subsequent periods.[212]

This is to be explained by the psychological capacity not only of human individuals, but of the human species in general – to distinguish law from lawlessness and to feel and distinguish justice. Positive law is not a phenomenon encountered only among some peoples in a particular epoch, but a phenomenon that accompanies human life constantly and emerges wherever there is human life. It grows together with all cultural life spontaneously from dark pra-foundations and only slowly and gradually becomes the subject-matter of conscious interpretation. Spontaneity created organizations and institutions, but they responded to conditions and requirements in such a way that finally formed a logical whole.[213] Therefore, the universality and permanence of law is confirmed in a series of agreements and similarities which we encounter in positive laws of all peoples. The assertion of the Historical School that every people must have a separate law adapted to its individual life conditions and therefore legal systems must be different from one another is not fully upheld in studies of legal phenomena on a world scale. They showed that the greater part of the principles and institutions of law of various peoples have much in common.

[212] Del Vecchio, note 6 above, p. 24.

[213] Del Vecchio, note 9 above, p. 401.

Various researchers of comparative law, especially Post and Kohler, pointed to this similarity. In Post's opinion, a large general human link exists in the life of peoples; there is a large range of customs and views which are the common heritage of mankind.[214] There are certain legal institutions which all possible peoples on Earth have so often repeated that they should be regarded as the common heritage of mankind.[215]Kohler shares a similar view. In his opinion, the deeper the studies penetrate, the more clear it becomes that all mankind, notwithstanding national distinctive features, is guided not only by the same genes but also embraced by identical creative aspirations in law, in the development of folk norms and customs. As a result, a legal analogousness exists between peoples which had nothing in common between them and which developed their cultures completely autonomously.[216]

Development shows common identical human tendencies and occurs similarly in various peoples which temporally and spatially are separated from one another. It is not even necessary to refer to a unity of origin in order to explain this universality of similarities. The common origin does not explain the similarity of all the phenomena observed, and ultimately in many instances it does not exist. We encounter similarly stages of development of various peoples which have no historical juncture between them.[217] In law general human features increasingly predominate over national distinctive features as a higher level of development is achieved. The certain closed and confined nature of national systems over time cedes to an abstract understanding of the mater and the universalist trend towards a mutual rapprochement of peoples in the domain of law is based on this rationalization.[218]

e) *Natural Comparability and Universality*. Given the state of affairs described above, it seems that the entire theory of natural comparability has been undermined. But in fact the theory of the universal similarity of law is merely a consequence of the theory of the analogousness of all of Indo-European law. From the

[214] Post, *Über die Aufgaben einer allgemeinen Rechtswissenschaft* (1891), p. 17.

[215] Ibid., p. 19.

[216] Kohler, note 32 above, p. 274.

[217] Del Vecchio, note 9 above, p. 402.

[218] Ibid., p. 404.

assertion that all European law is analogous it is only a step to the view that all law is analogous. It was even easier to say that because empirical law continues to manifest conceptual identity. It would be clearer to say that variant solutions of vital questions are relatively infrequent. When vital issues typical for identical cultural conditions were actually identical and the resolution of these questions differed little and in a number of instances completely independent from one another were similar, it is not surprising that the question arose of the similarity of law on a world scale, just as Del Vecchio postulated.

In reality, even accepting that the assertions about the universal similarity of law is exaggerated and has relative value given that it in comparison with differences in details is not great and concern only the principal types of legal forms which beyond this differ in details – one may agree on the whole that certain general analogies in the laws of all peoples truly exist. The historical material presents in addition to individual differences that clearly appeared especially in Antiquity when peoples had no active links between themselves, certain common features of analogousness, and this cannot fail to be noted.

However, this analogousness should not be accepted as grounds for the classification of legal systems. It is so general that within its confines differences of principle may exist and the comparison thereof must take them into account. This relates especially to historical materials of the earlier surveys in which national differences are evident and insuperable.

On the contrary, as regards modern times, the gradual coming together of systems and likening of civilizational conditions influences the fact that the significance of the ethnic group is lessening somewhat. Natural comparability recedes to the advantage of artificial and incidental comparability as the coming together of different systems ensues throughout history and especially as law likens by virtue of parallel historico-civilized development of socio-economic conditions, which leads automatically to identical or similar solutions of identical or similar questions advanced by life.

From this it follows that natural comparability has meaning basically if one speaks of the comparison of historical systems and institutions. Rabel expressly said that historical comparison has the purpose to trace historical relations in legal orders in the light of which one may assert similarities that can be reduced to a common origin, borrowing, or autonomous factors operating in parallel.[219] The kinship of institutions and the development of various cultures and races also is affirmed with the assistance of comparative studies besides the relativity and changeability of positive law. These similarities should not be reduced too the direct chain of imitations and influences, and although Del Vecchio may be correct in pointing to the unity of the human character as the reason for the analogy – but one may come to cognition of the truth only with the assistance of comparative studies.[220]

Unlike historical comparison, which operates basically with national laws, contemporary dogmatic comparison is linked to a lesser extent with the issue of natural comparability. Kaden does not expressly recognize the request by Rauchhaupt to compare only comparable laws dogmatically. In his view, all contemporary European laws and the laws which emanate from them are so proximate that they may be systematically compared.[221] It is evident that here one enters the game of artificial and incidental comparability, which in the course of history approached ethnically alien systems to such an extent that the issue of the comparability of contemporary, primarily codified, laws is not very complicated. Nonetheless, individual groups of laws exist and will exist hereafter despite a certain coming together for a long time as proximate complexes of legal systems.

## 3. ARTIFICIAL COMPARABILITY

Artificial comparability is a consequence of the kinship of legal systems, branches, or institutions which arose by the implantation or acceptance of foreign law.

a) *Forced Implantation of Foreign Law.* The introduction or implantation of foreign law is usually conditioned by a certain political advantage of one State over others which makes such material interference possible. It arises most naturally when the metropolitan establishes laws in its colonies or similarly controlled State, for example, a mandate. Therefore, in general by implanted

[219] Rabel, note 77 above, p. 281.

[220] Ibid., p. 284.

[221] Kaden, note 14 above, p. 18.

law should be understood foremost colonial law. Colonial law is adapted to the requirements of the population and differs greatly from the law of the metropolitan when the population differs racially. For example, Indian law is codified, whereas British law is in the best case merely consolidated.[222]

An organized colony which developed under the cultural and legal influence of its metropolitan retains the legal system received from it even when it becomes autonomous or passes under another form of domination. In the first instance the laws of former colonies and the metropolitan will slowly, in an evolutionary manner, depart from one another while preserving similarity for an extended period; in the second, the old law manifests significant stability. The Spanish provinces of America which acceded to the United States in the nineteenth century moved away from Spanish law slowly. There are remnants of Spanish law to this day in Texas, California, and Louisiana.

Foreign law may be implanted forcibly on a weak or less-civilized State such as, for example, Egypt in 1875 by the French. This may affect the entire system or relate to a certain sphere of privileges which the stronger State secures by treaties. In the last instance the imposition, as an entirely external phenomenon, does not concern the internal structure of local law. The difference between this kind of imposed foreign law and voluntary, albeit mechanical, reception is that the imposition of foreign law excludes or limits the will of the respective State.[223]

To the category of not entirely voluntary taking of foreign law belongs the introduction of foreign law under the influence of political pressure of one State on another. The implantation of Islamic law in Albania, Bosnia, and Herzogovina emerged only as a consequence of Turkish expansion. It is interesting that it has been retained to this day even though Turkish dominance has long been thrown off and Turkish law has, moreover, been modernized.

Napoleonic codifications were at one time disseminated under the influence of French hegemony duly facilitated, in truth, by the clarity of method and modernity of codified French law. The radical method of Napoleonic codifications, which consisted of the introduction in place of collections of law in force of ordered

[222] Rauchhaupt, note 76 above, p. 163.

[223] Ibid., p. 164.

autonomous, closed codifications by branches of law when the simultaneous cessation of the operation of the old prescriptions, was received and imitated, duly furthered too by the political expansion of France. Together with the method in part or as a whole, legal ideas were borrowed, especially in Spain and in Spanish America. The Napoleonic codifications were introduced in Belgium and Luxembourg, provisionally in Italy and Switzerland, and their influence was felt in Holland, Poland, and the Balkan States.[224]

Only over time, when the brilliance of France had faded a bit, was the method separated from the content and, given the later changes of the codifications, was the borrowed French law replaced primarily by national law.[225]

A separate category of artificial comparability is the not entirely voluntary introduction of foreign law under the constant geopolitical pressure of another State. Here the invisible influence is taken into account of the hegemony of one State on the surrounding legal systems. In America, where commercial policy was always decisive and had priority over politics proper, an invisible influence was preserved of the United States on the entire western hemisphere. Europe once more was before the Second World War under the political hegemony of France and England, and this influenced legal relations between States. As a consequence of the Second World War, the hegemony of the United States recently began to grow throughout the world, and by its scale and universality is reminiscent somewhat of the impact of ancient Rome on the civilized world of that time. The United States will as a result have a certain influence on the structure of many countries which take American ideas.

All the said types of artificial kinship and artificial comparability from the flagrant imposition of law by one State on another up to the imperceptible influence of a mighty power which by its brilliance but also by direct, albeit invisible interference, forms legal life in the desired direction – they all have one thing in common: to a greater or lesser degree they exclude the free decision of a weak people.

[224] Rauchhaupt, note 208 above, p. 339.

[225] Rauchhaupt, note 76 above, p. 167.

b) *Reception of Foreign Law.* In addition to such artificial kinship, foreign systems may approximate one another also by the voluntary reception of foreign law. Such reception may be purely mechanical or may be a consequence of the absorption of foreign law as a result of recognition of its superiority. In the first instance, foreign law is introduced by an act of the government without preparation and without the existence of an organic foundation, whereas in the second, one is concerned with the objective science or practical evaluative activity by the legislator.[226]

1) *mechanical.* The mechanical reception of foreign law occurs only between States having a different culture. The introduction of Eastern States into the European community of peoples led to the reception of European law by them. Typical is the Europeanization of Turkish law in 1856, which the introduction of French law completed. Having received a constitution at the instigation of France, Turkey also received part of the French commercial code which in a free translation from the French language into Turkish became the law in force in relations with European States. It is interesting that together with the Turkish text there also existed a French translation of the received law and this text had the same force of law as the Turkish. Also of interest is that the French translation of the Turkish text of the commercial law did not correspond word for word to the formulations of the last but was closer to the original French code. How shaky and unstable such mechanical reception is was shown by the fact that Turkey later case French law aside, and the Young Turks Movement in reforming Turkish law introduced the 1907 and 1911 Swiss Civil Code in 1926 in a French formalization.[227]

The influence of Swiss law is to be explained by the fact that Switzerland was the center of the League of Nations and various international organizations, on one hand, and on the other that the Swiss code permits, in the absence of a provision, the use of customary law and even allows law to be created for a concrete instance instead of the legislator.[228]

In addition to Turkey, Japan and China have mechanically borrowed law, partially from the French and partially (commercial

[226] Ibid., p. 164.

[227] Ibid., p. 165.

[228] Rauchhaupt, note 208 above, p. 339.

law) from German law. Moreover, there are mechanically received civil and commercial law in Haiti and the Dominican Republic, who appropriated French civil and commercial law verbatim.

In all the said instances we are concerned with the mechanical taking of foreign law, the States concerned belonging to a completely different cultural milieu and the law taken not directly satisfying the internal needs of the peoples, instead having the task of civilizing their legal life and adapting it for world relations.

2) *organic*. The appropriation of the law of a State of the same cultural milieu is not mechanical borrowing, as was the case of Uruguay and Paraguay, who received the commercial code of Argentina, or with Bolivia and Costa Rica, who introduced virtually verbatim the Spanish commercial code. In this instance the internal requirements of these countries corresponded to the content of the norms of the acquired codes, which should have been merely a legal model for organizing the existing *de facto* relations. The legal life of the countries did not change because of the appropriation of foreign codes, as had occurred in the case of Turkey, where the new prescriptions created new forms of European legal relations. It by its style corresponded to the spirit of the appropriated law.

In Europe the voluntary appropriation of foreign models occurred on a large scale in the field of constitutional law. It is characterized since the seventeenth-century revolution in England and the eighteenth century in France by democratic forms of a certain type in which the initial idea is the sovereignty of the people, and the organizing conception of power is its separation into legislative, executive, and judicial. These ideas and principles were taken by other nations as the people's awareness grew of being a sovereign subject during the nineteenth century and caught on in organic consistency with the conditions which merely by their emergence in the struggle against absolutism led to the introduction of foreign models. The European continent, full of historicism and tradition, was not appropriate for the unanimous acceptance of the French or English models and demonstrates great diversity in their State systems. Republics exist side by side with a few old monarchies, and the doctrine on the separation of powers is not always and everywhere identically and precisely realized. Then in America, where free States were constructed under the direct influence of the idea of the sovereignty of the people, the foundations of popular rule are preserved, possibly, in identical and pure form. The taking of models of institutions from the same sources by all States made constitutional law the most comparable law of all the branches of law.[229]

Second in comparability is commercial law, which, just as constitutional law, is a consequence of policy, only in this case, commercial policy. Commercial policy is rooted in internal conditions and, depending on these, regulated in one way or another. However, under the present constant preference of foreign trade over the domestic market, external economic relations have great influence on its formation. There is active and passive influence of own norms on foreign norms, and *vice versa*. In order to lay a path for economic relations, the interested States seek in their joint interest by means of treaties to achieve a mutual equalizing or adaptation of legal prescriptions, and this leads to a likening of law, which ultimately allows its comparability.

For all this, trade policy measures do not affect the integrity of national systems which for commercial matters have separate commercial codes. Even commercial law preserves its national face because it remains linked with the integrity of the civil law of a particular State, irrespective of whether it is autonomous or subject to the last. The early autonomous codifications of commercial law recognize in principle its subsidiary, auxiliary role with respect to civil law, and commercial law is applied only when civil law does not offer solutions for a concrete instance.[230] Since the mid-nineteenth century the growth of trade imparted greater importance to commercial law and this led to its autonomy. The new versions of the commercial code interpret commercial law as an autonomous branch, and it has preferential use in trade turnover, leaving to civil law an auxiliary role to fill in possible gaps in commercial law.[231]

Being the most dynamic of all civil law, commercial law demonstrates the greatest ability for large-scale adaptation. The Nordic States (Denmark, Iceland, Norway, Sweden, and Finland) achieved a mutual approximation of commercial law with the assistance of a series of jointly adopted laws. After the World War, even certain civil laws were coordinated.[232]

[229] Ibid., p. 343.

[230] Ibid., p. 344.

[231] Ibid., p. 345.

[232] Ibid., pp. 340-341.

The taking of law also is proceeding in Europe and America, basically along earlier links between the former metropolitans and colonies: between England and North America, and between the Iberian Peninsula and South America. In the Anglo-Saxon world, despite the kinship of legal systems, there is no significant influence, but in the event law is insufficient in one system certain solutions in another serve as an orientator. As between Hispano-American States and the old motherland, legal exchange has acquired evident forms. Between 1900 and 1905, treaties were concluded between Spain, on one side, and a series of South and Central American States on the other, on the basis of which the academic degrees of one State are recognized by other States.[233] This is a vivid illustration of how closely the legal systems of the contracting parties have organically harmonized their cultures and needs.

There also are examples in history of how organic the reception of law by another culture may be. Of interest is the reception of Roman law in Spain and Germany by way of scientific studies. In Spain this taking occurred in the second half of the thirteenth century. The time cannot be precisely ascertained in Germany. At first, Roman law was perceived by scholars and gradually found proponents in broader circles of jurists and legislators. Roman law was assimilated by this means gradually and organically, and through the introduction therein of the ideas of Germanic law a synthesis was achieved. Their complete merger require centuries; however, they did not exist in mechanical separation from one another, but were in a state of constant merger. This was so exceptional, that it should be separately emphasized. Only the colonies of North America received English law in the same unnoticed manner. It was simply gradually brought there by jurists educated in England. But in this last instance the culture and traditions were identical, whereas the reception of Roman law by Germany, given its exceptional nature, is the sole instance of the organic merger of two different systems.[234]

It should be noted, however, that Roman law throughout its development received much foreign and thanks to this became to comprehensive and flexible, and this in turn may have made its appropriation by other peoples easier. The discovery of monuments

[233] Ibid., p. 342.

[234] Rauchhaupt, note 76 above, p. 166.

of the Ancient East generated hopes that one would succeed in identifying the chain of the reception of law from Babylonia through Persia, Greece, and to Rome.[235] These suggestions did not find positive confirmation; however, the question of the possible influence of the law of the ancient Eastern world on Roman law remains topical to this day. In the law of Egypt of the Roman period the intersection is confirmed in any event of Roman, Greek, and local Egyptian law, and this preserves topicality of the problem of the mutual influence of law in the ancient epoch.[236] The chain of succession extends even farther into the dark past because studies have shown that Babylonian-Assyrian law is not a homogeneous phenomenon because individual autonomous cultural groups and strata have been discovered on clay tablets.[237] In this connection one cannot speak of the unanimous development of ancient law. Mechanical imposition occurred together with voluntary and organic succession. In any event, the likening and mutual approximation of law occurred uninterruptedly through the entire ancient epoch, creating comparability.

This also affected Roman law. Except for the influence of Attic law, it cannot be determined precisely which ancient laws were received by Roman; however, the entire development of Roman law indicates that foreign law had a serious influence on its formation. The Romans did not impose their law directly, but only as their dominions expanded did they receive from new citizens to a certain degree their practical legal institutions and incorporate them into their own system.[238]

The development of Roman law begins at a time when the Italians receive the civil laws of Rome. The task then arises for the science of law to crate the law of the country from the city law of Rome. The citizens of Italian communities sometimes occupied important State posts and brought with them views which they attempted to realize. A conflict occurred because of this between the new and the old trends, and only gradually were these views approximated thanks to the work of jurists.[239] The apex of the

[235] Lautner, note 11 above, p. 30.

[236] Ibid., p. 32.

[237] Ibid., p. 33.

[238] Bernhöft, note 46 above, p. 30.

[239] Ibid., p. 31.

flourishing of the science of law came at a time when Roman citizenship began to be granted to non-Italian peoples. Then Italian law was transformed into imperial, world law, and the coming together of views ensued between different peoples of the Roman Empire, obviously under the guidance of Roman jurists. The Code of Justinian fully completed the unification of the law of the Roman Empire and a change of the legal system. Virtually all the works of the ancient Roman epoch were eliminated and replaced by new legislation structured on Imperial law.[240]

To be sure, because of this one cannot speak of Roman law as a synthesis of the law of the ancient world because even the Roman law of peoples cannot be regarded as a product of all the laws of the ancient world. Although it arose to a certain extent under the influence of legal opinions of subject peoples, in fact it was Roman law created by proceeding from Imperial requirements.[241] But despite this, one may speak of the succession of Roman law from the laws of the Mediterranean Basin, which occurred gradually and so organically that Roman law now seems to us to be a monolith.

As we see, the taking of law between States, especially of one culture, is and was rather active. It creates comparability to a greater degree, especially if one speaks of States belonging to a narrower cultural group such as, for example, Scandinavian. There were exceptional instances when the laws of different cultures so approximated one another that they over time merged into a monolith. This, together with the imposition of law on colonies or weak States, expressly and directly or under the significant or quiet pressure of the Great Powers created an extensive artificial base of comparability, which possibly over history acquired greater weight than natural comparability. When today one refers to the fact that all European laws in many respects are comparable, the principal reason for this is the voluntary or forced taking of foreign law. This succession destroyed ethnic groups and linked national laws to such a degree that few legal systems can be said to be completely isolated in all respects. One may trace in all laws the crossover of influences, and this moment provided an extensive basis for comparison.

[240] Ibid., p. 32.

[241] Lautner, note 11 above, p. 35.

## 4. INCIDENTAL COMPARABILITY

The second reason for the comprehensive comparability of all civilized laws is incidental comparability, which helps the previous, seals and perfects, and ultimately may lead to the general approximation of all laws.

Incidental comparability, unlike natural and artificial comparability, does not rely on any link between the laws to be compared. It is characterized by incidental similarities of legal views which developed independently of one another, without any linkage between them and without any mutual influence. The emergence of these incidentally analogous laws, as a rule, is conditioned by the similarity of conditions or needs, and above all by a similar cultural and social development. There are certain legal institutions inherent to determined cultural conditions and repetitious among all peoples at the respective level.

a) *Parallelism of Law in Antiquity and at Present.* Thus, the lawless status of a stranger and the gradual legal protection thereof is an independent phenomenon in all systems of all times and formulated identically in principle in identical cultural conditions.[242] The institution of blood vengeance also is responsive to a certain cultural level, being encountered among peoples of completely separate races such that there are no grounds, as a rule, to speak of any influence. As culture develops, the institution of vengeance softens and is changed in general depending of the unique properties of peoples. The institution of witnesses in introduced among various peoples independently from one another and in accordance with the state of culture with unique, autonomous formal rules. Later a written form of legal actions is required, despite its heterogeneity, also being evidence of certain prescriptions arising simultaneously under determined conditions of culture (when writing was already known) without any linkage between them. This illustrates how a degree of culture influences the incidental similarity of legal norms.

Other analogous institutions are a consequence of certain relations. Among peoples, for example, where the power of the ruler is strong, he performs the undoubted function of a judge. In other instances the power of a judge is performed by the public itself

242 Bernhöft, note 46 above, p. 33.

or through their representatives.[243] Given the technical, economic, and political similarities of modern times, legal prescriptions are especially developed in an identical direction, rising from identical foundations of life. These similarities even lead to international adjustments in certain spheres, such as currency turnover, communications, and others.[244] Most recently, the process of rapprochement between peoples on an identical *de facto* foundation of life conditions has gathered pace, and this evidently has and will have increasing influence on the coming together of law, which now reflects the identical cultural-civilizational and economic questions throughout the world.

The idea of an international-legal community of peoples especially serves the process of the mutual coming together in the political sphere. This is manifest in the creation of various large and small unions of peoples and States with a view to jointly undertaking common tasks and policies for the joint benefit of each of the allied countries. Among such unions were the former League of Nations and the present United Nations, which unite nations into a universal territorial and subject-matter embrace, and the British Conference of Dominions or the Pan-American Union of the western hemisphere. The conception of a United States of Europe is seriously being considered increasingly and mention is even made of a world government.

In parallel with this, the economy is developing on a world scale – so it could be said that the national economy has become strongly dependent on the world economy. Enlivened economic and political links facilitate the rapprochement of all other spheres of life, mutual cognition, and rapprochement, recalling the art and culture of daily existence with its fashions, customs, and style. This general growing rapprochement naturally gravitates toward such rapprochement in the field of law, which under conditions of similar economic, cultural, and vital issues of all civilized peoples will further provide, as the organizer and regulator of this life, similar decisions to a greater or lesser degree. The growing analogousness of the life style of peoples wil be reflected in the analogousness of their law.[245]

[243] Ibid., pp. 34-35.

[244] Rauchhaupt, note 76 above, p. 168.

[245] Rauchhaupt, note 208 above, p. 332.

b) *Relation between Parallel Development and Natural and Artificial Comparability.* The assertion that the development of legal institutions occurred or is occurring among various peoples in parallel and independently of one another obviously is contrary to a certain extent to the assertion that genetic similarities by ethnic groups are traceable in the legal systems of peoples. Therefore, it is understandable that the greater the degree one considers the prevailing factors in the development of the law of various peoples to be in parallel and autonomous, the less probable is the hypothesis that similarity of law is drawn from a general law which was the pra-origin of all later and for this reason (and also because of mutual influence) related institutions. In this instance similarity would have been the result not of genetic kinship or historical mutual relations, but of the operation in parallel of identical factors among all peoples.

This issue has significance of principle not only for comparability (see Chapter VII, 2(e) above), but for the origin of the comparative method in general, and therefore should be considered again. The Historical School from the outset, unlike the school of natural law, asserted that there is no eternal all-embracing and immutable law; there exist only different national laws changeable throughout history. The Historical School survives so long as it is advisable to overcome natural law. The comparison of law should have performed the task which the Historical School did not perform (namely, to trace the law of all peoples), and as a result, it takes the same ideological positions as the Historical School. Therefore, the fact that law displays a universal similarity irrespective of kinship and historical links as a consequence of the operation of parallel, identical factors – is simultaneously the principal foundations of the historical and comparative schools. Thus, they are very close to the affirmation of natural law, that man has an innate law, identical for all peoples and races. In this case, the law of all peoples would by its nature be similar and comparable, and the comparative method itself, conditioned by distinctions, would disappear into the air.[246] The question depends primarily on the interpretation of the concept "factors operating in parallel".

It may be said that these factors should be understood as objective conditions determining the state which do not depend on

[246] Bernhard Rehfeldt, *Grenzen der vergleichenden Methode in der rechtsgeschichtlichen Forschung* (1942), p. 5.

the character and nature of man: cultural level, social and economic relations, and others. The question, however, cannot be considered to be exhausted given that culture and all social relations are themselves human products and not incidental independent phenomena coming from without, such as, for example, rain. It seems that only as an exception and with certain reservations may one consider such factors as climate, geographical conditions, and technical adaptations to be objective conditions. The last especially may be regarded as an objective factor because, even though they are human products, there is no direct lawmaking link between them and individual legal institutions which are the subject-matter of comparison. Beyond this, law is in its social function directly an organizer of mutual relations of people and as a social phenomenon also is a human product together with all social phenomena. In ascribing to humans an undoubted role of a subject of the creation of law, we may merely put the question of to what extent it is determined by human properties. One must accept first and foremost that man, as such, everywhere has identical basic indicia, and namely those which characterize him as a person, beginning with the Hottentots and cannibals to the cultured Greek and Roman or to the present civilized individual. All humans at every cultural level determine by their human nature the scale of all possible states, actions, and relations between themselves and with respect to things.

This scale is basically identical, embraces all variants of a possible relation with other humans and the external world, and by this determines the quantity, type, and quality of legal formalizations of these relations. The fact that the scale of legal problems is limited is confirmed undoubtedly by experience. The principal types of legal institutions emerge in principle identically throughout the planet when we refer to a determined quantity of social and State structures and private relations of humans between themselves and to things. Comparative studies of times past showed even that the similarity of basic legal questions goes so far back that one may imagine analogous pra-forms of law common to all peoples, identical stages of development, despite whether they were related or had a direct link between them, if any. The forms of law demonstrate at the same time a large degree of diversity conditioned by national conditions. The diversity, however, is preserved within limits of the changeability of a universal type of legal phenomena inherent to an identical essence and to similar basic requirements of individuals of all peoples and races.[247]

The number of types of institutions is limited by the scale, identical for all peoples. Within these types a variation of difference exists through time and space. It also, however, is not infinite, being preserved within certain limits. Various factors determine these limits, for example, the idea of reciprocity, which in its day required to interpret slavery as an unjust institution because it provided benefit without reciprocity. In any event, cultural rights do not know the acquisition of benefit without mutual service, and one may suppose that the idea of reciprocity might influence a limitation of the variants of legal formalizations of relations acting in an identical direction for all time and under any conditions. A similar idea of the unconditional value of the human individual and in this connection the idea of the freedom of the individual and the sovereignty of a people, which have now become unconditional components of a legal order, operated in parallel in all systems of all times, having a general trend towards likening.[248] Finally, the gradual rationalization of law, especially noticeable in the epoch of codification, setting for law the task of equalizing individual and group interests, influences and levels by this reasonable element simultaneously the laws of various peoples independently of one another.[249]

This objective rational element in every law that seeks first and foremost a fair and advisable resolution of a vital issue often identical in essence among all peoples, influences the fact that foreign peoples may and want to take foreign models. Just as at one time the Germans took Roman law, the Slavs took German city law, so in modern times Japan introduced the new German commercial law. A rational moment in all instances decided that although they received together with foreign law also foreign influence and life was not structure on local style, peoples did not cease to be themselves and did not lose their national distinctiveness. In the most foreign laws, the common human element creates a natural bridge for links with other peoples.[250] Moreover, at present

[247] Ibid., p. 6.

[248] Del Vecchio, note 6 above, pp. 472-473.

[249] Rehfeldt, note 246 above, p. 7.

[250] Ibid., p. 8.

the contemporary, civilized, vital forms with industrialization and world turnover create especially convenient conditions for the emergence of unification trends in law. Therefore, incidental comparability, that is, comparability which is a consequence of the spontaneous parallel development through history based on the similarity of the human character, and in modern times also a consequence of the unification of civilization – does not exclude or deny ethnic and historical comparison. It is merely a broader base of comparability in juxtaposition with them; the similarities of variants within the frameworks of similarities of universal types are specified anew.

Thus, the question of factors operating in parallel may be resolved without denying natural and artificial comparability, and the more so without disturbing the foundations of the comparative method. The parallel development of the law of all peoples by reason of identical human nature provided only an analogy of the types of legal problems on a universal scale. These universal types in principle are the subject-matter of studies of the general science of law, if we speak of the formal aspect. The material aspect of this problem and, consequently, the question of the vital content of legal forms typical for mankind and the reasons for this depend on various factors; the development and further trends belong in their comprehensive complexity to the typical questions of sociology. Moreover, the extent of the interests of the science of law and the matter, bypassing the general science of law which is interested only in the theory of legal phenomena, is narrower and more specific. The science of law, in addition to typical forms of law, is interested in variants of decisions within various types. Positive prescriptions diverse in details especially interest the science of law, and their study augments the content of the different branches thereof. The comparison of law in particular does not confine itself to a determination of the typical legal forms, but (except for ethnological-comparative studies, which for their own reasons have a tendency to categorize phenomena into types) enter into details that develop the comparative method, the deeper, the better. This kind of parallel development is not contrary to genetic and historical similarity, which determine, in addition to the similarity of types, the similarity of variant decisions.

As regards parallelism which is a consequence of similar contemporary civilizational conditions, it should be noted that it is a consequences of historical processes which linked various groups of peoples, races, and continents and brought closer together their forms of life so strongly that now universal parallelism is noted within not only types, but also variants of law in certain branches. This event, which is based on technico-communications world dependencies, is in no way a denial of genetic and historical links, but the augmentation and completion thereof.

All three types of comparability are competent and irreplaceable in their sphere. Genetic, historical, and, finally, universal-civilizational kinship interchanged with one another, and although recently civilizational parallelism has proceeded to the first level, both first kinships have not lost topicality. The comparison of law should take into account all categories of comparability if it wishes to be successful.

## 5. COMPARABILITY OF NON-COMPARABLE SYSTEMS AND CERTAIN SPHERES

In addition to legal systems which are comparable in principle on the basis of natural, artificial, and incidental similarity, there are also non-comparable legal systems. The contradictions of legal systems may be so fundamental and principled, that it seems that comparison cannot give a positive result. Despite the fundamental contradictions of systems, however, in individual spheres the boundaries are not necessarily insuperable. Since the Napoleonic codifications the active exchange of legal ideas and laws between States has led to the fact that even between completely unique laws something mutually comparable can be found.

However, laws for which natural, artificial, or incidental grounds of comparison are not sufficient even in individual parts cannot be contrasted so long as a certain approximation and likening ensues on the basis of these three principles. The contradictoriness of legal systems follows basically from ethnic differences and only slowly disappears thanks to gradual approximation. A typical example of such fundamental contradictoriness which partly is gradually eliminated is the evolutionary approximation of Romanic and Germanic law.[251]

Romanic and Germanic law have their own indicia. Roman law, the source of all Romanic laws, tracing its origin to the remote past

[251] Rauchhaupt, note 76 above, p. 168.

and developing gradually as the might of Rome grew, preserved its unity and transparency thanks to its abstractness, which is traced basically in obligations. Unlike Roman law, Germanic laws have a newer origin and have not achieved such crystallization and order which distinguishes Roman law. Nonetheless, they have demonstrated an ability to adapt to the requirements of time without losing their properties. English law has still preserved this property. The principal branches of Germanic law are family law, for the family was closely linked with the land, and land law. As for obligations and commercial law, these spheres should have been augmented by provisions of Roman law because of their being underdeveloped in Germanic law. In Germany the approximation and merger occurred over centuries and finally created the present organic system of German law.

On the whole, the contradictoriness between Romanic and Germanic law began to weaken from the time of the Napoleonic codifications, which simplified written law.[252] Until then, the legislator attempted to encompass all law and to place it in a single work, ordering the material so that the historical retrospectivity was made obvious of the foundations of law being dependent on their age and the frequency of the usage of law. Napoleon liberated law from its historical bonds, orientating its possible future development. Thus arose the closed codifications of individual branches of law, among them constitutional, criminal, civil, commercial, and procedural law, and they became a model for other States. This system withstood the verification of life thanks to an ability to adapt law to the extensive expansion of economic functions and links. The economic and parallel political relations in the world were called upon to cleanse the national peculiarities in law.

The great changes of which the nineteenth century was rich made the world the single focus of interest and also influence respectively the traditional legal views of the Romanic and Germanic worlds. Law was gradually freed from the genetic burden and serves, if not exclusively, the basically as the material law of the future. This revolution was noticeable, in addition to France, also in German codifications from 1900.

It should be further affirmed that thanks to international cooperation, the Napoleonic codifications ceased to be the final

[252] Ibid., p. 169.

resolution of the problem of the source of laws and thereafter the further mutual adaptation of the material laws of different countries became a stage in the development of law. Possibly the present process of the approximation of foreign law is a new, genetic period.

From the standpoint of having grown out of the old European, Romanic, and Germanic laws, the new extra-European laws have come to the forefront and Romanic laws are now represented by Spanish-American, and Germanic – by Anglo-Saxon law. The economic and political tempo of our time in a new world is overcoming to a certain extent the traditional contradiction between Romanic and Germanic law, mutually bringing together both systems instead of waging an implacable struggle. Both systems, in aspiring to merge two continents in Pan-America, are creating the prerequisites for unification especially in public and private international law, and also in international commercial and transport law. As measures to ameliorate differences process in these spheres, one may hope on the further approximation of both systems within the framework of Pan-American solidarity. It is natural that such an outcome would be an impetus for the approximation of laws also in Europe.[253]

Approximation might occur also between individual spheres of law; however, this should be evaluated against the background of the relations of entire system with one another. The comparability or non-comparability of certain parts may follow directly from the comparability or non-comparability of entire legal systems, the more so that this may depend upon the linkage of this part with a national system. From the standpoint of the stronger or weaker linkage of individual parts with the entirety of the system one may divide the parts of law into two groups: one group of laws is more abstract and international-homogeneous in character, and the second group of laws is national in character.

To laws of an abstract character are relegated constitutional law, which in monarchies of the recent period and republics is based on the sovereignty of the people who, through their constitutional representation, have decisive influence on legislation and administration. Commercial law has the same abstract character; it grew in all States from identical requirements and thanks to international commercial relations achieved great

[253] Ibid., pp. 171-172.

likening, although certain difficulties may exist for comparison because certain systems interpret commercial law as the primary and others as a second source of law with respect to civil law. In any event, the international approximation of abstract laws is so advanced that the comparison of law between them to a significant degree is achieved despite the absence of the fundamental comparability of systems.[254]

Legal institutions, which despite a certain similarity between themselves, have no natural, artificial, or incidental linkage with foreign law may be understood only in connection with a whole national legal order. This applies, for example, to land, family, or inheritance law, which often preserves national distinctive features and for these reasons may be compared only within an ethnic or other linkage. But in these instances too comparative law may lead to some likening of laws.

The law of nations, despite its formal universality, demonstrates particular differences depending on the cultural groups to which States relate and shows that if one refers to the law of war, there are often differences of understanding. From this foundation, just as with private international law, one should act according to general principles.

Thus, it seems that the cause of comparability lies in details. They are ordered according to criteria of comparability on the basis also as in general relations of systems.

Therefore, when evaluating the theory of comparability as a whole, it should be acknowledged that it is the basis and the summit of the comparison of law. By using the criteria of comparability, one may order the material for comparative studies so that the result gives us a clear image of the dependencies of changes in law. When classifying law according to criteria of comparability, one may among the changeability of empirical reality determine the basic factors of the dependencies in the history of law, and when one refers to dogmatic contemporary comparison, one may by analysis of the most advisable solutions determine the prospects for the further development of law. Comparability is the principal element of the comparative method, which not only gives it transparency, but, most importantly, the sense. Without distinguishing comparable laws and without a classification of the quality and

[254] Ibid., p. 172.

type of comparability between them, the comparison of law would not give such precision of analysis. It would be the accumulation of analogies and style of Post without taking into account the dependencies between them and without the investigation of the historical and vital laws of societal development. Therefore, the core of the theory of comparison should be considered to be the criteria of comparability presented and analyzed above.

# Chapter VIII. Ethnological Comparison



## 1. PROBLEM OF ETHNOLOGICAL LAW

Ethnological comparison, which has been analyzed above (see Chapter V(b); Chapter VI(2)), engages in comparative studies of legal phenomena within the confines of ethnology. By reason of its interests, it delves deeply into the field of ethnology, from which it differs because it investigates solely legal phenomena. The concept of legal phenomena is construed broadly in ethnological comparison, bearing in mind that ancient social forms did not know the now precise differentiation between customs, morals, religion, and law. Whereas it is easy to say of contemporary cultured peoples that they have law because there are accessible, clearly formulated sources of written and customary law, among primitive peoples it is difficult to separate law from other manifestations of social life. Therefore, when presenting the legal order of primeval peoples, their way of life, beliefs, and customs which do not relate to legal phenomena in the narrow sense have to be described over and over again. Science, however, should extract from this material all that may relate to the sphere of law and for the same purpose legal concepts should be used. But this aspiration cannot always be achieved, and in the absence of a sufficient transfer of tradition, ethnological studies of law will remain at the edge of historical quests,[255] because historical studies in general occupy a prominent

[255] Trimborn, note 8 above, p. 417.

place in the comparison of law as introductory works for the undertaking thereof.

This fact inspired Ernst Immanuel Bekker (1827-1916) in his day to protest against studies of individual laws being placed in a journal for the comparison of law. In his view, they were purely historical studies and should not fall within the competence of comparison.[256] But comparative studies become possible only when the historical material is systematically studied, and taking into account that the Historical School confined itself earlier solely to studies of German and Roman law, the comparative orientation should have engaged in the preparation of material for comparison in scientific works devoted to individual laws. In the introductory article to the *Zeitschrift für vergleichende Rechtswissenschaft*, Bernhöft also said that "in order to understand the ideas of other peoples well, one should understand their law well, just as was achieved with respect to Roman and Germanic law".[257]

If we speak of ethnological law, it is understandable that knowledge is gathered from second hands, especially from ethnological material assembled in passing by travelers, hunters, and missionaries. These sources are by their nature fragmentary, dilettantish, and unscientific. They were, however, in their day the sole sources from which facts were gathered for ethnographic comparison. It is another matter that incompetent individuals also undertook comparison; that is, not familiar either with ethnology or law. Therefore, it is no surprise that the early ethnological-comparative works encountered reproaches for the unscientific nature and dilettantism. Attraction cannot replace fundamental knowledge of the laws to be compared or conceal the superficiality of the comparison itself.[258]

Therefore, the early works, to recall those of Post, have only limited significance. The comparative method, just as ethnology, relies on induction, and this means that every assertion must be empirically proved. The early works do not meet these requirements. At that time, ethnology not enough full empirical substantiations to support deductions. Instead of the systematic study of the life of peoples and groups thereof, only descriptions

256 Bekker, note 84 above, p. 90.

257 Bernhöft, note 46 above, p. 37.

258 Bernhöft, note 46 above, p. 91.

of incidental ethnological details were permitted.[259] Therefore, the early works could not have full scientific value. Their importance was that they provided a certain survey of ethnological-legal material for raising problems for ordering and for orientation. However, they did not provide either ethnological or legal truths.

Kohler in his review of Post, *Die Grundlage des Rechts und die Grundzüge seiner Entwicklungsgeschichte* (1884), pointing to the significance of this kind of synthetic work as an essential transitional phenomenon, determined as a further task of the "comparative science of law" the study, with the assistance of special works, on the legal life of all peoples. Only after this preparatory work is completed will it be possible to ascertain with assurance the principles of the evolution of law.[260]

The tasks set by Kohler for ethnological comparison have so far not been fulfilled. The synthetic works by Kohler himself in this sphere have not radically changed the matter even though many detailed preparatory studies have since been undertaken. The results of these works synthetically presented by Kohler are merely an introduction to the final study of the subject-matter, and this task awaits someone to perform it.

Analytical preparatory works have moved forward. The comparative method has been developed more precisely. The delusions of early ethnological-comparative studies of law have been analyzed. All this charted the path for further work which might to a greater degree than the previous works of Post and Kohler be considered to be a successful performance of the tasks set for ethnological-comparative works in the field of law, including the design of a universal history of law.

## 2. UNRELIABLE SOURCES AND UNRELIABLE RESULTS

That which concerns the comparative method is discussed elsewhere in this work. The general rules of comparison should be adapted to ethnological studies of law, especially all that concerns the comparability of laws. Here we engage only is a discussion of

259 Schmidt, note 161 above, p. 370.

260 Ibid., p. 372.

how to approach accessible sources of ethnological law in order to ensure the scientific quality of the results of comparison.

In ethnological studies one should to a greater degree than in another science critically and with special care evaluate the sources when studying the material. The cooperation of ethnologists and jurists is essential for ethnological studies in order to reduce possible errors to a minimum. Ethnology, including legal ethnology, is forced to use incidental sources, such as descriptions of ethnographers, geographers, missionaries, officials, and others. It is evident that such sources must be precisely verified in order to develop a true image of reality.[261] The critique should consider the reliability of the author, draw all possible conclusions from such facts as the time and place of composition, the time and place of observation, and seek any possible dependence of various sources.[262] In addition, one should consider the reliability of the described details on the basis of the data of the description itself and by comparison with other sources.[263]

This introductory work makes it possible to ascertain undoubted facts for a determined place and time. These individual details should then be linked into a single whole, grouping them in a causal-historical perspective. Such a synthesis of legal phenomena should be undertaken earlier with respect to a single people. It should not only link individual legal phenomena, but also take into account all properties and changes of social life in which law is merely one component. This kind of causal linkage of legal institutions in time provides historical succession and logical completion. Only now, after the systematic study of individual laws, is it possible to commence comparison; that is, to link phenomena spatially up to a universal history of law.[264]

One should be aware, however, that even under the most severe and pedantic consistency in ethnological comparison, one cannot be assured of the results thereof. Obviously, it is easier to compare written laws and even customs because the memory of them has been better preserved. Unlike this, ethnological works are to a large degree confined to probabilities because they are based on

[261] Trimborn, note 8 above, p. 421.

[262] Ibid., p. 422.

[263] Ibid., p. 425.

[264] Ibid., p. 429.

unreliable data and incidental descriptions of mostly incompetent individuals. Therefore, this data can only be applied conditionally and interpreted as relatively true. But it cannot be completely cast aside, for it is hardly advisable to reject evidence of ancient writers which has come down to us in a miserly few, albeit fragmentary, copies.[265]

That science should use all accessible existing sources, studying them with the assistance of scientific methods, and accept the results of these works as true until they are refuted is not subject to doubt. This conforms ultimately to scientific principles according to which every assertion resting even on insufficient evidence making it merely plausible may be accepted conditionally so long as it is not contrary to other facts.

All this relates to the comparison of law in general, and especially to ethnological comparison, which by its nature has more non-conformities in evidence than other forms of comparison. Every even weak study in the sphere of ethnological law just as in every other may temporarily fill a gap and, having been accepted conditionally it value on the basis of a critical evaluation of its results, all the same can form a certain view on a certain matter. But this clearly does not justify instances when comparison is undertaken carelessly. When comparing law, one should proceed correctly and scrupulously as circumstances permit. Taking into account, however, the massive amount of material to be compared, especially having regard to unreliable ethnological sources, one should not be surprised that mistakes occur.[266]

Nonetheless, the unreliability of results in the comparison of law is no greater than in other sciences where mutually contradictory views and theories exist. Every science has moved from one mistake to another, and this is also permitted in the comparison of law which has in the ethnological material, taking special objective difficulties into account, special justification.

## 3. MAJOR MISTAKE OF EARLY ETHNOLOGICAL LAW

To a certain extent mistakes of principle are also justified which were committed by the pioneering researchers of ethnological law.

[265] Bekker, note 84 above, p. 91.

[266] Ibid., p. 92.

Using the comparative method, they *a priori* proclaimed certain assertions not fully substantiated and insufficiently proved by empirical material. They proceeded on the basis of hypotheses of the then scientific worldview led by the idea of evolution and were convinced of its truth, and they sought merely the confirmation thereof in ethnological material without endeavoring sufficiently to find the truth objectively. In a completely human way, they paid tribute to the ideology of their time.

Ultimately, from the outset both ethnology and the comparative method were captives of the natural worldview. Ethnology immediately after its emergence as a separate science fell into the group of nature-descriptive sciences. This was a time of Darwinism, and naturally the idea of evolution became an integral part of the method of the new discipline, the more so that the ideas of Hegelian historiosophy proceeded in the same direction. Ethnology as a science, just as history, could not close itself off from the ideas of evolution which had taken hold at that time in all natural sciences and under the influence of Hegel been embedded in the humanities.

The same factors influenced the development of the science of law (see Chapter II(8)). It too could not cast aside the idea of evolution, the more so because it had principally rejected the obsolete natural law.[267] The Historical School was at a turning point, having introduced the evolutionary ideas of Hegel on the science of law and imparted to the last the character of an inductive science. Although the horizons of the science of law expanded in this way, in fact the Historical School remained, together with the inductive method, within the confines of Roman and Germanic law. Only slowly under the influence of linguistics did historical studies of law expand to foreign systems. The decisive turn in the direction of expanding legal studies to all peoples of all times was given by the comparison of law, then called the comparative science of law. It created extensive opportunities for the science of law.[268] Ethnology and the comparison of law were born of the same ideas. The theory of evolution, as a revolutionary idea of that time in all the sciences, closely combined ethnology with the comparison of law. Ethnological comparison by its origin was entirely within the ambit of the natural sciences and only the separate comparative

[267] Schmidt, note 161 above, p. 352.

[268] Ibid., p. 353.

method separated the ethnological study of law from it. Legal ethnology, although during the time of evolutionism was among the natural sciences, pursued its own methodological paths and this separate it in particular and gave to it the indicia of a separate science.[269]

Albeit natural in essence, the theory of evolution negatively encumbered the comparison of law, especially ethnological comparison, which at the time was the principle domain of the application of the comparative method in law. The ethnological study of law was formed at a time when the theory of mechanical evolution exerted great influence on the historical sciences and all the pioneers of the comparison of law: Bachofen, Post, and Kohler. It is another matter, and this must be acknowledged, that in its day evolutionary theory facilitated the creation of the conception of the universal history of law,[270] and without this conception the comparison of law would not have attracted researchers, as in fact occurred, and without universal searches science would have merely had several monographs on the law of primitive peoples. Thus, not for the first time in science a false theory provided the beginning for other ideas which are firmly preserved at the time when it is refuted by criticism.

## 4. THEORY OF NATURAL EVOLUTION OF LAW

Post in his works most fully set out the theory of natural evolutionism. He resolutely supported the idea that ethnological-comparative studies should be included among the natural sciences because natural scientific views began to be applied also in the life of a people and the social sciences were discovering a trend towards becoming a natural science of social life – ethnology.[271] Post plainly opposed *a priorism* and abstractions, and therefore under the influence of Darwin attempted to base his assertions in the field of law on natural empiricism.[272] He believed that ethnology – a new science at the time – would deepen the science

[269] Trimborn, note 8 above, p. 416.

[270] Ibid., p. 430.

[271] Post, note 59 above, I, p. 5; Trimborn, note 8 above, p. 431.

[272] Post, *Die Grundlage des Rechts und die Grundzüge seiner Entwicklungsgeschichte* (1884), p. iv.

of law because it used the natural science method of research.[273] In the spirit of natural science, he wrote all his works reducing all phenomena of life to natural biological factors.[274]

The carrying over of the natural science method to the ethnological study of law, as Post insisted, led to a simplification of the problem and to casting aside searches for the concrete reasons for individual phenomena.[275] When interpreting every legal phenomenon according to the model of the natural sciences – as a type in which a certain rule is realized –the typical and homogeneous absorbed the individual and distinctive. But the natural science method aspired to exactly that outcome. In the view of Post, the comparative method so used economizes a mass of unnecessary work which a historical study undertakes in order to study details entirely unimportant for eliciting the essence. Such work is reminiscent by its uselessness of the senseless efforts of the botanist to establish every form of a flower of a certain type.[276] For ethnology, which should find typical phenomena, individual differences and chronological clarifications have only local significance solely in a particular ethnic milieu, but for they have no importance for the wholeness of an image of degrees of development because the phases of evolution are interpreted schematically as standard forms.[277] The variants of these universal forms of law present among individual peoples as a consequence of the distinctiveness thereof have no autonomous significance, but merely establish the limits of types.[278]

This typization of social phenomena is a result of the adaptation of natural science causality to ethnology. Just as in the natural sciences, which are engaged in non-organic, vegetative, or comparatively non-complex fauna life, mechanical causality suffices to concisely and exhaustively explain the linkage of phenomena without entering into unique deviations – so too, in Post's view, should ethnology through comparison determine

[273] Post, note 59 above, p. 2; Trimborn, note 8 above, p. 432.

[274] Post, note 272 above, p. 183.

[275] Trimborn, note 8 above, p. 433.

[276] Ibid., p. 434.

[277] Post, note 169 above (1880), p. 17.

[278] Post, note 59 above, p. 7.

only the typical in social facts. A comparative-ethnological study should provide cognition of the reasons for social forms by way of contrasting analogous or similar ethnic phenomena, wherever and whenever they emerge, and by way of formulating conclusions relative to their causes on the basis of these analogies.[279] This method tacitly applies the assumption that identical or similar phenomena of the life of peoples must necessarily have an identical cause because only under such an assumption can comparative studies of this kind provide the required outcome. Comparative science, according to Post, should find natural laws of the history of peoples excluding its arbitrary formation.[280] These natural laws explain the entire causality invariably guiding the history of peoples.[281]

In this mechanical understanding of history, the human species was a homogeneous mass with an identical psychic structure and with an identical trend of development. This view of history was linked with a respectively adapted method.[282] Ethnology sees mankind guided by large, strictly regulatory processes of development that over centuries and millennia proceed by their own paths without glancing at small historical events which here and there act as symptoms of this large process of development. In view of this, it is evident that the method of research should be directed chiefly, if not solely, towards identifying this large all-embracing law of the process of development.

This law of societal development in the mechanical evolutionism of Post was linked with the assumption that the human psychic structure is identical and in this connection the causes of actions are identical. In his view, the comparative-ethnological method demonstrated the deep parallelism of the legal life of all peoples on the planet. This parallelism is not accidental, but is an emanation of a common human nature.[283] The unity of the human species manifests itself at a time when world links unite the peoples of the

[279] Post, note 169 above (1880), p. 13.

[280] Post, *Einleitung in eine Naturwissenschaft des Rechts* (1872), p. 2.

[281] Trimborn, note 8 above, p. 435.

[282] Ibid., p. 436.

[283] Post, note 59 above, p. 4.

entire planet. At that time, science affirmed that common laws exist for all mankind.[284]

Kohler also surrendered to the impact of the theory of evolution. Although he linked it with the development of culture and juxtaposed his philosophy as the idealistic one, to positivism and materialism (which, in his view, describe phenomena in external mechanical dependence on the bedrock, while he acknowledged the leading role of the ideals of the cultural epoch of each time in the forming of law);[285] however, he considered every law to be valuable which corresponded to the requirements of a particular cultural epoch. The history of culture was for him a development in which a change of law occurs automatically and in parallel with changes of culture. This mechanical nature of the inheritance was close to the cult of all that time brings, so that despite theoretical idealism, Kohler is ascribed to the ranks of evolutionists of the natural scientific type.[286] In the aspiration for a universal history of law, Kohler valued the significance of monographs which might create the foundations for synthesis.[287]

Early ethnological comparison is characterized by natural science evolutionism – as Post saw it and Kohler in part.

## 5. DELUSIONS OF THEORY OF NATURAL EVOLUTION OF LAW

The ethnological-comparative method, as Post presented it, in determining consistently only the basic features of similarity, was characterized first and foremost by a formal-logical delusion, classifying very different phenomena into a single category. Thus Post relegated to tribal organizations all the same community with the matriarchate law, a totemic clan, and a patriarchal family – phenomena very heterogeneous in essence.[288] With the assistance of such a generalization classifying socio-legal phenomena,

[284] Post, *Studien zur Entwicklungsgeschichte des Familienrechts: Ein Beitrag zu einer Allgemeinen vergleichenden Rechtswissenschaft auf Ethnologischer basis* (1889), p. 3.

[285] Kohler, note 29 above, p. 7.

[286] Binder, note 41 above, p. 960.

[287] Trimborn, note 8 above, p. 437.

[288] Post, note 284 above, pp. 1, 21, 43, 47, 52.

evolutionism interprets the entire human species as a psychically homogeneous aggregate which develops identically according to laws of social development.[289] The entire early comparative-ethnological method rests on this assumption and evidently together with this assumption it is preserved and entering into decline. The last occurs when it is to be proved that the distinctive individual development of a separate essence is possible. In any event, the mechanical homogeneity of manifestations of the human will as evolutionism assumes this is contrary to the empirical facts of human behavior, which differs greatly and is not encompassed by the scheme of mechanical laws of societal development. Even determinism explains the obvious heterogeneity of history by the difference of character because of a different heritage, nurturing, cultural conditions, and the like which, together with various external conditions which every people has, excludes the *a priori* generalizing method of research.[290]

Despite this, the natural scientific interpretation of law enables one to mention in a study the observation of numerous minor chains of causality in individual instances and is satisfied by the determination of the most general homogeneous features, calling them natural laws. On the contrary, a scientific study should avoid *a priori* normative assertions, studying in each instance combinations and complexities of volitional acts in which the heterogeneity of objects of history and circumstances of each time are portrayed. In this contradiction the nature descriptive understanding of the laws of the societal development of culture should demonstrate that, although the psychology of man is homogeneous in basic features, one cannot prove an absolutely identical reaction to identical causes, and even if one accepts the causal conditionality of acts of human will, the real evidence of this can be only provided by detailed studies – to which extent the history of culture is a result of the internal laws of societal development of a human character and the homogeneity of its reaction to external motives.[291]

This evidence the ethnological-comparative method did not provide. The *a priori* and universal system of the history of law constructed on the basis of the acceptance of the natural scientific laws of societal development of history rested on false

[289] Trimborn, note 8 above, p. 442.

[290] Ibid., p. 443.

[291] Ibid., pp. 444-445.

assumptions. The adherents of evolutionism, when adapting their extrinsic method to the universal studies of legal history, were forced to fill in its shortcomings with psychological-reconstructive hypotheses, which in the absence of precise evidence should have combined individual ethnological facts into an integral *a priori* thought out evolutionary theory. The psychological conclusions of Kohler testify to how the fantasy of the evolutionists helped them create a single system: "of course, the development of a herd state proceeded in the direction of monogamous marriage and the separation of individual couples occurred so that a male chose one female and thus separated her from all the others".[292] Or: "Everything belongs to the State and tribe, and no one wants something for himself or herself".[293] Post clearly recognized that his approach to ethnological material in his works was *a priori* reconstructive. One year, he said, he spent in consistent reflection in order to combine these fragments found in isolation into a single structure of development.[294]

In the comparative study of law, this approach would be correct: in asserting factually the numerous analogies in legal forms of various peoples, one should determine beforehand whether and to what extent one may rely on genetic and historical mutual relations between them. And they may sometimes arise thanks to the joint heritage from one kinship line, and further through travels, borrowing, imposition, conquest, and so on. When all these and similar possibilities have been established through historical and comparative studies, only then will it be possible to carefully assume as probable that the other analogous phenomena are a result of a common process of development.[295] And in this case it should also be determined to what extent this analogy is not incidental as a consequence of identical geographical or technical relations which independently led to similar legal forms. Only after the determination of genetic, historical, and incidental similarities on the basis of evidence may an assumption be allowed with

[292] Kohler, "Die Anfänge des Rechts und das Recht der primitiver Völker", in P. Hinneberg (ed.), *Die Kultur der Gegenwart. Ihre Entwicklung und ihre Ziele* (1914), II(VII), 1, p. 8.

[293] Ibid., p. 12.

[294] Post, note 272 above, p. vi. Evidence of this approach also is found on pp. 38, 43, 45, 48, and 59.

[295] Trimborn, note 8 above, p. 449.

respect to other analogies that they are the result of an identical human nature developing in a single direction.

When evaluating the mistakes of early ethnological comparison as a whole, the assertion is necessarily made: the lack of the use of criteria of comparability when comparing, together with the assumption of mechanistic development, had led to the conscious or unconscious erosion of differences between legal phenomena, on one hand, and on the other, did not impart to comparative works clarity and transparency in conclusions and consequences. A partial explanation of these delusions is the universalist orientation of the researchers who sought a synthesis prematurely, even before performing the preparatory work relating to the analysis of legal phenomena of individual peoples and groups of peoples.

It seems, however, that ethnological comparison will continue first and foremost to be the study of types of legal forms. There will be various reasons for this. The shortage of precise sources forces one to rely on various fragmentary retellings which by their nature present law only in its general features. Great temporal and spatial differences of the ethnological material to a significant degree diminish the genetic and historical influences between the objects to be compared and for analogies remain basically the general frameworks of typical, logical forms, which can be drawn from identical conditions of life or, at least, from an identical human nature. These moments will continue to predetermine that ethnological comparison will present broad pictures of general analogies, leaving to historical and dogmatic comparison precise comparative analysis which the sources make possible, being rich in details in these types of comparison. Ultimately, ethnological comparison also is set the task of investigating the origins, causes and evolution of law, defining with this formula its tasks in directing searches for typical universal phenomena. Conditioned by the type of sources, the tendency of ethnological law to seek the most typical in phenomena of law also explains why early ethnological studies led scholars directly to a universal history, irrespective of whether this was facilitated by their scientific worldview. The material investigated directed them on the whole to a universal interpretation of phenomena, and interests proceeded along this line, leaving all other moments aside. Delusions arose, and general comparative assertions made that lack scientific solidity because the generalizations and classifications of legal phenomena remained unproven. This eliminated the services of ethnological law. They were significant, and ethnological comparison deserves to be considered separately.

Now, when the comparative method has been improved and ethnographic material is more solid, and certain preparatory works in the field of ethnological comparison have been made, the time are more appropriate for synthesis. The lack of interest in this kind of work is being felt, however, because, on one hand, the most general and sensational truths in this field are known to all, and, on the other, comparative studies have other spheres for study, namely history and, especially, dogmatics. The attention of researchers is being directed there, and ethnological comparison, after a brilliant commencement, is being developed in the quiet and shadows, awaiting a great synthesizer who would finish the task of which Kohler at one time thought.

## 6. UNIVERSAL HISTORY OF LAW CONSTRUCTED ON BASIS OF ETHNOLOGICAL LAW

Also awaiting realization is the conception of a universal history of law, which once was closely linked with the ethnological comparison of law. Proposed at one time by Post and later substantiated by Kohler, who even tried to positively realize it, finally it found substantiation in the theoretical works of Del Vecchio. The realizer of this conception has yet to be found.

That the early idea of a universal history of law was linked with ethnological comparison and may be said to have developed on the basis of ethnological studies at the time was reflected in the construction thereof so strongly that there are grounds to discuss this together with ethnological comparison. The entire scientific worldview of a comparative orientation is reflected in the conception of a universal history of law of the old school, and this brings it close to ethnological comparison.

The foundation of a universalist understanding of law is the assumption that all people have an identical nature and therefore law develops everywhere identically. As a result, it is in principle so similar that law can be reduced to common fundamentals and with the assistance of the comparative-ethnological method an integral image presented of the history of law of all mankind. A universal history of law built on ethnological comparison was orientated entirely to search for these foundations in pra-forms of law and in their evolution. The searches for the typical in law characterize the early universal history of law based on the conception of a single evolution of mankind should proceed in one direction.

a) *Universalism in the Works of Post and Kohler*. This presumption Post viewed as a fact proved by the then comparative works in the field of ethnological law. The object of history in his understanding was mankind, in which peoples were merely fragments with all their distinctiveness not essential for mankind as a whole.[296] It creates unity, the basis of which is an identical human nature. This nature originates in the parallel legal life of all peoples developing according to general laws identical for all peoples.[297]

As we see, the universalism of Post rests on a natural-science mechanical foundation which understands legal phenomena as articles that may be systematized according to external analogues, determining only the principal standard forms because they are directly products of one pra-cause, namely, identical human nature.

Wherein lies the confusion in Post's thinking has been demonstrated above. The template interpretation of legal phenomena which sees only standard forms cannot comprehend differences that exist within universal types. This template classification which theoretically should be the foundation of comparison distorts the grounds of empiricism. An empirical approach should dictate a detailed analysis of phenomena with the determination of genetic, historical, and incidental analogues. Only after ordering similar features in law according to these criteria of comparability can one have a correct view of the universal foundations of law which emanate from identical human nature.

Post interpreted analogy in law *a priori* universalistically and, having proposed a universalist hypothesis, only searched for facts confirming it. Given this hasty and unscientific approach, he not only did not prove his basic assertions, but undermined confidence in such a pseudo-empirical method.

Kohler also did not earn this trust, for he, similarly to Post, proved the universalism of law and in this connection the

[296] Post, note 169 above (1880), p. 17; Post, note 59 above, p. 7.

[297] Post, note 59 above, p. 4; Post, note 284 above, p. 3.

possibility and necessity of a universal history of law. Although he proceeded from historiosophical thought in the spirit of Hegel, he adhered in his main assertions to the theory of evolution, which despite idealistic phraseology did not differ from the natural mechanistic theory.

The point of departure for Kohler was the stable development of culture, which conditioned the development and progress of law to the same extent. The evolution of culture, in his view, was contrary to the theory of natural law because although human development is based on animal psychological laws that are always immutable in their profound essence, something different and new arises from the mixture of different forces, and one cannot draw a permanently identical and immutable natural law from the uniformity human character.[298]

Hegel's theory of evolution, especially the "comparative science of law", showed the powerful development of law and therefore affirmed that law is diverse in time and space, and no legal forms can be eternal. Any identical laws of the development of law in the nature of justness, equality of interpretation by the legal system of living phenomena from which no one can be privileged or humiliated, and so on – are merely templates which every cultural period fills with its own content. Each epoch decides what is good and bad, what is advisable, what is inadvisable, that is just or not, and the aforementioned abstract principles merely confirm the assertion that law is developing in dependence on the conditions of a period of culture and law becomes that which is considered to be law at a particular time.[299]

Even such apparently most correct criteria for the evaluation of law as the dignity of labor is nothing other than a general place which the dominant world outlook interprets distinctly, Certain types of occupations in olden times were not regarded as labor in the full meaning of this word, were neither honorable nor worthy of a free man. For example, the calling of a theater actor was until recently an occupation to which, in the view of authoritative circles, a self-respecting person should not devote himself or herself. Labor as a general evaluative and normative criterion of

[298] Kohler, note 29 above, p. 3.

[299] Ibid., pp. 4-5.

law was reflected in law only in that form which responded to the state and degree of the development of culture.[300]

The aspiration for happiness and well-being of the public similarly cannot be regarded as a normative factor of law. The realization of aspirations and the achievement of public satisfaction as a dynamic factor of culture cannot explain its development because it often emanated independently of the well-being of individuals and the masses. Not the consumption of benefits but only cultural achievements determine its place in history.[301]

Having regard to all that has been said, law is not an incidental, external product, but is rooted in the psyche and character of a people who in the aspiration to develop improve and create constantly new legal institutions in accordance with the dominant views and conditions. Law thus should be evaluated only from the standpoint of the state of culture and its consumers, and only this criterion may determine the ideal of law for a particular time. Law grows from the foundations of culture with which it develops together, having a different appearance in each epoch: statically it represents the past epoch and at the same time prepare the path for a new epoch.

The philosophy of law, from the standpoint of historical development, becomes a philosophy of ideals and, in counterbalance to positivist and materialist philosophy, which considers a scientific view on the essence of phenomena to be impossible and describes them in external-mechanistic dependence from the materia – determines a leading role in the formation of law for the ideals of the epoch.[302]

The philosophy of law formulates a goal of the cognition thereof by the method of comparison of the results of the history of law against the background of the entire cultural development. Only the universal range of law can provide the grounds for the philosophy of law.[303] Studies of law in the world aspect are therefore essential, for law does not exist outside human life as, for example, nature does, but just as language, is a human product developing

[300] Ibid., p. 6.

[301] Ibid., p. 9.

[302] Ibid., pp. 6-7.

[303] Ibid., p. 9.

together with man. Every legal structure is an expression of a cultural formation of its time, and observation of the changes thereof is an indicator of the cultural processes in history.[304] The universal history of law, also called the comparative science of law, has the purpose to study the law of all possible peoples, living and deceased, old and new, cultured and primitive.[305]

As we see, universalism in law is closely linked in Kohler with comparative studies that, at the time, ethnology undertook. Kohler argued it basically by asserting the historiosophy of Hegel, the cultural-philosophical reflections which determine his programmatically as an idealist. With his emphasis on evolution, however, Kohler remained a prisoner of this mechanistic positivism against which he convincingly struggled. The core of Kohler's evolutionist theory was the degrees of development through which all mankind passes within the framework of individual nations in a dense dependence on the development of degrees of culture. The entire development of all peoples, basically independent from one another and, allowing for local deviations, homogeneous, in Kohler's view undergoes these degrees. Instead of the concept "standard forms" used by Post, Kohler suggested "degrees of development", but he did not change the mechanistic essence of the natural science understanding which he had decisively rejected from the outset. The automatism of the development of law is especially evident in Kohler's emphasis that law in every epoch was called forth by the cultural conditions existing and was justified by the fact that it was responsive to the ideals of the time. In this sense Kohler's evolutionism coincided with the assertion of materialism on the inevitability of the developmental trends in which every degree of development is an orientation point for the future, each positive law being the correct law for the particular degree of culture. In this understanding, all law was a good decision, and all that will be is correct because development, taking into account the state of culture, found and finds all the best legal forms, automatically giving the respective law corresponding to the degree of culture.

With this emphasis on the automatism and mechanism of development, Kohler rejected his own idealist foundations and, standardizing them into periods and degrees of development,

[304] Ibid., p. 14.

[305] Ibid., p. 16.

came to a paradoxical denial of his own assertion on the differences of human forms.[306] Therefore, the universal works by Kohler placed in the Holzendorff *Enzyclopädie* and in *Die Kultur der Gegenwart* did not differ materially from Post's works. The same spirit of positivism and evolutionism unites their works which, being a review of ethnological comparison of that time, by its simplification of the problems share the same confusions. For this reason, among others, their works did not perform the tasks set by their authors, and the universal history of law advanced by ethnological comparison is to date represented by nobody.

b) *Theory of Del Vecchio.* Del Vecchio sought to raise the question from a more theoretical vantage point of the universal history of law built on a comparative basis. He tried to resolve the contradiction into which Kohler fell – between typization of facts investigated with the assistance of comparison and attention to the differences between them – and upheld the position of natural law rejected by historical and comparative schools on the unity of the human character and law.

Whereas Kohler in acknowledging theoretically the national differentiation of laws, saw in the evolution of culture a universal bridge between them, whereas Del Vecchio expressly suppported the assertion of the old natural law about the homogeneity of human nature of all times, which he modernized. He simultaneously found within the universal conception a place for national distinction.

He accepted the logical homogeneity of law as proved and explained it by the fact that human nature is homogeneous (see Chapter VII(2)(d)). In his view, identical conditions and requirements of human nature throughout the world influenced the logical similarity of law on a universal scale.

However, even if it seems paradoxical, the unity of human nature was for the old theory of natural law not an adequate foundation for the discourses and conclusions, and hence all the confusions. It actually drew the ideal of law, despite its assertions, not from the marks of man, but only placed on the pedestal of eternal natural law the actual or apparent legal forms of those systems known to theoreticians of the old natural law.

And therefore the old natural law is merely a deceptive speculative and abstract theory. It is evident upon closer

[306] Binder, note 41 above, pp. 959-960.

examination that it is based on ideas borrowed from Roman law which at the time was the sole historical and dogmatic foundation of law in force. Complete agreement between universal and absolute old natural law and Roman law evidently reveals it as a speculative construction and is reduces it to the real foundations.

Del Vecchio did not doubt that all the mistakes of the old natural law were a consequence of a narrow and one-sided worldview of its theoreticians, who without extensive and profound knowledge of world legal phenomena constructed their own theories, relying on the one-sidedness of the close facts known to them. The historical school ultimately committed this same mistake as the school of natural law, which despite its general principles, occupied itself thereafter only with Roman and German law.[307]

In order to avoid the delusions of the old theory of natural law and at the same time to be in a position to acknowledge as a natural fact every positive law, Del Vecchio distinguished two meanings, two understandings, of the concept of natural law.

In his understanding, every positive law is natural in the sense that within the framework of causal laws of societal development it performs a purpose conditioned by the natural data of its time. In this sense positive law is a phenomenon of nature and may be understood and studied only in connection with the natural data of its period. This does not mean, however, that positive law represents nature in a higher, supra-empirical understanding. Positive law can be interpreted as a natural necessity, as a reality, fact, which norms law and duties in accordance with requirements and conditions of a particular time, but it is not obliged to conform to the ideal of law. On the other hand, one also can trace law from absolute human nature, and this law, based on the essence of human personality, as a legal duty and subjective claim, has significance higher than any positive reality.

Thus, Del Vecchio distinguishes two interpretations of natural law. In his view, one cannot refuse to some legal institution a naturalness if it does not correspond to the ideal of law and, on the contrary, it would not be correct to refuse recognition to an ideal because it was not fully realized within a legal order. The ideal of

[307] Del Vecchio, note 9 above, p. 227.

law by its nature is above the world of empirical reality and retains a binding truth even when it does not correspond to fact.[308]

It is undoubted that slavery was a legal institution determined by empirical conditions, and in this sense it was a natural phenomenon. Being a law, however, it did not realize the ideal of law because it could be extracted from the idea of the absolute human personality. Slavery was a concept of law, but it was not consistent with an innate human aspiration for freedom as a natural ideal, an unconditional requirement of its realization burning in the essence of man irrespective of any norms of positive law.

No dogmatism has the power to push into the background that which is unjust in the history of law, and natural law in its ideal sphere remains immutable in content, become clearer when positive law is contrary to it. On the other hand, unjust law is also law and should be analyzed as a logical quality, as a formal legal construction, and also as a causally conditioned phenomenon of nature.[309]

Natural law so defined by Del Vecchio made it possible for him to coordinate the changeability of empiricism with the theory of the eternal and immutable law. By this means he simultaneously and successfully resolved the issue of agreeing standard, universal forms with the fact of the existence of differences in law in time and space. He formulated on higher grounds the theory of the comparative method and a construction of the universal history of law.

On the assertion of the existence of the unity of human spirit manifest in the universality of the development of law, he founded, using his words, the "comparative science of law". The source of law is contained in human nature because each consciousness is capable of rising above its own personality and creating a just attitude towards others. This absolute requirement of truth rooted in each subject leads to all positive systems always reflecting an identical human nature to such a degree that law spontaneously, despite all the differences, forms itself into a similar logical whole.[310] This imparts basic comparability to it.

308 Del Vecchio, note 6 above, p. 467.

309 Ibid., p. 468.

310 Del Vecchio, note 9 above, p. 401.

Del Vecchio further alleged that only comparative studies provide a full and comprehensive knowledge of the development of law. Individual national systems display their individual properties and only the comparison of law can present a comprehensive and integral image. An integral and universal history of the development of law can be reconstructed by contrasting and comparing various national laws because their historical development is asynchronic, non-simultaneous, and therefore the augmentation and reconstruction is possible of past periods of contemporary systems on the basis of discovered monuments of law of other ancient systems or collected contemporary primitive orders of uncultured peoples. Moreover, the ancient law of any people is never a complete survival, but certain remnants of times past are preserved which may be studied and understood by means of the comparison of law. Legal thought of the past never disappears completely; it is held in later additions and intertwined in new forms and one way or another lives in modern times.[311]

With the assistance of attentive consideration it is possible to a certain extent to demarcate mixed strata of different legal systems at different periods of development and reconstruct the history of the construction of a particular system. This reproduction is possible, *inter alia,* because certain fragments of law which as remnants of a past period create a certain incorrectness in modern times by means of comparison with legal institutions of peoples of another degree of development and culture may be fully studied and understood because in the last they are preserved as fully-fledged and organic parts of the system thereof.

Similarities are discovered in the process of comparison between externally different systems and remnants of historical legal institutions which appeared to be completely independent and separate and they are reduced to a mutually reinforcing whole, thereby filling unknown gaps in the system of law. Thus, a series of material indicia of legal life were clarified which identically characterized both the most ancient legal periods of modern civilized peoples and contemporary legal orders of primitive tribes. The historico-ethnological and comparative methods are mutually reinforcing, making possible the systematic reconstruction of historical development of law and the construction of a universal history of law.

[311] Del Vecchio, note 6 above, p. 22.

Post and Kohler effectuated such an all-embracing presentation of the legal orders of all peoples on the basis of logical, non-chronological ordering.[312]

The universalism of Del Vecchio is evident in the aforementioned observations. The basic comparability of all systems makes possible, in his view, a synthesis by way of comparison of the logical forms of all times and peoples. This historical-comparative analysis within individual systems, while explaining the development of law therein, provided basic material for a universal history of law. The need for attentive investigation of individual national laws to which Kohler had drawn attention Del Vecchio specially linked to his universal theory. Relying on the foundation of the natural homogeneity of law which arose without any direct dependence of one system on another by the very fact of its human origin, he could not ignore the numerous historical instances of the borrowing and imposition of foreign law. Recognizing this fact as a historical phenomenon, he explained the possibility of the appropriation of foreign law by the unity of human nature and the similarity of legal forms, which facilitate historico-legal relations of that type. Every people may adapt the law of another people because in essence law is not exclusively a national phenomenon, but a human product. Every law has certain universal traits and can be accepted by another people with a certain adaptation to its requirements.

The classical example was the acceptance of Roman law by the Germans. This was not an isolated event. Every people was to a greater or lesser extent in its development under the influence of a law of another people. And Roman law also during its development absorbed the laws of Greece and of the Mediterranean basin. In more recent times there is the appropriation of English parliamentary institutions by other States.[313]

This ability to carry over legal norms from one soil to another raised the level of the particular law. The laws and customs of highly cultured peoples extend beyond the limits of their homeland and relatively rapidly and easily are domesticated on another's soil despite the existence of old local law. The legal thought of one people thus becomes the ownership of another and after a certain reworking becomes an organic integral part of another

[312] Ibid., p. 23.

[313] Ibid., p. 24.

legal system. In this event the value of legal institutions is a reason of the appropriation, and this moment dominates the historico-national conditionality of the high-quality law. Although it grew within a specific nation-State milieu, because of internal value it acquires an autonomous existence, which is the reason for the further adaptation of these thoughts in other milieus. Thus, legal institutions as an expression of the universality of human nature which breaks its way through national traits may be interpreted ahistorically.[314]

And so the carrying over of law from one people to another is not contrary to the idea of the homogeneous development of law. On the contrary, the inculcation of law is possible because a natural basis exists in the homogeneity of human nature. A common human character is reflected in every law, and therefore individual laws may be mutually inculcated.[315] Both the internal development of the law of each people and the exchange of legal thought between peoples leads to universalism of law. The comparative, universal science of law which makes visual and establishes the phases of this trend is itself an instrument of the unification of law. It is higher than the history of law because of its universal character, which proposes in historical facts to see the supra-historical, eternal human individual who identically is reflected in new and past times. In world law, which as positive law is relegated to categories of phenomena, are reflected eternal values of human nature – identical for all times and peoples. Individual empirical positive resolutions of legal problems are subordinate in all instances to the idea of justice, to this absolute ideal of man.[316] This makes possible with the assistance of the comparative method an understanding of contemporary and past institutions of various peoples as one universal system.

The difficulties in constructing a universal history of law with the assistance of the comparative method lay, for Del Vecchio, not in the underlying strata, but in the practical possibilities.

The study of universal legal phenomena will never be fully achieved. Many peoples have disappeared from history, leaving weak traces of their existence. Many monuments have been lost,

[314] Del Vecchio, note 9 above, p. 403.

[315] Del Vecchio, note 6 above, p. 25.

[316] Del Vecchio, note 9 above, p. 406.

many legal customs have passed into oblivion. It is now impossible to reconstruct the legal systems of peoples who did not achieve the legislative or scientific elaboration of their law. These difficulties can be partly overcome with the assistance of detailed labor.[317]

Other difficulties impeding the adoption of a program for a universal history of law, according to Del Vecchio, are the prejudices of jurists. Above all, national exclusiveness ascribing to one's own law a pre-eminent significance is an obstacle to universalism. In simple form it is now less in evidence, but concealed in refined form it is an obstacle to comparative studies requiring great objectivity. The idea of a chosen people having its origin in primitive religious systems surfaces later in various forms and is found even in completely contemporary developed philosophical systems. It is a reason for certain confusions in the science of the Italian, Giambattista Vico (1668-1744), and one need not recall how harmfully it influenced the philosophy of the German, Hegel.

As an idea connected with any system limited by its data and facts, Del Vecchio showed by using the example of Roman law. Roman law influenced the science of law to the greatest extent. This may be explained by the fact that it was the principal source of existing legal systems and, thanks to its technical perfection, the transparency of its constructions, and the succession of its development, was the greatest monument of legal thought of mankind. Moreover, it is known in its most developed form. This law, known as the oldest, had such features as, for example, a clearly designated patriarchal family, developed forms of procedure, and so on which indicate that it was the result of lengthy but unknown development. This ancient period may be traced among other peoples, ancient or new, but with a lower culture than in the ancient Roman period.

The perfection of the system of Roman law is an obstacle to interpreting it as a model of law in the universal aspect. Roman law, just as any other, is a historical phenomenon and in this sense it is merely a special effectuation of the idea of law whose content could not be confined to Roman law.[318] Other legal conceptions are of equal value, although they do not represent such a perfected system as the Roman.

317 Ibid., p. 224.

318 Ibid., pp. 226-227.

Del Vecchio's reflections on Roman law relate to all systems, each of which has its own national traits and historical explanation. In order to find a universal system, however, one must look above all systems without exception and see in them only the non-transitional and the eternal, in reality.

One also should cast off the fetters of positive law as such. Jurists are not free of illusions which overestimate the significance of existing facts, ascribing to them virtually absolute value. The positive law of a people and the time to which it belongs strongly influences jurists. In devoting their attention and labor to the law in force, they are inclined to ascribe a perfection thereto and to interpret positive law not as a law which somewhere or sometime obliged or obliges, but only in the laws of their motherland. For these reasons, jurists cannot see the gaps and shortcomings of the law in force presently in force. Confining their interests to the existing legal order, they cannot go beyond this closed range of the now and the motherland. Only moving beyond the range of some individual system and evaluating legal phenomena from a higher elevation can provide an understanding of their relativity in which they are merely one variant and neither the beginning nor the ultimate completion of law.[319]

Thus did Del Vecchio assess the difficulties facing a universal history of law. This practical analysis of the possibilities of creating a conception of a universal law showed Del Vecchio to be a sober researcher who, in aspiring for the heavens, was aware that he was on earth. This sober approach also is seen in his attentive interpretation of real heterogeneous historical facts which he, unlike Kohler, not only separated out in a programmatic matter but also generalized in their totality, deeming them to be a virtually parallel factor in the creation of law by the side of the universal-homogeneous development of law. The ease with which Del Vecchio combined the assertion concerning the parallel development of law as a general human phenomenon with the fact of national diversity imparted to this theory significant persuasiveness. One does not find a center of gravity in his conception, as in Kohler and Post, exclusively in identical or similar degrees of culture of types of development, but it falls equally into logical identical forms and national variants which are, as he said, only a "special effectuation of the idea of law" and not an ideal thereof.

[319] Ibid., p. 225.

This, so to say, dualist view of Del Vecchio on the question of the unity and diversity of law was developed a bit later in the cautious and restrained assertions of Rabel. In his view, comparison demonstrated simultaneously, on one hand, the relativity, conditionality, and changeability of positive law and, on the other, showed the impressive kinship of the institutions and development of different cultures, peoples, and races. These similarities should not reduce to a direct chain of imitations and their impacts (although Del Vecchio is more correct in pointing to the unity of human character as the reason for analogy); however, the principal task of the comparison of law is the cognition of truth.[320] This truth, in Rabel's opinion, may be cognized by finding a similarity on the basis of a common origin, reception, or autonomous factors operating in parallel.[321] Only in this way can one find plausible general human analogies (see Chapter VII(2)(e) and (4)(c)). Regrettably, Del Vecchio did not express a clear view on this aspect of the question.

Therefore, although his assertion on the question of the universality of law finds fresher confirmations, from the standpoint of comparison of law as a whole it is not entirely correct. Del Vecchio, of the view directed in priority to the universality of law for the construction of which comparison should be a useful means, was not in principle interested in the details of comparative analysis, although unlike Post and Kohler, he did not close his eyes to national differences. In his opinion, the parallel development underlies all changes which, as reasonable and logical categories, were reflected in all variants of the homogeneous nature of man. In this understanding, genetic and historical similarities for him are merely a function of the universal. Ultimately, Del Vecchio said that the borrowing of foreign models and their absorption are evidence that law contains general human elements above all. This position possibly is understandable from the standpoint of universality, but for the comparative method it is harmful. The precision and transparency of comparative analysis requires the good faith application of all the criteria of comparability which guarantee that not only the typical and the gross, but also the special and the precise, will be determined in law.

[320] Rabel, note 77 above, p. 284.

[321] Ibid., p. 281.

In assessing the general significance of Del Vecchio for the comparison of law – and the last in time of his basic studies was based almost entirely on ethnological studies – it should be acknowledged that when ascribing to them an auxiliary role with respect to the universal history of law, the researcher cognized their value for knowledge of law in historical studies and philosophical reflections. The passion and convictions of Del Vecchio speak now to the reader who allows himself to be captivated by the integral existence of the image of law without the unpolished natural science evolutionism and mechanistic dogmatism. Del Vecchio differs in this theory from the old ethnological comparison and from the universal constructions of Post and Kohler. The reason is probably the contemporary construction of natural law used by Del Vecchio. It gave him better philosophical foundations for theoretical reflections than his predecessors. They vacillated between a natural science worldview and an extra-worldview legal positivism, whereas Del Vecchio took an autonomous legal worldview which gave him more freedom and confidence of expression.

As for the old universal conceptions as a whole, it should be noted once again: they were densely linked with the ethnological studies of the time. Therefore, all the confusions of the old ethnological school are also discovered in the attempts to conceive a universal law. Only Del Vecchio, although an adherent of ethnological comparison, thanks to his modernized philosophy of natural law, does not rely on natural science evolutionism.

Although the theory of universal law had confusions and was not realized, as already noted its all-encompassing construction greatly influenced the development of comparative studies of ethnological law. It inspired and preserved the interest of researchers in the study of ethnological legal phenomena far from the forms of all positive laws of the time around which the entire science of law revolved. Now, when the old construction of the universal history of law has been cast aside based solely on ethnological comparison and instead or together with it a new conception has emerged relying on historical or contemporary systems together with a universalist shift of interest in a newer period of history, ethnological comparison was moved to the back burner and became a veteran instead of a leader of the comparative method in the study of law. The comparative method wants to determine in law not only typical phenomena as ethnological comparison had done (and a universal history built on it which had a natural inclination to a search for a typical), but also as many analogies and differences in details as possible, which make legal forms interesting and expressive. The wealth and diversity of life capture more than monotypal homogeneity.

# Chapter IX. Historical Comparison

1. Comparative Method in Historical Studies. 2. Limits and Scale of Studies in Historical Comparison. 3. Universal History of Law as Synthesis of Historical-Comparative Studies.

Whereas ethnological comparison and the universal history of law based thereon provided (and one may suppose will continue to do so) especially general surveys of an analogy of typical legal forms, historical comparison has to a large extent natural data to determine analogies and differences of variant solutions of legal problems within the confines of the types side by side with similarities of the latter. More precise and rich than ethnological sources, historical sources of law provide substantial material for historical-comparative works and broad scope for scientific conclusions. Therefore, historical-legal comparison quantitatively dominates ethnological.

But historical comparison differs from ethnological not by method, but by subject-matter. When ethnological comparison was engaged solely with ethnological law, historical comparison had the purpose to encompass the entire breadth of historical phenomena in law. In this sense, ethnological law is part of the history of law.[322]

## 1. COMPARATIVE METHOD IN HISTORICAL STUDIES

Historical comparison is closely connected with historical studies; they strongly overlap. It differs from the history of law basically in that when using, as a historical science, in equal degree the methods of analysis and synthesis, it aspires to provide a cross-section of legal phenomena in that time as the history of law explains their continuous development. Historical comparison puts forward the question of the link of legal phenomena in space, studying them according to the criteria of comparability. The history of law is engaged basically with the question of the temporal

[322] Trimborn, note 8 above, pp. 417, 420.

grouping of law, determining the dependencies influencing the change thereof. Throughout all this, the history and comparison of law are intertwined and tend to provide in a synthesis a universal history of law this time structured not only on ethnological, but also on historical-comparative studies in all their breadth.

Comparison may be historical for the history of law itself.[323] The comparison of law ultimately uses by default every historical study. The development of an individual historical institute of law at various times provides a crosscut after comparison of all periods and a full image of the changes in time. This link between comparison and history should not be considered accidental, and it should be interpreted as a result of the close relation between the historical school and comparison.[324] But the comparative method is useful when investigating a certain legal system not only by comparing its individual epochs, but also their comparative contrasting with respective epochs of other systems. Comparison of the results of the study of sources of one law with the respective sources of another provides useful additions and confirmations for conclusions and suggestions which arose during the investigation of the sources. In so doing, one should only use the general rules for comparison.[325] When investigating some ambiguous fragment in history, one may compare analogous parts of other legal systems according to the criteria of comparability. With the assistance of these cross-sections of genetic, historical, or cultural-civilizationally analogous laws (or even whole series of such comparative cross-sections), one may explain or fill gaps of sources of the law being studied.

It is evident that under this kind of comparison certain petty differences remain aside and there is reliance on typization to a certain degree of forms and a search for analogous complexes or fragments.[326] However, the simplification of problems with the assistance of typization in historical comparison occurs on a small scale in matters less petty than in ethnological comparison. For comparison, the problem is formulated as broadly as necessary in the particular instance, and may take into account only a

[323] Bekker, note 84 above, p. 90.

[324] Adam, note 67 above, p. 2.

[325] Lautner, note 11 above, p. 65.

[326] Ibid., p. 71.

small fragment. Within those limits in which it is determined as a comparative object it becomes a type insensitive to insignificant deviations.

This trend towards typization in the comparative method may be neutralized thanks to attentive historical analysis. In order to cognize any law, one must study its history with care. The more profound is the study, the more precise and comprehensive will be the knowledge of that law because only comparison of its various changes in time provides a basis for evaluating its present state. Every state of development preserves in itself all preceding changes. Each epoch includes beside the innovations of its time also the remnants of past periods.[327] The past lives in the contemporary in some way further, often in latent form, and in a mixture with the contemporary. Attentive observation, however, may differentiate various layers of time. Some remnant of the past may explain an unknown gap in the system, and one formula preserved by an unconscious tradition may make possible the reconstruction of legal relations of a past epoch. Such a reconstruction will be especially successful if some preserved fragment in the background of the law in force of a particular system as a deviation exists in full harmony with the entire system in some other legal structure of a different people having a lower state of culture.[328]

In this case, a good faith and detailed analysis within the system, with the assistance of comparison of individual changes in time locates the problem, defines it, and makes it the object of further comparison with respective parts of other systems. Only if this comparison discovered an analogy, can a reconstruction of a legal institution from the remnant of a tradition acquire the character of scientific evidence. Such is the consistency in historical-comparative studies. /

They must be objective. The researcher must eliminate a "natural science" attitude toward the objects of comparison, ethically disarm himself, and evaluate phenomena impartially and "amorally". Only then can both cannibalism and witchcraft be understood, and other phenomena rejected.[329] Only then can one evenly and objectively evaluate the laws to be compared.

[327] Del Vecchio, note 9 above, p. 230.

[328] Ibid., p. 231.

[329] Ibid., p. 229.

The general basis of historical comparison is that a certain law should be studied first and foremost on the basis of own sources. Comparison must in so doing be an auxiliary and supplemental means. One must be very careful when applying the criteria of comparability. Among three factors making the law of different systems similar, one must be especially attentive to parallel development arising on different territories and at a different time independently of one another thanks to identical cultural, economic, and social relations.[330] Taking this aspect into account, one should not in each instance consider very minor analogies as evidence of the inculcation of law. Analogies do not prove reception; for this additional data is essential such as, for example, that a particular legal institution which in one law creates an organic whole with the system comprises in another a completely solitary part. On the other hand, one should take into account that the borrowed institution is so adapted to the conditions and customs of a people that the initial differences between the old and the borrowed law erode and they grow into an organic whole. It happens that the borrowing occurs through the appropriation only of legal formulas, especially when the peoples of a low culture encounter the developed law of an old culture, for example, the Germans with Roman law. Then the borrowing is easy to confirm. More difficult are peoples who have an identical level of culture, for the borrowing is more difficult to ascertain.[331]

## 2. LIMITS AND SCALE OF STUDIES IN HISTORICAL COMPARISON

In historical comparison in general, unlike ethnological comparison, the question of the reasons for an analogy is more difficult to resolve. Whereas ethnological studies of law have clear tasks: to determine the pra-foundations of law and the most ancient legal institutions and, consequently, typical forms of law, historical-comparative studies to a great extent have the purpose to establish the reasons for variations of universal types.

When investigating, for example, contemporary trade law, one cannot compare it with the trade exchange of an African tribe. This comparison would provide at best gross analogies which

330 Koschaker, note 10 above, p. 191.

331 Ibid., p. 195.

demonstrate the typical and eternal in trade turnover without illuminating at all the complex machine of contemporary trade relations. Ethnological studies above all provide analogies of types, historical and contemporary, directed towards the details and nuances of legal forms.[332] Therefore, the comparative method should rely not on general, formal, logical criteria because they provide only analogies of types of legal forms, but on certain scientific criteria for the classification of material – those which make it possible to consider the laws different in detail.[333]

In historical comparison one must apply solidly and carefully the criteria of comparability which have a specific application, unlike ethnological comparison.

Whereas in ethnological comparison the elements of kinship are limited basically to incidental and universal factors, in historical comparison they are fully represented. By its nature in ethnological comparison in doubtful instances, and this means when one cannot prove a natural or artificial kinship, parallel development is assumed with confidence, which in turn reduces to common human nature as the basis of all analogies. In historical material, as was mentioned, such a proposition cannot be considered to be reliable because analogies may identically be the result of either borrowing or original formation, and therefore there must be other evidence besides analogy itself to establish the type of kinship.

Analogy within related peoples is a separate problem. The question is whether these similarities are the result of jointly inherited but already formulated legal institutions or, possibly, a consequence of mental and cultural kinship which, as a joint foundation, influenced the development of law in one direction. In other words, should the similarity be relegated to a historical fact of the existence of a common law in antiquity and hence all later analogies drawn, or should they be considered the consequences of parallel development of these jointly inherited spiritual inclinations and traditions. In this second instance, what comes into play is not the so-called natural comparability, but rather the random one, which ultimately and essentially in this case would also be natural in the current sense of the word.[334]

[332] Rotondi, note 96 above, p. 18.

[333] Ibid., p. 19.

[334] Rehfeldt, note 97 above, pp. 11-12.

The question raised ultimately has significance not only from the point of view of historical comparison, but also affects basic aspects of the theory of comparison. Therefore, we must occupy ourselves with this again (Chapter VII(4)(b)). This problem may be explained by analyzing the relationship between the comparison of law to comparative linguistics.

The comparative method was introduced into the science of law under the influence of the triumph which it experienced in comparative anatomy and especially in comparative linguistics. The last especially greatly influenced comparative studies in law.

Under the influence of comparative linguistics, the comparative method in the science of law proceeded along the line of the reflections of linguistics. The basic idea of this method was the suggestion that if two magnitudes are similar to one another, then in the event of doubt the similarity proceeds from a third, and namely from that to which both owe their origin. This means that if when studying the similarity of a large number of phenomena one may with confidence exclude the origin of one from the other or borrowing, then one must accept the existence of one more phenomenon common for all. It had at some time together all those properties which later were found in individual transformations of inheritance into different variants, and the similarity of these properties is evidence of a common origin.[335]

Such was the principal evidentiary consistency of the comparative method. It had significant indicia of the evolutionist orientation, and this definitely characterized the method. In the field of law, the comparative method actually took into account the possibility of mutual influence and allowed for independent parallel development of law, especially as a consequence of economic parallelism, which according to the rule that identical causes should generate identical consequences, might influence independently in an identical direction. Despite, however, these theoretical cautions in comparative studies, historical facts were involuntarily interpreted as decisive evidence, and the problem was simplified so that in the event of a similarity of legal institutions, it was assumed they were rooted in joint origin.[336]

[335] Ibid., p. 3.

[336] Ibid., p. 4.

This was, as already noted, an imitation of the progress of comparative studies in the natural sciences and linguistics. The contrasting of law with languages, which according to the Romanticists, should originate identically from the spirit of peoples and, having a source of origin therein, should for this reason be identically considered, led to the complete borrowing in studies of law of the comparative method elaborated in linguistics. Thus, the question of the competence of the comparative method in the investigation of law as an historical phenomenon depended on the answer of to what extent language may be contrasted with law.

When considering this, one is struck that despite a certain similarity between language and law based on the incontestable fact of the close link of these phenomena as social products, there is a material difference between them. Despite the fact that they are in equal measure not only a product of psychology and vital requirements (joint feelings, views, and aspirations), but also an organizer and regulator of daily life, they differ in the scale of possible variants of manifestation, each phenomenon to its own sphere. The number of possibilities of expression in language is infinitely greater than in law, and although it serves for the expression in all languages of the same things, concepts, and actions, in its individual formulations, separate languages, it theoretically is so large as the combination of sounds is numerous. Law is limited, not only, as in language, by the logical and vital substrata, but also by the means of expression of possible legal formulations of human life (see Chapter VII(4)(b)). Not only the types of legal forms are limited, but also their variations.

This all contributes to the fact that the difference between laws of peoples is not too great, or in any event not so great, as between languages. There are numerous analogies between ethnically and culturally kindred peoples.

Linguistic kinship itself materially facilitates the similarity of legal institutions. In every language certain concepts correspond to determined words which pra-ancestors, having formulated them once, bound following generations. In this sense language is satiated with a certain traditionalism of the "spirit of ancestors", and therefore linguistic kinship is also a spiritual and cultural kinship significantly deeper than language itself. For this reason, law also should be interpreted as a product of a certain spirit of the past also encompassing ethnic kinship.[337] This ethnic kinship seals a joint pra-language which, as the bearer of joint views and actions, passes this common tradition to new centuries. In addition to a direct tradition, even common roots of a language themselves through a similar legal terminology were influenced in an identical direction when creating legal concepts, bringing together ethnically close peoples in connection with a similarity of law by closer links than the comparison of the laws of completely foreign peoples shows.[338]

These considerations inspire the thought that the comparative method cannot be applied in the historical sciences as in the natural or even the ethnological sciences. Historical comparison does not produce so easily undoubted evidence for determining the type of kinship and then the type of comparability, which as noted above, are the grounds for the comparative method in law. Especially difficult in view of the question raised at the beginning of this subsection on the origin of analogies among kindred peoples.

On this basis one may only suggest a relative rule of plausibility. The more that two ethnically-kindred peoples become alien from one another, the more likely it may be assumed that existing similarities are a produce of a common pra-law. Likewise, the more that two peoples are ethnically and culturally close to one another, the less one may extract similarity from the historical origin of legal systems from one law, for to the same extent analogies may be a product of the parallel influence of a common tradition and similarity of ideas, culture, and civilization.[339] Thus, similarities existing between Hindus, Europeans, Romans, Slavs, and Germans rather point to the existence of a common Indo-European law (evidently if the possibility is taken into account of a homogeneous general human development of types of legal forms). Analogies between individual branches of peoples may be the result of parallel development stimulated by these cultural-civilizational aspects, and, if so, should not be reduced mechanically to a common genesis, but their explanation should be sought in similar spiritual-psychic prerequisites.[340]

[337] Ibid., p. 9.

[338] Ibid., p. 10.

[339] Ibid., p. 13.

[340] Ibid., p. 14.

That the question of the similarity of the law of peoples of one tribe is advanced from the historical stratum to the psychological, and actual similarities are explained not only by the ancient fact of their joint historical existence, but also by inherited joint psychological inclinations based on identical ideological and cultural traditions. In view of this, in the historical comparison of the laws of one tribe it is appropriate to distinguish between natural and accidental comparability; that is, similarities drawn from a common origin and parallel development – the middle type of similarity. It combines natural and accidental comparability so that the common origin, without providing natural comparability directly, is the psychological basis for parallel development. Thus there arises, so to say, natural accidentalness characteristic for the historical comparison of the laws of a single tribe.

The introduction of another type of comparability determines for historical comparison, especially the comparison of the laws of kindred peoples, narrow limits. It may be justified within limits determined by ethnological comparison, on one hand, and studies from the field of the psychology of peoples and sociology, on the other. The domain between these two categories of investigation encompasses purely historical phenomena, and therefore may be accessible to the historical-comparative method. If, however, the limit of ethnological studies is precisely determined, the limits of the competence of psychology and sociology are not defined. Only when these sciences are capable of resolving the question of whether the similarity of the norms of kindred peoples is a consequence of an internal law of societal development or the result of historical fate can one distinguish parallel development from the consequences of tribal kinship and determine the ability of the comparative method on this unestablished boundary.[341]

The question of the type of comparability within systems of single-tribe peoples does not find a precise answer. Historical comparison is at the stage of quests and improvement and conceals ever greater possibilities. In any event, the scale of the problem of historical comparison is far more complex than in ethnological comparison and is discovering a trend towards specialization. This is forming a duty for basic and cautious studies which will interpret empirical facts simultaneously, well-foundedly, and carefully, expressing any possible conclusions with caution and

[341] Ibid., p. 16.

hypothetically, in any event so long as it is not possible to combine them into a whole.

## 3. UNIVERSAL HISTORY OF LAW AS SYNTHESIS OF HISTORICAL-COMPARATIVE STUDIES

This does not mean, however, that historical comparison adheres or should adhere exclusively or primarily to data which may beyond doubt be empirical. Just as any type of comparison, historical comparison aspired and will aspire to synthesis. Such breakthroughs will not happen at once, as was so in ethnological studies in which the general formulas of the legal phenomena being studied and the ideological positions of the researchers were directed towards an all-encompassing universalism; and possibly will not emerge so promptly in finished form. The great difficulties of historical comparison, on one hand, and the failure of premature attempts to synthesize comparative work of ethnological law, on the other, caution against attempts of this kind in the field of the history of law.

They do not have the strength to refrain from plans of this type. The intention to continuously aspire towards a universal synthesis of the history of all law will hereafter engage the minds of comparative jurists. Proceeding from empiricism, facts, and their close causal linkage, they will aspire to a synthesis, to the creation of a universal system of the history of law, despite the difficulties and the lack of a large number of links binding into a whole the facts already known and investigated. No science, even the most empirical, can confine itself to a narrow range of the undoubted and aspire to an expansion of its boundaries, formulating hypotheses and construing synthetic scientific structures. This provides a more precise purpose to researchers and enables the highest meaning to be seen in the fragments being investigated.

For these reasons historical comparison within the entire comparative orientation has not resisted the aspiration for universal constructions, and in its sphere there also have been proposed, somewhat timidly and cautiously, courageously indeed, the conception of a universal history of law.

The reflections of Rotondi are characteristic of the approach to this question. For him, the point of departure when building a universal conception is the aspiration to discover the laws guiding the development of law. The method of researching these laws should, in his view, be simultaneously historical and comparative and also be related to dogmatics, as is comparative linguistics to grammar. The joint operation of these two methods ensures the cognition of legal phenomena after their release from temporal and local links and provides knowledge of general law outside of time and peoples.[342] A relativist understanding of legal phenomena is obliged to the historical method of the science of law. It enables the remnants of the old or the embryos of the new forms to be seen in each historical fact; these together reflect the development of a legal institution. The connected links of changes reconstruct past law, establishing the sequence of forms determined by causal mutual relations. History, determining trends, also opens the prospects for the future. This all imparts significance of the first degree to the historical method.[343]

If, however, the science of law wants to be an all-encompassing science, it should be augmented by an extensively cut out and systematic comparison of past and existing legal systems.[344] It should not be an accumulation of raw material, but aspire to building a comparative history of law on the model of comparative linguistics. Just as it developed on the base of Romanistics, the comparison of law also should develop its own method, chiefly studying Roman law, which has a long tradition, and those contemporary laws based thereon. Thanks to the wealth of sources from various epochs, significant reworking, the possibility of observing a lengthy development, comparative studies of Romanist law are especially suitable for working out appropriate methods of comparison that may be later applied to other legal systems.[345] Only after achieving this purpose is it possible to aspire comparatively to link various historical forms of law in equal measure according to common indicia and origin into kindred groups. Upon the completion of these studies, the science can approach a universal vision of the history of law.[346]

342 Rotondi, note 96 above, p. 15.

343 Ibid., p. 16.

344 Kaden, note 13 above, p. 17.

345 Rotondi, note 96 above, p. 21.

346 Ibid., p. 22.

So appears the program for a universal history of law built on the basis of historical studies. It reflects the purpose of every universal conception: aspires to a greater synthesis and an integral image of the existence of law in which all variations would create one highest whole above time and space. From a conception based on ethnological law it differs insofar as it is based on the historical study of material and places the emphasis on an investigation according to groups of law. Whereas the conception of a universal history of law on the basis of ethnology broke through at once to a full and integral synthesis (which, *inter alia*, was not successful for this reason), the plan for a universal notion of the development of law with the assistance of historical material was approached more carefully, determining at the outset narrower tasks: to achieve a historical-comparative synthesis by groups of laws. Having achieved results in the group of Romanist law which to researchers seemed most suitable for such studies, one may hope for similar successes in other groups of laws. The synthesis of these studies will be the completion of a universal history of law.

That the idea of a universal history of law rests on historical studies directly influences the content of the conception itself. The old universal history of law built on ethnological law, in aspiring theoretically to encompass the law of all peoples by synthesizing the results of comparison, in fact was constructed especially under the gaze of studies of the pra-causes and pra-forms of law and attempted to determine the principal elements and major developments of the law within the law of primitive peoples. In this it followed the trend of ethnological comparison, of which it was a superstructure.

The historical base of the universal history of law advanced interest from the ethnologically and sociologically interpreted problems to the historical transformations of law. History and comparison were occupied with addressing them. Comparison provided a cross-section of a preliminarily historically studied material, presenting an image of the problem or stage in space. The universal history of law combined these cross-sections in temporal and logical succession and created a new lengthy cross-section, being primarily a history built in this case on an extensive comparative foundation.[347] The historical method

[347] Lautner, note 11 above, p. 40.

in this way was interlaced with the comparative, taking time and space into account.

These two methods are not actually covered in this symbiosis, although they are mutually reinforced. Above all, the bedrock of law is studies within an individual system by a method of analysis, after which there should be a comparison of individual phases of changes and a final synthesis. This synthesis provides the basic ideas which in comparison with the synthesis of other systems produces an image of the development of law throughout history. This process of the study of material is by the comparative method. It may theoretically identify similarities on the basis of the criteria of comparability; that is, when individual laws have a common origin, when they are linked by borrowing or are similar as a consequence of independent parallel development. The scheme of such comparison takes equally into account the natural flow of development, as well as its artificial or forcible phases. Moreover, the investigation of the universal development of law by its nature draws attention to the natural flow of changes in the laws of peoples, and therefore the external causes take into account these changes as both the non-material and accidental factor. Therefore, of the three grounds of comparison, only two have direct application to universal studies: the common origin of law and the independent autonomous development. A similarity which arose by means of mutual, voluntary, or forcible influences has for the harmonious development only indirect significance as a factor which interfered in the successive natural development, and therefore is on the back burner of research. That the general history of law differs from the comparison of law not only conceptually, but also methodologically, does not mutually overlap the comparison of law, does not exhaust all the possibilities which the comparative method provides.[348]

Therefore, the comparative method is capable of filling gaps of the historical method. The comparative method, in studying the historical material of law according to the criteria of comparability, is engaged in the resolution of those problems which remain unresolved when crating a universal history with the assistance of only the historical method; that is, an analysis and synthesis. Moreover, the comparative method expands the foundation of the historical synthesis, which usually rests only on temporal

348 Ibid., p. 43.

historical material, on space, seeking analogies in cross-sections. By its universal attitude towards laws, it orders legal systems and their sources under a common angle of vision and thereby provides a large guarantee of objective and even interpretation of different laws. The comparative method thus in combination with the historical is capable of providing new and comprehensive syntheses without being subjected to the risk of one-sidedness which might arise if, when applying only one historical method, would have been adopted by the force of inertia as the point of departure for studies of the legal ideas of merely one system.[349]

Researchers are not satisfied, when analyzing law in the perspective of time or space, only with fragmentary knowledge, but rather aspire to an integral image of the foundation. Having a single worldview position and adopting certain sociological or philosophical criteria, they endeavor with the assistance of the comparative and historical methods simultaneously to achieve their purpose as, for example, Kohler did.

To perform this task with the assistance of the history of all laws is complex, and is far from having been realized. Aware of this, they narrow the universal program, determining closer and narrower goals whose achievement seems easier. We refer to the idea of first a synthesis within certain groups of laws. Pursuing this thought, Julius Georg Lautner (1897-1972) considered the problem of the universal history of law by stages, expressing the view set out above of a universal history of law as the final goal – secondary in connection with the plan for building an integral antique history of law as a part thereof.

The universal antique history of law should have been a stage for realization of the idea of an entire universal history of law. The conception of an antique history of law in which side by side with Roman law the law of other antique peoples would be considered by way of comparison has its own history. It was proposed in 1904 by Leopold Wenger (1874-1953), who advocated the idea of such a history of ancient law in which Roman law would merely have been a component part. This view was formed after an investigation of papyruses showed a close link between Roman law and the East that led to an expansion of the temporal and spatial limits of research on Roman law.[350] It was declared simultaneously in

[349] Ibid., p. 66.

[350] Rotondi, note 96 above, p. 28.

connection with studies of the ancient history of the East that, in view of the great differences in the races and cultures of the ancient East, the unified development of law in these spaces was excluded and one cannot speak of the usual construction of a single history of law. Therefore, the history of antique law is possible only as part of a universal science of law. With the assistance of comparison of the material being investigated, its purpose would be to identify the principal phases of the development of law on a universal scale.[351]

When creating such a construction of the general history of antique law, the concept of "antiquity" needs to be understood broadly. Old Germanic and old Slavic laws should be added to such a general ancient history of law.[352] In and of itself, Graeco-Roman history of law cannot create a real general ancient history of law. Even Indo-European law would not exhaust the general material of law in view of the fact that agreement has been discovered of the principal features of law not only among the Indo-European peoples, but also among the peoples of other groups, at a minimum, Semitic, who in antiquity were in active cultural contacts with the Aryan peoples.[353]

In this perspective it is practically very complex to realize a general history of the law of antiquity even though much it is much narrower than a general universal history of law. This complexity, however, does not exclude the theoretical possibility thereof, and monographs on individual laws of antiquity may provide a real foundation for the full realization thereof.[354] It is evident that the final realization of the history of the law of antiquity will be the result of the respective application of the comparative method for the creation of a final synthesis.

One possible task of the comparison of ancient laws would be to find a link between the history of Roman law and the history of other laws of antiquity on the basis of a unified approach to legal phenomena of the ancient world. Within the limits of a history of the law of antiquity, Roman law would, on one hand, be deprived of isolation in which, as a science, it is, and on the other, being the

351 Ibid., p. 34.

352 Ibid., p. 37.

353 Ibid., p. 38.

354 Ibid.

greatest and best preserved monument of ancient law, it would be a basic part of the history of the law of antiquity. In connection with such a program, one would investigate the relation of Roman law to other systems of antiquity and determine the influence of ancient Eastern, Greek, and Hellenic laws on Roman and, in later times, the reverse influence of Imperial Roman law on local Eastern law. The principal idea of these studies would be to prove that legal and State development of the Mediterranean world of antiquity which finally became part of the Roman Empire was mutually connected, and that Rome completed the synthesis of the legal forms of antiquity. The ultimate result of such studies would be resolution of the question: did Roman law at the time of the Empire have a purely Roman nature or was it under foreign Greek or Eastern influences; were these influences weak or so significant that they decisively influenced the transformation of urban Roman law into Imperial; can Roman law at the time of Justinian be called Roman law; did the synthesis of Roman and Hellenic law differ in the East, where Graeco-Eastern factors manifested themselves to a greater degree than in the West, where the Roman influence was stronger. In the domain of private law, the mutual influences of the East, Greece, and Rome are still an open question. In the field of the development of State law the dependence of Rome on the influence of the East and the Hellenic world has been shown to a certain extent.[355]

Taking Roman law as the focal point of comparative studies of the laws of antiquity, we grant to it the most favorable position; however, using all the means of science, chiefly comparison, one must embrace as fully as possible all past legal forms of all peoples in order to re-create a true universal history of legal thought.[356]

From this point of view, the comparative science of ancient law may be a preparatory stage for a universal history of the law of antiquity. It provides cross-sections illuminating individual stages of the development of law in space. The synthesis of these comparative analytical studies and their linkage into a temporal and logical whole will give a universal history. Thus, it completes the achievements of comparison, which in and of itself is not directed towards one end, but provides finished material for

[355] Ibid., p. 54.

[356] Ibid., p. 67.

every possible conclusions that may be made from the asserted comparative dependencies.[357]

So the conception of a universal history of law built on an historical-comparative basis presents itself. It is characterized by the fact that in order to resolve the task set it is taken in stages, attempting to produce a synthesis at first within groups of laws. Roman law is interpreted conventionally as the core of a universal construction of the history of law. In all instances side by side with comparison the basic historical studies are taken into account, and only the results thereof become the subject-matter of comparison. This comparison produces cross-sections which take into account part of the analogy in the material arranged in temporal sequence. Moreover, historical comparison is undertaken with due attention to the criteria of comparability, defining the types thereof within periods.

All this makes historical comparison and the universal history of law build thereon a more scientifically solid adaptation of the comparative method to an investigation of law than was so in ethnological comparison. A genuine large synthesis has not been achieved in historical comparison, but the fragmentary historical-comparative studies are undertaken with scientific solidity, and this provides grounds to believe that the soil for further synthesis is assured and stable. No doubt in the field of historical comparison much needs to be done, and many researchers will find in it a favorable scope for scholarly work. It will serve not only as an addition to historical studies, explaining dark places of some system or confirming certain assumptions, but also will be a contribution to the cognition of pure legal thought without national and temporal fetters. Historical comparison in particular may have significance for dogmatics, familiarizing the science of law with various legal ideas of different peoples. Historical comparison thus will produce material by its own conclusions for theory and practice while performing the true task of the comparative method in the field of law.

[357] Ibid., p. 68.

# Chapter X. Dogmatic Comparison



## 1. PROBLEM OF DOGMATIC COMPARISON

Dogmatic comparison studies law conceptually and systematically. It sees in laws logical constructions which interlinked create a system. Dogmatic comparison, when considering law, interpret it as finished, data, abstract formulas which have or had binding force. In interpreting law so, dogmatic comparison becomes more abstract, extra-historical, and to a certain extent an immeasurable type of comparison. Whereas ethnological comparison seeks and researches initial standard forms of law in time and space, and historical comparison attempts to provide spatial models of law at individual stages of time, seeking in so doing to spontaneously produce a universal history of law as a synthesis of its studies, then dogmatic comparison emphasizes the conceptual aspect of law, leaving history and time aside. The very fact of comparison, taking space into account, dogmatic comparison interprets as supplementary, although a necessary factor, drawing attention to legal formulas themselves. Although all types of comparison are linked by the material of positive law and sociological background in which it arose in each instance, both ethnological and historical comparison were interested primarily in the development of law, and dogmatic comparison is interested only in the internal and external conditions of a particular time and instance.[358] It maximally eliminates all kinetics, seeking to illuminate the essence of law in abstract, static forms of legal prescriptions in force.

For this reason, dogmatic comparison draws virtually exclusive attention to contemporary, primarily codified, laws which as isolated integral systems are seemingly outside time: unified,

[358] Petraschek, note 86 above, p. 671.

self-sufficient, and exhaustive. The tendency of dogmatics to see rational formulas in legal norms leads to exclusive and closed codifications being considered the highest types of system.

This orientation of dogmatics towards abstraction led Rotondi to assert that only a full and organic system is subject to scientific interpretation. In his view, the law of primitive peoples cannot be the object of comparison because it is not a whole. Even Roman law of the period of the first written sources is not suitable, in his view, for comparative studies because it has large gaps. Such laws in the eyes of Rotondi are disqualified because they do not comprise closed systems and do not provide the possibility to cognize the basic and general principles on which they are built. A closed, especially contemporary, system does not have this shortcoming, and therefore it may be the subject-matter of scientific, dogmatic, and systematic studies. A contemporary legal system has two traits: it is complete and has internal unity. A system is complete and integral if some positive order can provide a decision for each possible instance on the basis of prescriptions and the interpretation thereof. One may speak of an organic and unified system when individual norms can be reduced to a few main grounds so that individual laws and their consequences must be drawn with the assistance of induction and deduction.[359]

It is evident that advancing such requirements for the scientific interpretation of systems is excessive. Rotondi himself, consistently pursuing his ideas, ascribed to the Italian system the capability to be the subject-matter of dogmatic interpretation because it, by a provision that in the absence of a respective prescription a judge should find it in the general grounds of law, makes possible the resolution of every case and consequently is a whole and closed.[360] By such a raising of the matter, suggesting Italian law as an ideal, Rotondi deprived all systems of scientific value which have no clause in positive law relating to the lawmaking role of the judge. Not only ancient Roman law cannot be the subject-matter of scientific studies, but contemporary French and German law as well.[361]

[359] Rotondi, note 96 above, pp. 6-9, 11.

[360] Ibid., p. 12.

[361] Stoll, note 177 above, p. 368.

The exclusively dogmatic interpretation of law may lead to such consequences. This clearly demonstrates to what extent dogmatic interpretation of law in and of itself may be one-sided and narrow. The logical-conceptual understanding of law cannot, on one hand, exhaust the entire problematic of law and, on the other, may easily permit mistakes.

The identification of scientific interpretation with conceptual dogmatics is completely false. The lack of wholeness and fragmentariness of any system may not be an obstacle to the scientific interpretation thereof. Roman law before Justinian was fragmentary, but one cannot refuse it scientific interpretation for this reason. By synthesizing fragments of law one may come to the general foundations of law and order law methodically and in a unified manner. The prescriptions of positive law are not essential for this activity. Dogmatism, however, combined with positivism, is capable of seeing only conceptually finished forms in polished prescriptions of positive law which should exhaust the entire content of law. This ahistorical, atemporal, abstract understanding of law is dangerous and false.

Friedrich Lenz (1885-1968) drew special attention to the danger of an extremely dogmatic treatment of law. He believed the view to be mistaken that with the assistance of the systematic study of the bedrock one can come to a pure theory of the subject-matter that provides absolutely true knowledge. A historical moment can never be eliminated as immaterial for pure cognition: all the temporal is occurring and special; having diversified the essential, it erodes the absolute.

However, the dogmatic for methodological reasons excludes for better cognition the factor of time from studies. Thus, the static is separated from the kinetic, and theory is juxtaposed to practice.[362]

Moreover, the elements being investigated are not in and of themselves absolute qualities. They have been placed in time and space, and only the last are real categories. Individual phenomena are merely temporal forms of an, in essence, single reality. Even time and space ultimately do not exist for themselves, but are linked by a mutual relation. Reality exists as a substantive whole in time and space and may be only represented therein. Therefore,

[362] Friedrich Lenz, "Prinzipielle Abteilung der historisch-systematischen Methode", *Archiv für Rechts- und Sozialphilosophie*, XXXV (1942), p. 95.

any absolute cognition is possible only in the historical-dogmatic perspective.

For these reasons a dogmatic or historical understanding of phenomena in and of itself is meaningless. This relates especially to dogmatics when it excludes the historical factor. A historical approach always silently uses dogmatic concepts, such as the State, people, possession, contract, and so on. Systematic studies without taking the historical factor into account may be absurd. Therefore, the final condition of every study must be the substantive unity of the historical.[363] Dogmatics directed towards the rational aspect of law in principle do not provide such conclusions, although in practical life the historical elements in law must be taken into account, especially where they cannot be avoided.

Dogmatic comparison, therefore, going beyond the insuperable requirements of reality in which all laws are the result of history, could not in practice divorce itself from tradition. However, through its extra-traditional propositions it attempts to reduce the historical encumberment of law to a minimum, hoping over time in general to free itself from the fetters of historicism. The method of integral codifications, which as closed systems exclude historical material and direct law to future development, facilitates to a great degree the dogmatic, atemporal interpretation of law. Certain branches especially, such as trade or transport law, discover a trend towards an abstract, ahistorical, worldwide formation that in the view of dogmaticians will give to dogmatic comparison in the future especially convenient conditions.

But in fact dogmatic comparison is not cut off in a revolutionary way from the historical foundations of law. This is impossible and obviously harmful. Therefore, the theoreticians of dogmatic law, among them Rotondi, make a concession to the historical-dogmatic interpretation in the case of comparison. In order to harmonize this essential concession, Rotondi distinguishes two understandings of law: as a regulator of human relations and as a natural phenomenon of social life. Law as regulatory norms is researched methodically and systematically, but as a natural phenomenon may and must be researched historical-comparatively.[364] Other theoreticians of dogmatic comparison, approaching the matter primarily from a practical vantage point, have not worked with the theoretical

[363] Ibid., pp. 101-102.

[364] Rotondi, note 96 above, p. 366.

constructions which would have removed the contradictions immanent to dogmatic comparison. They expressly endeavor to take into account the historical factors in dogmatic comparison within the limits necessary for dogmatic comparison to make sense.

So Rabel, in defining the scientific tasks of systematic comparison, strove that law was evaluated principally in connection with the entire legal order, part of which it is. It follows under dogmatic comparison, in his view, that the entire historical and life background should be taken into account in order to actually compare law, and not paragraphs. Law is a phenomenon of culture, and therefore cannot be independent of its causes and influences.[365]

Rauchhaupt fully realized these requirements, having constructed a theory of comparison especially from the viewpoint of contemporary dogmatic comparison. This was the more necessary because dogmatic comparison, stimulated almost entirely by practical requirements, was drowned completely in positivism, with no concerns for large scientific constructions or even systematics, which above all is required for the systematic study of material. Interest directed towards current practical use of the conclusions of comparison was liberated from theoretical reflections.

Practical interest also led to dogmatic comparison taking a leading place in the comparison of law in general. This meant that the contemporary comparison of law, unlike ethnological and historical comparison under the mark of theoretical and scientific quests, was as a whole under the influence of life requirements and claims. Contemporary comparison sees only the law and the practical side of life. As a result, despite a large number of comparative-dogmatic works, dogmatic comparison did not suggest either breath-taking theories or great constructions. All attention was directed towards positive prescriptions and their application. It is therefore not surprising that under such development the summit of theorizing is the search for the most practical and advisable decision in the laws being compared. Indeed, this is happening also with practical purposes, namely to find the best models for imitation or for verification of the advisability of own legislation. Critique, the politics of law, and

[365] Rabel, note 77 above, pp. 281-282.

legislative needs – these are the stimuli for use of the comparative method in dogmatics. To these purely practical reasons are added even more practical ones: the vital need to know foreign law – because in present active mutual relations between nations jurists often encounter foreign laws.

Dogmatic law, however, cannot avoid theory. In dogmatic comparison material needs to be studied systematically. And this is possible if undertaken in accordance with some system, according to some plan, according to some criteria which guard comparison against the senseless accumulation of analogies. In order to achieve a transparent ordering of similarities and to order comparative data and conclusions, dogmatic comparison uses to an equal extent other types of comparison worked out and tested by the theory of comparability.

As mentioned, this theory was proposed at one time by Bernhoft, and adapted specially for dogmatics by Rauchhaupt. He drew special attention to the historical aspect of the problem. Soo that dogmatic comparison had a clear field, an individual type of comparison engages in all genetic and historical problems of the objects to be compared. It was conceived as the preparatory stage in the application of the comparative method during dogmatic comparison.

The idea elaborated by Rabel is the main idea of this operation, that laws should be compared within entire systems and also within individual branches. To this end the development of each legal system must be studied within those confines it is planned to undertake dogmatic comparison. One should find the laws of past periods which remain binding, trace the possible influences of foreign systems, identify the state of codification, and, if regional laws exist, find the conflicts norms (Chapter 6(3)). Thus, the entire kinetic will be studied; that is, the historical background of the system, and conclusions drawn which are necessary to clarify and understand the positive law in force; that is, the static of the legal system. Genetic conclusions within one system should be compared with respective parts of another comparable system in order to establish possible mutual relations. If comparable material is contrasted individually by branches in order to be convinced whether and to what extent it was or is, irrespective of the system, genetically related, all the preparatory work for dogmatic comparison will have been done.

In the process of these preparatory studies of the objects to be compared, a precise analysis must be done of the mutual relations of the systems and their branches according to the criteria for comparability. The theory of comparability is fully applicable in dogmatic comparison and is a decisive criterion for the genetic ordering of the material. In principle, all positive law is strongly encumbered by national tradition, and the genetic and historical similarities of the systems and branches should be taken into account fully and beforehand so that dogmatic comparison provides clear results. Even exceptionally when a similarity is the result of parallel development, dogmatic comparison must have precise data beforehand. Branches not linked by tradition with the national system such as, for example, trade law, also must be verified for their own comparability against the background of their system and with respect to other objects of comparison.

Thus, an attentive genetic-historical analysis precedes dogmatic comparison. It orders the material for dogmatic comparison proper; however, encumberment by tradition is not finally eliminated from the further operation. Historical-genetic factors emerge throughout further comparison even though after the Napoleonic codifications law was increasingly emancipated from historical links, becoming the material abstract law of the future. Dogmatic comparison is linked with this trend in the law, drawing attention by its nature basically to the atemporal, abstract, ahistorical, and the static.

## 2. UNIVERSAL LIKENING OF LAW

The undertaking of dogmatic comparison taking account of historical traditions only as a necessity, and comparison itself whenever possible solely in the stratum of rational and abstract concepts directly influenced the type of universality which is fostered within dogmatic comparison. Whereas in ethnological law there was a trend to build a universal history of law presented as a survey of the development of pra-forms of law, for studies of the pra-beginnings of law were the principal idea of ethnological law; and whereas in historical comparison the universal history of law acquired, according to its interests, the form of history built on a broad spatial foundation, dogmatic comparison, which separated itself as much as possible from history, did not present a similar conception.

Indeed, Heymann, in asserting the unity of law which in particular is developing against the background of present civilization in one direction and unites peoples to a greater extent than does language, recalled the idea of a universal history of law in which the law in force of all peoples should have been taken into account individually. However, this thought is not a result of a purely dogmatic approach, but inspired by the philosophical orientation of the researcher.[366]

The construction of a universal history of law did not arise among dogmaticians. Not only because of the insufficient interest in history was there no foundation (negatively received), but it has in dogmatic comparison a positive analogue which fully exhausts universalist trends inherent to each comparison in general.

Within dogmatic comparison, the role of a universal history of law is performed by the idea of the universal likening of law. It is responsive to the atemporal arrangement of dogmatic and provides instead of tradition a formula, a mathematic, which should regulate human life not according to habits and customs, but according to the key of rational advisability. Noticeable in the most recent development, the rationalization of law, that is, movement to the forefront ahead of traditionalism of the aspect of advisability in the formation of law, furthers the idea of the universal likening of law.

Likening has many stimuli, from the analogous nature of types of legal forms on a general human scale, through mutual influence during history, voluntary borrowing or forcible imposition, to parallel analogous development which against the background of contemporary cultural and economic world relations acquire ever greater significance. The likenings of legal systems which occurred spontaneously over history in and of themselves significantly expanded the limits of analogy previously enclosed within the framework of single-tribe groups. This slow process of the likening of law has accelerated significantly in our epoch of world turnover of spiritual and material benefits and the trend is speeding up.

The branches of law connected with international turnover especially encompass the trend towards a mutual coming together. In the world process of the likening of law of interest in particular is the emergence of parallel similarity of law which arises not

366 Ernst Heymann, "Auslandsrecht", in *Handwörterbuch der Rechtswissenschaft* (1926), I, pp. 425-426.

such much by way of direct influence of legal systems between themselves as it does as a consequence of the existence of identical civilized institutions and social needs. These institutions are created by identical conditions such as, for example, a parliamentary system or industrialization, which require identical laws.

Irrespective of this, the likening of law goes along the old path of the borrowing of law, especially in branches close to world turnover. Similar life conditions make possible the inculcation of foreign laws in branches which by their international character differ from others branches which grew from national tradition. Phenomena identical on a world scale have a tendency to be identically interpreted, and if the natural course of things did not lead to likening, then a mechanical reception completes it. This happens especially in trade law, but partly, though less noted, in other branches such as, for example, constitutional law. Rational advisability in these abstract branches with respect to national conditionality is decisive in the matter of borrowing those foreign models which seem to be best, most practical, and vital.

The process of world likening of law of recent times, being based on similar conditions of civilization, proceeded spontaneously on one hand by means of parallel development and, on the other, intentionally with the assistance of special intervention of the legislator appropriating the most advisable foreign models into his own system. In this process dogmatic comparison naturally has broad scope. The tendencies of the legislator to find the most practical law forces one to study foreign laws, and the best means to cognize them is comparison. The aspiration to improve law also dictates recourse to the comparison of law. All this connects the process of the likening of law with dogmatic comparison.

For this reason, the idea of the likening of law is proclaimed by dogmatic comparison programmatically as the final purpose of the development of law. Petraschek said that the comparison of law builds a road for the likening thereof. In this sense one may consider the comparison of law as the final goal – an attempt to create a world law.[367] Rauchhaupt fully supported this idea, asserting that after the present period of codification will come a period of unification of law as a natural completion of the development of law.[368]

[367] Petraschek, note 86 above, p. 272.

[368] Rauchhaupt, *Die Rechte Europas in ihrer rechtsgenetischen Gestalt und*

This thought he consistently developed in a separate study. The commencement of accelerated unification of law on a world scale he relegated to the discovery of America and Australia. Thereafter one culture took possession of the entire world, the center of which Europe became. This in a general understanding joint culture promoted the slow likening of law on a world scale. Now as a consequence of the improvement of communication even remote countries cannot stand aside from the likening process. To be sure, to these spontaneous universalist aspirations are juxtaposed the same spontaneous traditionalism of individual nations; however, the process of the likening of law proceeds all the same, although slowly, to various extents and in different combinations.[369]

The coming together of peoples in an international-legal stratum, on one hand, and world trade turnover, on the other, facilitate the process of likening. In addition to these two most universal and unification factors, a role is played by tribal and geopolitical factors which group peoples according to the ethnological and territorial principle or by range of common interests, and sometimes by all the causes simultaneously. Within these groups the coming together and likening of law occurs and a road is being built towards universal unification.

The League of Nations was the most universal coming together of peoples at the international stratum, and now the United Nations. Besides them, one may mention the Pan American group, the British Commonwealth of Nations, and tribal groups according to the scheme: Romanist, Germanic, and Slavic, and among them, even more closely, the Nordic. The likening and coming together of law, for various reasons and to different degrees of intensity, proceeded to a greater or lesser extent in these groups. The coming together ensued especially in spheres connected with international turnover, and one may believe that the process has not ended.

Of all the legal spheres, the most likening has occurred in private international law and the law of nations. Nonetheless, one must recall that this law is in essence national law constructed by taking into account the requirements of international turnover. A certain coming together ensued by the conclusion of various treaties and agreements. In America such treaties have been concluded within the Pan American Union. Various agreements have been concluded

---

*pragmatischen Auswertung* (1932), p. 92.

369 Rauchhaupt, note 208 above.

in Europe within the framework of the League of Nations and the Hague conventions.[370]

Constitutional law as the second in sequence [in this context] also displays a tendency towards likening because it is in significant measure analogous in its genesis. It is drawn from idea of the sovereignty of the people, based on the parliamentary models of England and France, and dates from the French Revolution. Both the origin and identical time of dissemination make constitutional law the most abstract law, especially now when the number of traditional European monarchies is being reduced. Contemporary constitutional law manifests a tendency to create a strong parliament and weak executive power in strong States; weak States have a strong executive and a weak parliament. But all this is more a consequence of a de facto state of affairs, and not a verbatim formulation.[371]

Whereas constitutional law is linked by common political institutions and trade law through trade turnover, this makes them similar. It is evident that trade law emanates from its roots in the national system and has been conceived with regard to internal conditions and requirements. But understanding and amelioration of differences has been achieved on many issues by means of treaties. This also concerns such branches as the law of bills of exchange and cheques, security, transport, and others.

In addition to constitutional and trade law, criminal law also is likening. The reason should be sought in criminal policy being guided to a great extent by factors of advisability, which in the criminal law is decisive from the time when the idea of vengeance ceased to be dominant. Identical theoretical grounds of departure borrowed by all cultural peoples, such as, for example, the idea of the greatest subjectivization of guilt and taking into account the human personality, on one hand, and advancing the public interest as a factor which adjusts strict justice, on the other, led to analogous criminal laws as a result. Rational factors in criminal policy further the likening of the criminal law of all peoples.

Whereas in constitutional, trade, and criminal law certain ideological and linguistic commonalities arose on a world scale, private law is rooted deeply in traditionalism. It is diverse and

370 Ibid., pp. 337-338.

371 Rauchhaupt, note 368 above, p. 92.

does not display an ability to liken. Individual systems created slowly throughout history preserve their own vitality not only within different States, but also within one State they stubbornly preserve individual particular regional laws. Another instance of traditionalism – is the existence of customary law not fixed by the legislator but still cherished by judges. Such is the image of Germanic law.

Romanic law also is diverse, but drawn from a common source, from Roman law, which is interpreted significantly or silently as an auxiliary source. The common origin of Romanic law and its codified nature make it to a significant degree comparable and capable of likening. The codifications in general which leave the traditional-historical factor aside should be considered to be a progressive phenomenon that provides a basis for the further development of law presently in the stage of universal unification.[372] Although civil law is very conservative, the coming together of trade law and the law of obligations quietly influences other parts of the civil law.

From the aforementioned, it is evident that, as a rule, one must accept the existence of unanimity in constitutional, trade, and criminal law. In civil law, however, most linked with the past, the process of likening is not felt.

The process of the coming together of systems will proceed. Above all, by means of territorial, economic, and political links. It will be a result of a mutual coming together, unilateral adoption or imposition, or ultimately will proceed simultaneously one way or another. In our times, when it seems that a world political system is being formed not by means of the cooperation of peoples but by the hegemony of one power, this is not a unification evolution, but the influence of one dominant system being decisive for unification. Who knows whether we will be witnesses to the return to the time of the Roman Empire or whether there will be a new world unifying center for world law. In any case, one may imagine that the organization of world government, now spoken of, if it were to arise would accelerate decisively the likening process of law.

Dogmatic comparison is playing at present the major technical role in the slow coming together of law. It is a slow erosion

[372] Ibid., p. 347.

process that flows unnoticeably, but systematically individual bodies of different laws gradually achieve the same level. This role is not dominant in the daily practice of dogmatic comparison. It undertakes practical goals of daily life and, as already mentioned, worries little about the future consequences of its work. But when any researcher using the comparative method to study contemporary legal problems, lifts his gaze beyond the everyday issues before his eyes the image of the world stratification of law is raised.

This does not mean that the image should be considered to be progress or a higher level of the development of law. Universal systems have existed in the past and fallen. Sometimes it seemed that within the "Roman world" the entire civilized world had been unified in all spheres also from the standpoint of law. Outside its limits were barbarians, exotic peoples of the fabled Orient, in any event elements considered to be marginal by the wise men of that time. This Roman world, however, collapsed and new peoples arose on its ruins who sometimes were subjugated and intertwined with the great Empire by the force of legions, but also by the skill of Roman administrators and politicians. After the fall of Rome, the Papacy was virtually a world State, and canon law, together with Roman, was a world law. In comparison with them, national laws were weak and underdeveloped together with the peoples vegetated in the shadow of the papal cross and the Imperial sword which competed in the struggle for dominance over the world. However, both the spiritual power of Christian universalism and the secular power of the Empire became transitional phenomena. Multi-national monarchies also collapsed, having within their boundaries undertaken the idea of the unification of peoples and laws. The contemporary era is under the banner of the sovereignty of peoples, which even during the First World War was the principal call of the War.

In light of these facts, the most recent unification phenomena realized either in practice or in the propaganda of ideas were nothing new. The building of some multinational system, whether voluntary to a large degree of not, becomes a repetition of the "Roman world", a new return to the past, and therefore in and of itself cannot be assessed as "progress". Moreover, this is not so because a more or less concealed hegemony of some power underlies the foundation; already this would indicate the transitory nature of this new Universe.

This question ultimately affects fundamental problems: on one hand, unity, and on the other, the complexity of the world in all spheres. Science is not able to say whether the world is at the stage of origin and development or in the process of decomposition and regression. This also relates to law. There are no grounds to assert that the unification of law is the final goal of development. In asserting that the likening of law is happening to a certain degree, one cannot generalize this and elevate the facts to the significance of a goal.

However, the hypothesis of the world process of the likening of law has scientific significance not because it is completely right, but because it is capable of linking legal phenomena in the broadest system and providing the possibility to encompass in a single view the questions of the existence of contemporary law in all its breadth. This makes it possible to see legal problems in the highest perspective and rescue them from wandering among the insignificant. Moreover, with the careful interpretation of the problem one may actually draw conclusions with regard to the likening of law where it actually occurs and may occur in the future.

With these reservations, one may consider the development of law from the standpoint of the unification of law. Dogmatic comparison is useful for daily requirements if it is undertaken with care. In resolving tasks at hand, it undoubtedly serves a larger purpose which, however, according to sociological laws is neither rationally predictable or desirable. The future comes for transcending human ideas and intentions because their actions and works exist as autonomous, objective phenomena of life. No doubt the practice of life has passed to the agenda over the theories because spontaneity was and will be the principal factor of social life.

# Chapter XI. Some Theories of Comparison of Law and Critique Thereof from the Kantian Position

Although the comparative method in essence remained empirical, it was at the same time often part of philosophical and theoretical quests in the field of law. It is obliged by its application in the science of law to philosophical interests, and although in later applications it served as a method of research for primarily practical purposes which in recent times have come to dominate over theorizing, but to a certain extent philosophical discourse was interested in the question of the comparison of law. Various authors attempted to ascertain the value of the comparative method for the absolute cognition of law or to determine the limits of its usefulness. In these attempts they evaluated the comparison of law from various standpoints, beginning with historical materialism and ending with extreme idealism. An approach to the comparative method basically from a theoretical viewpoint was characteristic for them all.

The ability of the comparative method to find an ideal, just law is the central problem in these theories. They respond to this issue variously, depending on their basic grounds. The ability of the comparative method to find the ideal law was assessed most positively by Franz von Liszt (1851-1919).[373] The point of departure for him is the axiom that the ideal law may originate only from existing positive law. The existing, as historically perfected, determines at the same time the future, which is the ideal. The identification of the future and ideal law leads Liszt to his understanding of the trends of development. In his view, the process of development does not depend on human activity. Human aspirations may merely impede or facilitate the natural laws of societal development. Thus, cognized developmental

[373] Franz von Liszt, "Das richtige Recht in der Strafgesetzgebung", *Zeitschrift für die gesamte Strafrechtswissenschaft,* XXVI (1906), p. 555; Liszt, [title not indicated], *Zeitschrift für die gesamte Strafrechtswissenschaft,* XXVI (1906), p. 91.

trends point to the future, which at the same time is that which must be; that is, ideal.[374]

In Liszt's view, however, despite this the actual development is not an entirely reliable expressor of life trends because under conditions of mutual influences of neighboring States the course of events does not form naturally, being subject to deviations from the historical path. Mistakes are possible when evaluating national development as a result of subjective attitudes, prejudices, and short-sightedness, which may cloud one's judgment. These factors, in Liszt's view, substantiate the need for the comparison of law. It makes possible the cognition of typical phases of development, especially standard legal systems. Only by means of cognition of standard forms of development on the basis of an objective assessment of the entire evolution of mankind can one evaluate national development and thereby indicate the future and the ideal thereof.[375]

By this attitude to the matter, Liszt defined himself as an adherent of historical materialism. He starts from the assumption that the development discovers a certain stability which consists of a chosen orientation stably preserved. Proceeding from these assumptions, it obviously would be unreasonable to resist the inevitable, the inexorable, and predestined. That which occurs, happens because it must happen, and therefore is good and desirable. In this formulation, development is a natural necessary law of societal development of the most positivist and materialistic orientation.

But despite the assertion that such an assumption has a purely empirical origin, it is based on a concealed metaphysical non-scientific presumption which accepts without objective grounds, that development proceeds constantly and necessarily from below upwards, and that in time later phenomena are materially more perfected.

Without acknowledging the truth of these grounds, one cannot consider Liszt's assertion to be correct on the possibility of deriving a just law from existing law. Ultimately, if the notion of developmental trends is correct, this does not justify the comparison of law, but replaces it. If on the basis of the existing

[374] Binder, note 41 above, p. 952.

[375] Ibid., p. 953.

one can judge the ideal and the future, one merely need follow the developmental trends in order to arrive at the just. Comparison of the law of peoples under the formulation of the question is superfluous.[376]

Despite the evident inaccuracy of such a view which Liszt presents, it is encountered more often than might be supposed. All references to evolution are close to a materialist worldview. As paradoxical as it may seem, the views of Kohler are close to the Liszt position. In his universalist understanding of the results of comparison, that law is just which resolves its task; namely, makes the development of culture possible; and valuable is that law corresponding to the requirements of the time.

That position is close to Liszt's assertion and is not subject to substantiation. Similar to the last, Kohler confuses the sociologically understood reality with an autonomous evaluation of its value. Moreover, if the relation of law to culture should have significance for comparison of law, one should accept that only that law is valuable which corresponds to a true culture. But in this way the question of the measure of value is transferred from the sphere of law to the sphere of the philosophy of culture without finding a solution. In reality, the views of Kohler should not be completely identified with the views of Liszt. His view should be considered rather an opinion that each cultural epoch together with its law leaves a certain trace of the just and correct, but it is difficult to find the measure of value which would give grounds for comparison. The orientations of development cannot determine the just. There have been periods of rise and fall in history, and there are no grounds to assert that history is direct invariable progress. Such a philosophy leads to opportunism, which does not oppose that which time brings.[377]

Radbruch was more critical of the ability of the comparative method to find the ideal on the basis of studies of law in force. As a result, he approached more attentively the empirical tasks of the comparative method.

In Radbruch's view, just as two concepts cannot be compared directly with one another but only mediately with respect to a third concept as a measure, so too individual national systems

[376] Ibid., pp. 954-955.

[377] Ibid., pp. 959-960.

should not be compared with one another because then the result will be conditioned by current national interests.[378] For comparison to provide atemoporal and non-national results it is necessary to undertake comparison with respect to a legal system above nations. Genuine supranational natural law as a conception belongs to the past, but in our day we may understand existing and ideal law separately, which in the theory of natural law were inadmissibly mixed together: the first as a type of law; that is, as a whole of usual properties of a legal system of a certain cultural group at a certain degree of development; the second as an ideal law; that is, as a system of advanced subjective claims with respect to the law of a certain cultural group at a certain degree of development of culture. Both criteria, having no claim to be eternally in force outside time and space, as was so with the theory of natural law, all the same are higher qualities of a supranational conditionality and therefore may be measures for individual national laws to be compared. On one hand, one may raise the question: what relation do national laws have to a type of law at a particular stage of development, in particular do they exceed or achieve this level, and on the other, in what respect are they an advanced ideal of law, and are they approaching such or moving away.[379]

In advancing these methodological orientations, Radbruch at the same time adhered to the view that the ideal law cannot be drawn from the law in force and that the consideration even of many existing legal systems cannot provide the correct law as a result. In his view, it is not worth repeating the mistake of Karl Marx (1818-1883), who imagined that if the development of law proceeds in a certain direction, this will necessarily lead to certain indicated forms of law. The developmental trends do not prove in and of themselves their justness, and are not automatically classified as the aim of aspirations. For these reasons, Radbruch suggested to compare law not in connection with logical necessity, but only with psychological advisability. Who experienced, as often in life it becomes true that previously did not come to mind, will with gratitude derive inspiration from the comparison of different legislative solutions. As a result of reflections, Radbruch ultimately concluded that the comparison of law cannot lead to

[378] Gustav Radbruch, "Über die Methode der Rechtsvergleichung", *Monatsschrift für Kriminalpsychologie und Strafrechtsreform*, II (1906), p. 422.

[379] Binder, note 41 above, p. 949.

finding the just law in a philosophical understanding; however, it may facilitate the politico-legal formalization of a better law.[380]

In evaluating the theory of Radbruch, Binder acknowledged the correctness of his last conclusions. But he did not agree that individual laws had to be compared with the assistance of their relation to a third factor. This was unnecessary because the task of comparison according to the last assertions of Radbruch is to give to the legislator all possible legal formalizations and decisions known to reality. Thus, Radbruch's legal type and legal ideal as general criteria for the comparison of comparable laws become completely subject-less. These criteria of comparison are rather doubtful concepts. When constructing a legal type from above, it is accepted that within a certain cultural group there exist certain, identical ordinary properties of law, and this would be proved beforehand by means of the comparison of law. As for the legal ideal which Radbruch presents as completely subjectivist and therefore relativist, in Binder's view, this ideal of law may be a measure of comparison; however, naturally, such an operation cannot have objective value. For these reasons, the theory of the comparison of law proposed by Radbruch does not, in Binder's view, withstand criticism.[381]

Just as Radbruch, Max Salomon (1884-1961) left the ethical value of the laws to be compared aside and, proceeding from the assumption that the science of law is not capable of finding a measure for the value of law, engaged more with the theory of comparison than philosophical issues. For him, the central problem was what makes the comparison of different systems possible?

Asserting that different laws of different systems of law evidently are distinctive, he wanted to find a point of relation which in general makes the comparison of a law possible from one sphere of law with a law from another sphere.[382] In Salomon's view, this point of relation is not a joint legal concept,[383] nor an

[380] Radbruch, "Rechtsphilosophie", *Zeitschrift für die gesamte Strafrechtswissenschaft*, XXVI (1906), p. 259; Binder, note 41 above, p. 950.

[381] Binder, note 41 above, p. 951.

[382] Max Salomon, *Grundlegung zur Rechtsphilosophie* (1919), p. 36; Binder, note 41 above, p. 956.

[383] Salomon, note 382 above, p. 38.

ideal, nor a cultural norm,[384] but only a legal problem,[385] which manifests itself in this, establishing a certain solution as legal and possible side by side with other possible solutions. Therefore, for the comparison of law, the legal norms of different systems are expanded attempts to resolve an identical legal problem, and comparative studies consider the solutions to this problem by different systems.[386] Salomon thus pointed out the question which the comparison of law should resolve, namely: what did individual laws do to resolve a concrete problem. Moreover, Salomon precisely affirmed that the science of law is not capable of creating a measure for the ethical evaluation of the law being compared. The value of ordering significance of the concept of the legal problem is a theoretical point of relation. The evaluation of the solutions of legal problems by various laws is beyond the science of law.[387]

Binder did not agree with Salomon on this aspect. He acknowledged the correctness of the last in that he reacted critically to the ideas to apply methods to the comparison of law analogous to mathematics and to the natural sciences,[388] to use experiment in the form of statistics,[389] legislative experiment,[390] or ultimately on the basis of the phenomenology of law to come to measure of value, which would make the comparison of law possible.[391] Experiment and statistics were relegated to the sphere of reality and therefore not suitable as a measure of the value thereof. The same applied to phenomenology, although it advanced claims that only it by virtue of its *a priori* concepts made the science of law possible, but it could not be understood how phenomenology might determine the measure of value if it could, by virtue of its properties, only

384 Ibid., p. 40.

385 Ibid., p. 41.

386 Ibid., p. 42.

387 Ibid., p. 49.

388 Ibid., p. 51.

389 Ibid., p. 53.

390 Ibid., p. 57.

391 Binder, note 41 above, p. 957.

point to the problem and never reach a sphere where the solution thereof might be found.[392]

Salomon, criticizing various possible approaches to comparison, refuted them as not capable of becoming the measure of value. Positive law cannot within its group determine the ideal of law.

Binder himself, in ascribing to empirical law the origin of the idea of law as a categorical intellectual claim, took a dualist position on this issue. On the question of whether empirical law could be just, in his opinion two points of view were decisive: ideological and teleological. Teleological points of view as a measure of the value of law change,, and certain legal provisions for a particular people and the conditions thereof may be just, and for another – which has a different life style – not. Therefore, the comparison of law should take into account the relation of the laws to be compared to the idea of law, on one hand, and at the same time consider, on the other hand, the relation to empirical purposes which law, having regard to typical conditions of peoples, must undertake by virtue of their institutions.[393]

Binder's position brings him closer to the view of Del Vecchio, who distinguished two valuations of law: one relative, and the other absolute. In the first instance, law performs its purpose against the background of the conditions of its time; in the second, law acts as supra-empirical, absolute truth. In both evaluations Del Vecchio interprets law as a natural phenomenon based on the unity of the human spirit which created analogy of law on a universal scale. These analogies make the comparison of law possible despite the existence of national differences.[394]

The connecting of natural law with the comparative method which one encounters in Del Vecchio is the most characteristic feature of the comparative method as a whole. Virtually in all discourses about it the link nearer or farther, openly or concealed, traces of the theory of natural law which in the case of Del Vecchio acquires clear contemporary forms. In the theories presented above, Liszt also referred to natural "laws of societal development", and Kohler spoke of the "development" of culture, and Radbruch applied the "degree of development" (rejecting the conception

[392] Salomon, note 382 above, p. 60; Binder, note 41 above, p. 958.

[393] Binder, note 41 above, pp. 961-962.

[394] Del Vecchio, note 6 above, p. 468.

of natural law), and Binder, emphasizing the teleological aspect, drew attention to change as a real fact. The idea of natural law revolves, then moves away, then approaches the question of the comparison of law, and never completely leaves it. Positivism and later the historical school struggled with it without result. A certain coarse truth resides in the theory of natural law which neither time nor its opponents have succeeded to kill. All the erudition and scientific weaponry of the idea of such great thinkers as Immanuel Kant (1724-1804) do not help overcome the gravitation towards an interpretation of legal phenomena as a natural human product.

The extent to which the ideas of Kant were without result is shown by the example of Felix Holldack (1880-1944), who despite the precision of argumentation adduced in his work on the limits of cognition of foreign law, could not convincingly cast aside an understanding of phenomena as a natural process.

The real substratum for Holldack's conclusions are his comparative studies of German, French, and Belgian law. When considering the concept of a "maritime journey" and "maritime travel" of the German civil code and the comparison thereof with analogous French and Belgian laws, together with their interpretation, Holldack was startled by the fact that identical prescriptions of the trade code of France and Belgium acquired different meaning in the science and practice of both countries such that even judicial decisions relating to identical cases of one country were interpreted differently than in the science of the other country. Not only identical laws but also judicial decisions acquired in two countries a different content despite an identical language. It followed that the legal life of both countries differed and identical legal prescriptions in both countries are not evidence of the similarity of law.[395]

In connection with these assertions, Holldack considered the limits of the cognition of foreign law with the assistance of the comparative method. Following the Kantian theory of cognition, Holldack took a negative position with respect to the ability of the comparative method to cognize a thing in and of itself with the assistance of concepts. The faith existing in the theory of comparison that this is possible is a consequence of a living memory of the theory of natural law which is obstinately preserved. Although Kant proposed the thesis of innate categories of thought

[395] Felix Holldack, *Grenzen der Erkenntnis ausländischen Rechts* (1919), p. iv.

which make empirical cognition illusory, the Aristotelian faith that phenomena find reflection in thoughts exists. The application even of metaphysics is found in the comparison of law, although it seemed that Kant expelled it from science. A reason is the fact that the comparison of law is under the influence of natural science, on one hand, and Hegelianism, on the other. Both these factors suggested each to his own faith in the legislator, who unseen draws up basically similar laws for all peoples.[396]

Legal conceptual dogmatism remained close to the natural scientific mentality. This was a logical consequence of the fact that the science of law was built basically on Roman law and on Roman philosophy. Following a Hellenic understanding of nature, Roman philosophy interpreted nature as something absolute and true, subject to the laws of logic and mathematics. This view extended to the science of law, which as a normative discipline was regarded as equal with them. This influenced the fact that the science of law began, following mathematics, to seek the identical in studies and to reduce the multiplicity of phenomena to general places. It is not surprising that the comparative science of law saw in the identical or similar legal forms the rational meaning of legislation, whose formulas should encompass different legal content. This view was based, as already noted, simultaneously on the notion of the law of nature that a reasonable law should and may be introduced everywhere and on the assertion of Hegel that in the process of changes an all-embracing Divine reason so clearly concretized in laws that the identity of universal indicia is seen in them. Thus, the assertion of natural law concerning the existence of the eternal and immutable built on the pure reason of law which as ideal law should replace the imperfect reality found contemporary reflection in the comparison of law, which by means of rationalization provided real existence to law, which only by its identical formulation and at first glance is analogous in another country.[397]

In the very process of the comparison of law one may distinguish two types of understanding and aspiration. One consists of the said unconscious application of the idea of the law of nature. This happens an awareness exists in the assumption of the researcher of a greater or lesser identity of the laws to be compared which

[396] Ibid., pp. 71-72.

[397] Ibid., pp. 48, 51, 53.

therefore seem to him to be forms of one legal type. The adoption of the reality of formulas rationalized from real life also make it possible to interpret individual laws as links in this *a priori* mutual relation not because such a principle is established by induction, but in connection with the suggestion of the said assumption. Thanks to a concealed faith in the existence of the unity of legal forms, the comparison of individual laws is undertaken as searches for confirmation of this. For this reason, the comparison is methodologically not justified because it, being directed to a search for analogies, always determines only similarities, and differences are considered on the second plane. Thus, the assertion concerning a similarity rests on superficial external analogies.

On the other hand, this approach is conditioned by the wish to encompass a multiplicity of phenomena, which is possible only if they are classified by groups on the basis of analogy. Thanks to this aspiration, individual externally similar phenomena remain in the consciousness as members of a homogeneous group. Such a classification generalization also is a search for analogies at the expense of attention to differences. For this reason, the comparative method, in Holldack's view, is not justified either in historical or in dogmatic comparison. It is retained everywhere only thanks to the fiction of the existence of a law of nature.[398]

In the field of history, the law of nature is manifest in the form of a universal history of law. Following concepts of the Aristotelian world according to which existence is reflected in thought as reality, it considers encompassing the thought of past law into one reality to be possible. Meanwhile, in fact the unanimity of cognition is retained at the expense of devaluing numerous distinctive features of the laws being compared in view of the fact that given the heterogeneous wealth of legal forms of the laws being compared, one cannot fully take into account the distinguishing nuances, and never with the assistance of comparison reduce to a single denominator the heterogeneous functions of individual, externally similar legal forms. Comparison units only externally homogeneous phenomena and therefore cannot take into account functional divergences of institutions. This neglect of internal contradictions in favor of external unanimity is to preserve the formula of methodological grounds of the comparative method.

[398] Ibid., pp. 45-46.

The matter is the same with respect to dogmatic comparison. The comparative method also when comparing contemporary law achieves a synthesis by intellectual speculation. Faith arises that in this way cognition achieved of different systems actually corresponds to reality. Moreover, the researcher unconsciously approaches a consideration not of law, but only that which, in his view, should be law. Because in reality the similarity of law is not the same as the identical content of laws. The legal life of a people is not precisely represented by a law: just as sometimes contrary to the faith of theoreticians of natural law it was not reflected by the forms of natural law. In fact, within the general limits of legal norm an individual legal reality arises which does not fully coincide with the content thereof. Just as it is unacceptable now to preserve laws constructed from pure reason without taking account of historical development and the conditions of life, one also cannot with the assistance of comparison of contemporary law and related intellectual speculation around the norms encompass the legal reality of individual peoples. No general formula of indicia of laws to be compared can fully exhaust the content of present legal life; a chasm exists between the legal reality contained outside the sum of laws to be compared and the formula which becomes the result of the comparison of norms. The lack of a critical attitude in such a formulation of the matter can only be justified by a deeply embedded influence of faith in the law of nature. Only a dogmatic prejudice cannot see that in all phenomena of human life there is a differentiation between the typical and non-personal and the individual and personal.[399]

Likewise, only a metaphysical desire, which is increasingly squeezed out of the science of law by a scientific orientation, makes possible the existence of the idea of the uniification of the law of different peoples. Because although, indeed, the comparative science of law discovers a certain coming together of national laws and is preparing this, but even the uniformity of laws in force in different States does not mean that the legal life therein is identical. Therefore, ideas concerning the comparison of law between nations without taking account of internal differences of legal feeling of different peoples is unfounded.[400] The idea that with the assistance

[399] Ibid., pp. 42-44.

[400] Ibid., p. vi.

of comparison one may research the legal past or the law in force and unify law contains a trace of the law of nature.

The comparison of law discovers a great similarity with natural law in basic points: it aspires to cognition of all legal phenomena by way of reflections with the difference that the law of nature is completely divorced from reality in its speculations, whereas comparison is undertaken on an extensive base of positive law. Therefore, natural law is a discovery, where the imagined existence acquires objective value. In comparison that which is accepted as objective is created by thought on the basis of reality so that, in the consciousness, the result of thought is confused with reality and an identity emerges between the real and the imagined. Moreover, in reality the result of rationalist operations in comparison provides a distorted image of legal reality. The reason is that not real life is the product of thought, but only legal concepts that are reality only in the mind of the researcher. If these conceptual abstractions are indeed true, they will find confirmation in real legal life, which in this instance empirically reinforces these concepts with content. Comparative studies in greater or lesser measure always are filled by real law, whereas natural law clearly juxtaposes imagined postulates to real legal facts. But the results of comparison also are close to the imagination because an identity is uncritically accepted between rationalized concepts and legal life. It does not change the matter here that the comparison of a large number of norms provides a large material base for conclusions. All the same, they will not fully coincide with reality and will not fully exhaust the content thereof. The use of an individual comparative method does not help here. Working with particular conditional material, it in fact provides only a hypothesis of an objective legal reality. Thus, the aspirations of comparative law reach merely metaphysical results. This explains why the comparison of law is so close to the philosophy of law. The influence of the law of nature negatively encumbers comparison.[401]

This may be overcome only by acknowledgement of the logic of Kant. A direct consequence of this will be especially attention to the differences of legal phenomena and acknowledgement of their non-repeatability. Thus, the imagined persuasion of almighty thought capable of inventing absolute law would disappear. The

401 Ibid., pp. 68-69.

sole real task of the comparative method, according to Holldack, would be to seek a better law.

So, proceeding from the philosophy of Kant, Holldack dealt with the great claims of the comparative method in the science of law.

His assertions concerning the encumberment of the science of the law with the idea of natural law and Hegelianism are completely correct (see Chapter 2(8)). However, he did not succeed in convincingly presenting arguments with whose assistance he wished to reject the influence of natural law within the comparison of law and the universalist theories which arise within the range of the latter, and confine the method itself to determining the better law.

Holldack's principal reproach against the comparative method directed more towards the practical results of comparison was that concepts can never cognize legal life because it differs from the letter of the law. This is, moreover, impossible because comparison is directed, in his view, principally towards the typical general and analogous; this does not adequately take account of the of the difference between legal laws and the legal life of individual peoples.

The questions which Holldack touched upon were the subject-matter of detailed consideration in the chapters on ethnological, historical, and dogmatic comparison. It was determined that one may indeed reproach ethnological comparison for the eposization of legal life, and that the danger of simplification of problems when comparing exists. This can easily be avoided, however (and in other forms of comparison it is indeed avoided), if comparison is undertaken not extensively, but intensively; that is, with all solidity and attention to all theoretical and living aspects of the laws to be compared. Many theoreticians of the comparison of law draw attention to the fact that one should not compare paragraphs; it is necessary to comparatively study a law against the background of whole systems and branches and take into account existing theory and practice in full.

Holldack himself does this, comparing certain concepts of German law with respective concepts of French and Belgian law. The disagreement between the legal life of both countries and the letter of their laws which Holldack demonstrated in his comparative analysis did not deny the potential of the comparative method, but confirmed it. The comparison which he undertook did not lead to confusing the typization of phenomena, but on the contrary, discovered nuances of differences in the understanding of individual systems. Every comparison may lead to such a nuanced analysis unless it is an application of templates and is undertaken with scientific scruplousness. The transparency of conclusions and clarity of their argumentation will be ensured if all the requirements of the theory of comparability are ensured. In dogmatic comparison, a model of which Holldack presented in the said work, needs genetic comparison of laws and their detailed investigation against the background of the entire legal system, both theoretical and practical. They prevent the errors which Holldack ascribes to any comparison.

Holldack's critical assault against the comparative method may be considered to be a knock on an open door. His assertions are basically correct, for hasty conclusions are unnecessary and one-sided. In justification of Holldack, however, it should be noted that, on one hand, when he wrote his work the theory of comparison was not so highly developed as now and, on the other, comparison was still under the influence of Post and Kohler – the pioneers of the comparative method and, at the same time, great typifiers of the legal forms of all peoples. The critique of Holldack may relate to them almost entirely if one discards his excessive scepticism relative to the suitability of the comparative method as a whole.

In addition to the critique of the comparative method from the standpoint of incorrect results in practice, which one may consider to be a misunderstanding, Holldack advanced in accordance with the grounds of Kant comments in principle relating to the abilities of the comparative method to achieve cognition of the truth with the assistance of concepts. In his view, concepts are merely the reality of thought which is only true insofar as it corresponds to real life, but is impossible to verify. In any event, comparison under the influence of science on the law of nature has some support in real facts, and the law of nature does not. Nonetheless, the results of comparison and confirmations of the law of nature, in Holldack's view, are fictions – some to a lesser extent, and others, greater.

This general denial of the possibility with the assistance of concepts to encompass reality appertains to the most fundamental features of Kant's philosophy and concerns the question of the limits of "pure" cognition. In philosophy it is relegated to the most complex issues and a significant literature is devoted to it. This problem is not closely related to law, which is concerned with phenomena, their systematic, and logical and ideological evaluation. Moreover, for the comparative method which in principle has modest tasks to determine similarities and differences in phenomena, the question of cognition of a thing in and of itself is beyond the limits of competence and interest. Researchers who use it aspire to certain practical concrete results that are true within human capacity to cognize the essence of things. The question of absolute cognition cannot concern the comparative method or, in general, the science of law.

So the problem of reproaches against comparison itself seems to us. As for the law of nature which was criticized together with comparison, it should be noted that Holldack thought about primarily the old law of nature which allegedly is derived exclusively from pure reason. Basically, for this reason he does not recognize it to be correct and for this reason believed that the comparative method, encumbered by the law of nature, is devalued for the science of law. Moreover, as it turned out, the majority of Holldack's arguments, namely all concerning the practical evaluation of comparison, pass into oblivion. The question of the law of nature is not so well-foundedly disputed as Holldack dogmatically from the outset accepted. To be sure, in its old form it is no doubt irretrievably buried, but something from its old arguments remained topical if it is so stubbornly embedded in the science of law, returning openly or in concealed form in various reflections. In various forms the theory of natural law is emerging anew, evidence of which was the theories of comparison considered at the beginning of the chapter that one way or another recognized the existence of naturalness in legal phenomena. Even if this question was not involved (as in Salomon), it was not denied in conclusions either directly or indirectly.

The link of the comparison of law with the conception of natural law is the main uncontested assertion which may be made in the field of philosophical grounds within the limits thereof.

# Chapter XII. Comparative Method against Background of Cross Influences of Major Orientations in the Science of Law

Capturing in one image the wholeness of the relation of various orientations in the science of law to the comparative method, one may assert that therein one finds them in organic and harmonious combination. It crystallized slowly. From the moment when the comparative method was introduced into the science of law, various schools determined their attitude towards it. Among these cross influences, comparison developed primarily by its own paths; however, one cannot say that the dominant views had no impact on its formation. The comparative method was the principal field of conflict between two orientations in the science of law: the historical school and the law of nature, whose influences in the field of comparison of law crossed. The struggle of these influences left a trace on the entire development of the comparative method. It tinged comparison, which was oriented to one or the other science, depending on which of them dominated at a particular time. Only over time was the confrontation softened, and the positions now are not directed one against the other, but one beside the other. But in the past they were formed within the confines of comparison as this responded to the prevailing opinion of a determined time.

The comparative method was introduced into the science of law at a time when the old school was the dominant orientation. This automatically determined the comparison of law on the side of the historical school. In this form the comparison of law was regarded by researchers then as a means of finally overcoming the old school of nature. The relativity of law, which was one of the results of the application of the comparative method, seemed to them the heaviest stone on the grave of the law of nature from under which it never should have been raised. The comparison of law fully confirmed the conclusions of the history of law that law is diverse, and if historical studies were capable of proving diversity in time, then it provided incontestable evidence of diversity simultaneously in time and in space; in doing so it even more supported the historical school in the struggle against the law of nature.[402]

In tandem with this, the comparison of law performed the role of continuer of those tasks in the history of law which the historical school faced. Namely, to study the development of law as a whole. The historical school had lost sight of this task to a significant degree, having been occupied with the old institutions of law in an antiquarian manner. Together with the comparative method, interest returned to living law, which indeed had its own past, present, and future. Moreover, the comparative method was connected with an expansion of the horizon of legal studies. The historical school, having drawn attention to the uniqueness of the law of every nation, in fact remained further within the traditional framework of indigenous law (in Germany, Germanic and Roman) just as the school of natural law, which although it suggested abstract theories, in fact drew them primarily from the old law in force within its circle. It is immaterial that it was primarily not real, but imaginary. The fact is that the old theoreticians of the law of nature believed that the ideal law which they propagandized once existed in reality. Thus, the Historical School, despite a theoretical confrontation with the old law of nature on this question and a declarative turn in favor of national laws, remained on the actual positions of the law of nature; that is, within the limits of the systems in force at the time.

The comparative method, in rectifying the flaws of the historical school and continuing its tasks, undertook to study laws of all peoples and all times. However, soon it imbibed ideas from the sphere of the law of nature which were not in full measure connected with the old theories of law of nature as an eternal immutable and absolute ideal, but by their concepts were to a certain extent close to the last. The results of comparative studies quickly brought scholars to the conception of the universal history of law, and within this conception began to reveal concepts of "natural development", "natural state", which under the operation of "natural laws" developed from the "nature of things", and so on.

402 Kohler, note 29 above, p. 4.

This terminology and concepts concealed behind it were borrowed from the natural sciences and from the naturalism of Kant and by their orientation were not linked with the science of natural law. However, by its emergence in the science of law, whence it seemed the entire spirit of natural law had been exiled, they confirmed by a certain means the requirement to study certain phenomena as natural. From such a development it was merely a step to introduce to the science of law the theory of natural law anew, this time in a new formalization. The comparative method which in its time facilitated the final triumph over the law of nature unexpectedly provided a basis for contemporary systems of natural law.

And indeed the results of the comparison of law fueled the theories of contemporary natural law. These results showed beside the great diversity of law simultaneously a great similarity at various times and on various territories. This provided a basis for the view that law is a work of identical human nature and, together with all life, develops according to a natural law of societal development. Individual national laws are variants of some natural types of laws which we encounter in somewhat different formalization in all peoples. Distinctive, it would seem, completely original, and separate national laws are, according to these ideas, in fact merely distinctive embodiments of one natural law. The division of law led to these views, on one hand, and, on the other, it began to a certain extent to build its own theoretical and philosophical superstructure. The idea, in particular, of a universal history of law and a universal likening of law find support in the newest philosophy of a law of nature.

The slow reorientation of the comparison of law towards a law of nature which occurred unnoticeably in the course of time (despite its initial definition as a follower of the historical school) did not suggest that things would take such a turn. Individual researchers used the terminology in passing from the field of the law of nature without a connection therewith, and often clearly delimited themselves from it. However, there were also processes and states in legal phenomena which should have been characterized as natural. A series of authors used the concept of the law of nature without sharing outside this such a worldview.

Bernhöft wanted, with the assistance of comparison, to find general laws of the development of law; that is, the idea of law.[403] These concepts, very close to a natural science understanding of the questions, created an invisible thread connecting the comparative method with the contemporary law of nature. The development, evolution, and law of nature were an arsenal of a modernized law of nature which with the assistance of these concepts acquired a field among, it would seem the camp most hostile to it.

The natural scientific naturalism of Post went towards these expansive trends of the law of nature, which for those same phenomena used designations from the sphere of the law of nature, and it is not important that he himself was a positivist. In his words, the comparative science of law should find natural laws of the development of law in the history of peoples excluding the arbitrary formation of the last.[404] This definition of the tasks of the comparative method broadly opened the doors to natural law once condemned to death in the science of law.

Kohler also continued to adhere to the basis of natural evolutionism, his position being in a full state of war against the law of nature. Although he did not recognize the existence of uniform legal laws,[405] he emphasized the development of culture[406] and thus was not far from the concept of a natural process.

We see in these examples that in an earlier time comparison was connected to the law of nature by tiny threads even though in principle it was in the camp of the historical school. These threads in the course of time became more numerous and stronger. The circumstance that the time had passed when in the natural sciences complete disappointment in the inductive method which previously had celebrated a triumph facilitated this, reduced the value of deduction, and also reduced the historical school to antiquarian studies. There came a wish to have an integral image of the results of science and the aspiration then emerged to synthesize various fragmentary results into a single whole, to

403 Bernhöft, note 46 above, p. 37.

404 Post, note 169 above (1886), p. 2.

405 Kohler, note 29 above, p. 5.

406 Ibid., p. 3.

create one integral worldview, to order the results of studies into a system which would explain all.[407]

This facilitated the reborn idea of a natural law which was more than any other system capable of giving an integral and clear image of all problems. This was easier because the historical school had not completely eliminated natural law. Friedrich Carl von Savigny (1779-1861) himself had drawn many assertions from the "nature of things", and although the law of nature was formally eliminated from the science of law, it unnoticeably retained its influence thereafter.[408]

It is therefore understandable that in the changed conditions the theory of the law of nature, having moved into the shadows, was reborn and began to find extensive application in the theory of comparison, which by its results provided arguments for the support thereof.

Del Vecchio fully took the positions of the new law of nature and most completely and convincingly harmonized the comparative method from a theoretical point of view with the philosophy of the law of nature. In fact, his interest was more turned to the attractive image of the universal history of law and the universal development of law, and therefore questions of the comparative method were not fully taken into account and explained; however, from the standpoint of coordinating the problematic of comparison with the philosophy of the law of nature, his argumentation was brilliant.

Rabel was under its impact, clearly inclined to follow Del Vecchio and to see the reason for analogies in law within the unity of the human character.[409] This meant the actual declaration of adherence to the theory of the law of nature, taking into account that its basic argument is the origin of all law from human nature, which from internal necessity creates law similar in all times and countries. Heymann also declared himself to be on the side of natural law; he believed that law, as a general phenomenon of human life, may be scientifically understood only as a unity simultaneously embracing all peoples and all times. Having studied it in all initial forms, through development and differentiation, through borrowing

[407] Berolzheimer, note 21 above, p. 16.

[408] Ibid., p. 232.

[409] Rabel, note 77 above, p. 284.

by one people from another, and their mutual influence on legal thought, one cannot fail to see the far-reaching loss of various laws throughout history. The growth of culture and civilization also influence this, which in developing in one direction in various countries influence the analogous formalization of law. From these assertions, Heymann drew the conclusion that indeed one may speak of the existence of natural law.[410]

The existence of natural law is passed over in silence by the convinced cosmopolitan, Rauchhaupt. His foresight that law will be universally likened because already in certain spheres it is coming together on a world scale[411] was made in the style of assertions of the theory of natural law. Petraschek also followed this line, foreseeing that the comparison of law will provide one world law as a result.[412]

If the last mentioned authors did not directly link the question of comparison with the law of nature, Rehfeldt (1902-1968) came to the conclusion in his reflections on the comparative method that it is no accident the ideas on natural law are not eradicated and constantly are reborn anew in somewhat altered form.[413] In the most alien laws the common human element creates a natural bridge to links with other peoples. In this aspect one finds the unexpected traces of the old law of nature and the eternal idea of law.[414]

It is evident from the foregoing that all the newest theoreticians of the comparative method have become more openly or indirectly taking the position of a contemporary law of nature.

This does not mean, however, that the views of the historical school and the historical method because of this have been defeated by the comparative method. On the contrary, it acts in full harmony, and also relying on the historical method. The historical method provides to the comparative method material of national laws studied to the finer points and saves comparison from the danger of the typization of phenomena. And the comparative

[410] Heymann, note 99 above, p. 425.

[411] Rauchhaupt, note 76 above, p. 154.

[412] Petraschek, note 86 above, p. 673.

[413] Rehfeldt, note 246 above, p. 6.

[414] Ibid., p. 8.

method, in turn, is useful in historical studies. Both methods assist one another and are mutually reinforcing.

The same relates to dogmatics. In its extreme purely positivist form, it also is cast aside and usually used by taking account of the historical background of legal systems. In tandem with this, it is useful both in comparison and in history to clarify concepts. On the other hand, comparison provides material to dogmatics for the preservation of concepts as fresh and further their renewal and clarification.

Thus, on the territory of the comparative method the contradictions of various approaches to legal phenomena are allayed. The juxtaposed positions have been overcome and life has found recognition for all positive assertions of each theory, having cast aside and avoided the excessive or extreme positions.

Ultimately, they never were so mutually opposed so that within their limits there were no indicia of combination. The most mutually-exclusive positions had points of juncture for agreement and compromise. The old theory of natural law, despite all the references to reason as the source of its grounds, additionally referred to the supposedly historical and positivist prescriptions of old times which should have confirmed the correctness of the deduction thereof. The historical school also, despite contesting abstract and eternally operating norms of natural law, gave tribute, on one hand, to positivism into which it fell against its own grounds, and on the other – involuntarily and unconsciously by reference to the natural development of law permitted concepts close to the contemporary theory of natural law. There are thus three major theories in the science of law: natural law, historical school, and positivism were in quiet connection with one another, despite an official confrontation. Invisible threads connected all the different approaches to legal phenomena into a single whole, emphasizing by this means that the life is one and indivisible, and that each scientific position is correct within certain limits. Being competent within the confines of its substantiation, it may be harmonized with another scientific approach with which it is not necessarily in a position of antithesis.

The concealed link of all three approaches to legal phenomena was preserved throughout the entire development of the science of law. Every period thereof, despite the emphasis on the priority of any one philosophical conception, discovered traces of the possibilities of other conceptions. Over time they came out of the shadows to the forefront, replacing one another so long as compromise and tolerance was not formed between them. The process of harmonization and synthesis of contradictions was most transparent within the comparative method, against the background of which they all found the limits of their calling without mutual exclusion.

The unity of the different is the highest cognition of the essence of phenomena. We observe this also in the science of law, in the coordination against the background of the comparative method of different orientations, sometimes opposed to one another. Faith in the law of nature as a universal phenomenon after its denial by the historical school, which in fact confined this faith to the limits of individual national legal systems, and finally skeptical positivism, which knew only norms in force without being concerned with the philosophical link of phenomena – this is the convoluted legacy of human thought from a large conception to lack of conceptuality. This line then arises to the old height, but this time without the struggle of views excluding one another, but only synthesizing them around a new formalization of a conception of natural law. The harmonization in particular of different views occurs against the background of the theory of the comparative method, which became the foundation of the synthesis in the philosophy of law of everything that can be preserved in mutual controversies. Thus, the comparative method facilitates the realization of the ideal of philosophy – the forming of an integral, all-encompassing scientific worldview. Despite all the benefit which the comparative method provides directly to practice and theory, this is possibly its greatest, albeit indirectly, service.

# Bibliography[415]

1. Adam, Leonhard. Franz Bernhöft zum 75. Geburtstage // Zeitschrift für vergleichende Rechtswissenschaft. 1928. Band 43.

2. Adam, Leonhard. Josef Kohler und die vergleichende Rechtswissenschaft // Zeitschrift für vergleichende Rechtswissenschaft. 1919. Band 37.

*3. Adam, Leonhard. Bemerkungen zu der Abhandlung // Zeitschrift für vergleichende Rechtswissenschaft. 1933. Band 47.*

4. Bachofen, Johann J. Das Mutterrecht: eine Untersuchung über die Gynaikokratie der alten Welt nach ihrer religiösen und rechtlichen Natur. Stuttgart, 1861.

5. Bacon, Francis. De dignitate et augmentis scientiarum. London, 1623.

6. Bekker, Ernst Immanuel. Aus den Grenzmarken der geschichtlichen Rechtswissenschaft // Zeitschrift der Savigny-Stiftung für Rechtsgeschichte: Romanistische Abteilung. 1885. Band VI.

7. Berolzheimer, Fritz. Die Kulturstufen der Rechts- und Wirtschaftsphilosophie. München: Oscar Beck, 1905.

8. Bernhöft, Franz. Uber Zweck und Mittel der vergleichenden Rechtswissenschaft // Zeitschrift für vergleichende Rechtswissenschaft. 1878. Band 1.

9. Binder, Julius. Philosophie des Rechts. Berlin: Georg Stilke, 1925.

10. Del Vecchio, Giorgio. Die Idee einer vergleichenden universalen Rechtswissenschaft // Archiv für Rechts und Wirtschaftsphilosophie. 1913. Band 7.

11. Del Vecchio, Giorgio. Lehrbuch der Rechtsphilosophie. Berlin: Verl. für Staatswiss. und Geschichte, 1937.

[415] The entries have been verified and clarified by O. V. Kresin. Entries in italics could not be located for verification.

12. Emge, Carl August. Vorschule der Rechtsphilosophie. Berlin-Grunewald: Dr. Walther Rothschild, 1925.

13. Fehr, Hans Adolf. Hammurapi und das salische Recht, eine Rechtsvergleichung. Bonn : A. Marcus & E. Weber, 1910.

14. Feuerbach, Johann A. Die Idee und Notwendigkeit einer Universal-jurisprudenz // Biographischer Nachlass. Leipzig: J.J. Weber, 1853.

15. Förster, Franz. Preußisches Privatrecht. 4. Aufl. Band I. Berlin, 1889.

16. Fortescue, John. De laudibus legum Angliae. London, 1442.

17. Fortescue, John. The governance of England: Otherwise Called the Difference Between an Absolute and a Limited Monarchy: A Revised Text / Ed. with introd., notes and appendices by C. Plummer. Oxford: Clarendon Press, 1885.

18. Gans, Eduard. Erbrecht in weltgeschichtlicher Entwicklung. Band I. Berlin: Maurersche Buchhandlung, 1824.

19. Guevara, Victor. Das Gewohnheitsrecht der Indianer von Peru // Zeitschrift für vergleichende Rechtswissenschaft. 1928. Band 44.

20. Haff, Karl. Institutionen des Deutschen Privatrechts auf vergleichender und soziologischer Grundlage, zugleich Einführung ins Bürgerliche Recht. Band 1. Stuttgart: Verlag von Ferdinand Enke, 1927.

21. Zivilgesetze der Gegenwart / Begründer von Karl Heinsheimer. Band 1. Mannheim, Berlin, Leipzig, 1932.

22. Heymann, Ernst. Auslandsrecht // Handwörterbuch der Rechtswissenschaft. Band I. Berlin, Leipzig: de Gruyter, 1926.

23.Holdsworth, William Searle. A History of English Law. Vol. I – III. London: Methuen and Co, 1903, 1909.

24. Holldack, Felix. Grenzen der Erkenntnis ausländischen Rechts. Leipzig: Verlag von Felix Meiner, 1919.

25. Ihering, Rudolf. Geist des römischen Rechts auf den verschiedenen Stufen seiner Entwicklung. 2 Aufl. Band 1. Leipzig: Breitkopf und Härtel, 1866.

26. Kaden, Erich H. [Рецензия на:] Walter G. Becker. Platons Gesetze und das griechische Familienrecht, eine rechtsvergleichende Untersuchung ... München, C.H. Beck, 1932 // Deutsche Literaturzeitung für Kritik der internationalen Wissenschaft. 1933. No. 38.

27. Kaden, Erich H. Rechtsvergleichung // Rechtsvergleichendes Handwörterbuch. Band 6. Berlin: F. Vahlen, 1938.

28. Kohler, Josef. Rechtsphilosophie und Universalrechtsgeschichte // Enzyklopädie der Rechtswissenschaft in systematischer Bearbeitung / von F. Holzendorff; hrsg. von J. Kohler. 7. Aufl. Band I. München, 1915.

29. Kohler, Josef. Lehrbuch der Rechtsphilosophie. Berlin; W. Rothschild, 1909.

30. Kohler, Josef. Chasaka und Ersitzung // Zeitschrift für vergleichende Rechtswissenschaft. 1914. Band 31.

31. Kohler, Josef. Über die Methode der Rechtsvergleichung // Grünhuts Zeitschrift. 1901. Band 28.

32. Kohler, Josef. Die Anfänge des Rechts und das Recht der primitiver Völker // Die Kultur der Gegenwart. Ihre Entwicklung und ihre Ziele / Hrsg. von P. Hinneberg. Teil II, Abteilung VII, Hälfte I: Orientalisches Recht und Recht der Griechen und Römer. Leipzig, Berlin: Verlag B.G. Teubner, 1914.

33. Koschaker, Paul. Forschungen und Ergenisse in der keilschriftlichen Rechtsquellen // Zeitschrift der Savigny-Stiftung für Rechtsgeschichte: Romanistische Abteilung. 1929. Band 49.

34. Kübler, Bernhardt. Griechische Tatbestände in den Werken der kasuistischen Literatur // Zeitschrift der Savigny-Stiftung für Rechtsgeschichte: Romanistische Abteilung. 1907. Band 28.

35. Landsberg, Ernst. Geschichte der deutschen Rechtswissenschaft. München, Leipzig, Oldenbourg, 1910. (Fortsetzung zu d. Geschichte d. deutschen Rechtswissenschaft 3. Abt.).

36. Lambert E. La fonction du droit civil comparé: Les conceptions étroites ou unilatérales. Paris: V. Giard & E. Brière, 1903

37. Lautner, Julius. Die Methoden einer antik-rechtsgeschichtlichen Forschung // Zeitschrift für vergleichende Rechtswissenschaft. 1933. Band 47.

38. Lenz, Friedrich. Prinzipielle Ableitung der historisch-systematischen Methode // Archiv für Rechts- und Sozialphilosophie. 1942. Band 35.

39. von Liszt, Franz. Das richtige Recht in der Strafgesetzgebung // Zeitschrift für die gesamte Strafrechtswissenschaft. 1906. Band XXVI.

*40. von Liszt, Franz. [*Название работы не указано*] // Zeitschrift* für die *gesamte Strafrechtswissenschaft. 1906. Band XXVI.*

41. Mazzarella, Giuseppe. Studi di Etnologia Giuridica: Teoria etnologica del matrimonio ambiliano. Catania: Tipografia di E. Coco, 1903.

42. Petraschek, Karl. Rechtsvergleichung // Staatslexikon. Band IV. Freiburg, im Breisgau: Herder, 1931.

43.Petraschek, Karl. System der Rechtsphilosophie. Freiburg im Breisgau: Herder, 1932.

44. Post, Albert Hermann. Grundriss der ethnologischen Jurisprudenz. Band I. Oldenburg, Leipzig: Schulze'sche hof-buchhandlung, A. Schwartz, 1894.

45. Post, Albert Hermann. Über die Aufgaben einer allgemeinen Rechtswissenschaft. Oldenburg, Leipzig: Schulzesche Hof-Buchhandlung und Hof-Buchdruckerei. A. Schwartz, 1891.

46. Post, Albert Hermann. Bausteine für eine allgemeine Rechtswissenschaft auf vergleichend-ethnologischer Basis. Band 1. Oldenburg: Schulze (A. Schwartz), 1880.

47. Post, Albert Hermann. Einleitung in das Studium der ethnologischen Jurisprudenz. Oldenburg: Schulze, 1886.

48. Post, Albert Hermann. Die Grundlage des Rechts und die Grundzüge seiner Entwicklungsgeschichte. Oldenburg: A. Schwartz, 1884.

49. Post, Albert Hermann. Einleitung in eine Naturwissenschaft des Rechts. Oldenburg: Schulze, 1872.

50. Post, Albert Hermann. Studien zur Entwicklungsgeschichte des Familienrechts: Ein Beitrag zu einer Allgemeinen vergleichenden Rechtswissenschaft auf Ethnologischer basis. Oldenburg: A. Schwartz, 1889.

51. Puchta, Georg F. Kursus der Institutionen. Leipzig, 1853.

52. Pütter, Johann St. Neuer Versuch einer juristischen Enzyklopädie und Methodologie. Göttingen, 1757; 2 Aufl. Göttingen, 1767.

53. Rabel, Ernst. Aufgabe und Notwendigkeit der Rechtsvergleichung // Rheinische Zeitschrift für Zivil- und Prozessrecht des In- und Auslandes. 1925. Band 13.

54. Rabel, Ernst. Das Problem der Qualifikation // Zeitschrift für ausländischen und internationales Privatrecht. 1931. Band 5.

55. Radbruch, Gustav. Uber die Methode der Rechtsvergleichung // Monatsschrift für Kriminalpsychologie und Strafrechtsreform. 1906. Band II.

56. Radbruch, Gustav. Rechtsphilosophie // Zeitschrift für die gesamte Strafrechtswissenschaft. 1906. Band 26.

57. Rauchhaupt, Friedrich Wilhelm von. Die wissenschaftliche Pflege des Rechtsvergleichung // Archiv für Rechts und Wirtschaftsphilosophie. 1929. Band 23.

58. Rauchhaupt, Friedrich Wilhelm von. Zustand und Fortschritte der Rechtsangleichung in Amerika und Europa // Archiv für Rechts- und Wirtschaftsphilosophie. 1932. Band 25, No. 3. S. 331 – 361.

59. Rauchhaupt, Friedrich Wilhelm von. Die Rechte Europas in ihrer rechtsgenetischen Gestalt und pragmatischen Auswertung. Leipziq : Verlag Fritz & Joseph Voglrider, 1932. 115 s.

60. Rechtsvergleichendes Handwörterbuch für Zivil- und Handelsrecht des In- und Auslandes / Hrsg. von F. Schlegelberger. Bd. 1. Berlin: Vahlen, 1929. IV, 1016 S.

61. Rehfeldt, Bernhard. Grenzen der vergleichenden Methode in der rechtsgeschichtlichen Forschung. Bonn: Bonner Universität Buchdr., 1942.

*62. Rotondi, Mario. Dogmatik und Rechtsvergleichung // Zeitschrift* für *vergleichende Rechtswissenschaft. 1933. Band 47.*

63. Salomon, Max. Grundlegung zur Rechtsphilosophie. Berlin, Leipzig: W. Rothschild, 1919.

64. Saleilles, Raymond. Conception et object de la science du droit comparé // Congres international de droit comparé. Procès-verbaux des séances et documents. T. 1. Paris: Libraire générale de droit et de jurisprudence, 1905.

65. Savigny, Friedrich Carl. System des heutigen Römischen Rechts. Band 1. Berlin: Veit, 1840.

66. Schmidt, Max. Die Bedeutung der vergleichenden Rechtswissenschaft für die Ethnologie // Zeitschrift für vergleichende Rechtswissenschaft. 1920. Band 37.

67. Schott, August Fr. Entwurf einer Juristischen Enzyklopädie und Methodologie, zum Gebrauch akademischer Vorlesungen. Leipzig: Heinsius, 1772.

68. Schönbauer, Ernst. Studien zum Personalitätsprinzip im antiken Rechte // Zeitschrift der Savigny-Stiftung für Rechtsgeschichte. Romanistische Abteilung. 1929. Band 49.

69. Schröder, Richard. Lehrbuch der deutschen Rechtsgeschichte. 6 Auf. Berlin, Leipzig, 1922.

70. A) Selden, John. Titles of Honour. London: By W. Stansby for J. Helme, 1614. B) Selden, John. The historie of tithes: That is, the practice of payment of them. The positive laws made for them. The opinions touching the right of them. A review of it is also annext, which both confirmes it and directs in use of it. London, 1618.

71. Stammler, Rudolf. Lehrbuch der Rechtsphilosophie. Berlin: Walter de Gruyter, 1923.

72. Stoll, Heinrich. [Рецензия на:] Rotondi M. Studi di diritto privato italiano e straniero. Band I // Archiv für die civilistische Praxis. 1931. Band 14.

73.Kohler, Josef. Nachruf an J.J. Bachofen // Zeitschrift für vergleichende Rechtswissenschaft. 1889. Band 8.

74. Trimborn, Hermann. Die Methode der ethnologischen Rechtsforschung//ZeitschriftfürvergleichendeRechtswissenschaft. 1928. Band 43.

75. Vico, Giovanni Battista. Principi di una scienza nuova intorno alla natura delle nazioni per la quale si ritruovano i principi di altro sistema. Napoli: Mosca, 1725.

76. Weiss, Egon. Griechisches Privatrecht auf rechtsvergleichender Grundlage: 1. Band: Allgemeine Lehren. Leipzig: F. Meiner, 1923.

77. Weiss, Egon. Die Rechtsvergleichung in der Rechtswissenschaft und Gesetzgebung. Prag: FS RANDA, 1934.

78. Wenger, Leopold. Römisches Recht und Rechtsvergleichung // Archiv für Rechts und Wirtschaftsphilosophie. 1920/1921. Band 14.

79. Eisler, Rudolf. Wörterbuch der philosophischen Begriffe. 4 Aufl. Berlin Verlag Ernst Siegfried Mittler und Sohn, 1930.

80. Wundt, Wilhelm. Grundriss der Psychologie. Leipzig: Wilhelm Engelmann, 1896.

81. Wundt, Wilhelm. Logik: eine Untersuchung der Principien der Erkenntniss und der Methoden wissenschaftlicher Forschung. Band 1: Erkenntnisslehre. Stuttgart: Verlag von Ferdinand Enke, 1880. Band 2: Methodenlehre. Stuttgart: Verlag von Ferdinand Enke, 1883.

# Biography, Diploma, and Examination Reports

## BIOGRAPHY

I was born in the Town of Stryi on 3 March 1912. I completed public school and a classical gymnasium in the proper time. Next I enrolled at the Legal Division of Lviv University, which I completed with the title magister of laws only in 1938 because by reason of arrest I lost four years. Then I worked as a clerk in a shop and a bank (in Krakow and Lviv). In 1941 I was arrested by the Germans and had been in a concentration camp until the end of 1944. Upon release, after the War I am working as a journalist.

Rebet Lev

Diploma of Doctor of Laws, L. M. Rebet

Q.F.F.F.Q.S.

UNIVERSITAS UCRAINENSIS LIBERA PRAGENSIS

ET NOS

IOANNES MIRČUK

PHILOSOPHIAE DOCTOR, PHILOSOPHIAE PROFESSOR PUBLICUS ORDINARIUS

H.T. RECTOR MAGNIFICUS,

LEO OKINŠEVYČ

HISTORIAE IURIS UCRAINENSIS PROFESSOR PUBLICUS ORDINARIUS

ORDINIS IURISCONSULTORUM H.T. DECANUS

ET

LEONTIUS ŠRAMČENKO

STATISTICAE PROFESSOR PUBLICUS ORDINARIUS

PROMOTOR RITE CONSTITUTUS

IN VIRUM CLASSIMUM

LEONEM ROMANUM REBET

E STRYJ IN UCRAINA ORTUM

POSTQUAM ET DISSERTATIONE, QUAE INSCRIBITUR: "PORIVNIAL'NA METODA V NAUCI PRAVA"

ET EXAMINIBUS LEGITIMIS IN UNIVERSO IURE SUMMA CUM LAUDE DOCTRINAM PROBAVIT,

DOCTORIS IURIS

NOMEN ET HONORES, IURA ET PRIVILEGIA CONTULIMUS IN EIUSQUE REI FIDEM HASCE LITTERAS

UNIVERSITATIS SIGILLO SANCIENDAS CURAVIMUS.

DATUM MONACHII, DIE XIX. MENSIS FEBRUARII ANNO MCMXLVIII.

RECTOR

DECANUS

PROMOTOR RITE CONSTITUTUS

Ukrainian Free University

Faculty of Law and Social Sciences

PROTOCOL OF EXAMINATION

History of Ukrainian law

Lev Rebet, student of the [...] semester of the Legal Division today took the examination with a good result.

Munich, 20.XI. 1947.

Signature of examiner [Lev Okynshevych]

Ukrainian Free University

Faculty of Law and Social Sciences

PROTOCOL OF EXAMINATION

Magister Lev Rebet, student of the ... semester of the Legal – Socio-Economic Division, took the examination today on the theory and history of cooperative societies with the result of very good.

Munich, 27. XII. 1947.

Signature of examiner [Iuryi Studynskyi]

PROTOCOL OF ORAL DOCTORAL EXAMINATION

Examination Commission:

Chairman of the Commission: Okynshevych L. O.

Members-examiners: Okynshevych L. O., for the history of Ukrainian law and the philosophy of law

Docent Dr. M. Stakhiv, for State law

Docent Dr. Iu. Studynskyi – member of examination commission

Doctoral candidate: magister Rebet Lev.

Born 3 March 1912 in Stryi.

Magister Rebet Lev, magister, having fulfilled all the provisions of the "Rules for Promotion to Doctor of Laws or Doctor of Social Sciences of the Ukrainian Free University", offered a doctoral dissertation on the topic "The Comparative Method in the Science of Law", which two professorial reviewers deemed to be satisfactory, and on this basis was admitted to the oral doctoral examination and he passed it today with outstanding success in these subjects: philosophy of law, State law, history of Ukrainian law.

Munich, 12.II. 1948.

Chairman of the Commission, Professor L. Okynshevych

Members-examiners: M. Stakhiv, Iu. Studynskyi.

REVIEW

of doctoral dissertation of Mr. L. Rebet:

«The Comparative Method in the Science of Law»

The work of the doctoral candidate on "The Comparative Method in the Science of Law" occupies a special place among those, already rather numerous, doctoral works submitted to the Faculty of Law and Socio-Economic Sciences of the Ukrainian Free University during the Munich period of its existence. This special work takes as the topic of this dissertation a broad problem of philosophical-legal and theoretical-legal content. This topic is far from fully explained in science; only the early, basic lines of development of the main principles and propositions of the comparative study of law have been noted. All this makes the task of the author especially interesting but, on the other hand, also especially complex.

Mr. L. Rebet on the whole has coped successfully with the task set and submitted a work in which a number of major and interesting problems of comparative jurisprudence have been touched upon. In Ukrainian legal literature this is the first attempt at such a detailed and attentive consideration of this problem, and in this respect the work can only be welcomed.

In passing on to those moments in the structure of the work of Mr. Rebet with which I cannot entirely concur, I note that the vast scope of the topic I consider not a positive, butrather a negative feature thereof which needlessly complicated the task of the author and in a number of instances led him to false constructions which he might have successfully avoided. To do so he had to confine the topic to the "comparative method in investigating the history of law".

Indeed: the investigation of the norms of positive law of the present day and the investigation of the processes of the origin and development of legal institutes so diverse in essence in their basic (and also methodological) positions that every time in the work addressing both topics one is obliged to speak separately about each branch. The author does not do this: for the most part, (to be sure – not in all) postulates are given which he applies to both the first and to the second task. This of the aforementioned reflections cannot fail to be false and in fact is an organic shortcoming of Mr. Rebet's work.

As regards questions of ethnological and historical research of law, here the author – in our view – on the contrary moves too far in the isolation of each of these branches. In principle the origin of a legal institute and the operation thereof in a primitive society and its further development into more complex and higher forms of social life are not problems completely independent of one another, but means the presence of certain specific problems and conditions of the study of each of them ("pre-historical" and "historical" periods), which does not provide grounds for their complete isolation into an autonomous branch. It is another matter when ethnological comparative research is understood only as preliminary attempts to identify and summarize data concerning certain institutes of the law of primitive societies. In essence these studies (including many of the monographs and surveys of a leading figure in the comparative history of law, Kohler) are not yet studies of a comparative character.

I absolutely do not agree with the denial expressed by the author of the views of Post and Kohler relating to certain trends of the development in the history of law leading to certain other general social organizations of states and periods in the development of dogmas of law. This criminal for the doctoral candidate "spirit of positivism and evolutionism" in fact was and is the sole leading ground for the scientific study of the history of law. In rejecting these positions, any attempt of the comparative study of the history of the development of legal institutes in essence from the beginning is excluded.

An undoubted weak aspect of Mr. Rebet's work is that he confines himself only to German literature. This comes to the point that the author mentions not a single word about the existence of a comparative school of the history of law which has fruitfully displayed itself, beginning with the works of Maine in England, Pollock, P. Vinogradoff, Maclennan, and many others.

I consider it necessary to note also an external but substantive side of the work: the language in which it is written shows that the author does not have a command of Ukrainian literary language and has not overcome in the language of his work regional peculiarities which are admissible in literary language only to a certain extent.

Notwithstanding these negative features of Mr. L. Rebet's work, it remains all the same one of the most valuable doctoral works submitted to the Faculty of Law and Socio-Economic Sciences of the Ukrainian Free University in recent years. This work displays the significant labor which the author spent in writing it. Written on a complex and difficult topic (especially for a young scholar), it definitely shows features of independent thought of the author. Of the work one may say that it enriches Ukrainian legal science with an investigation of a topic which this science had not yet experienced to this extent.

The Faculty of Law and Socio-Economic Sciences has every ground to assess the work of L. Rebet as a work deserving the conferral on him of the title doctor of laws.

Prof. L. Okynshevych

Munich, 12.2.1948.

# REVIEW

of the work of Magister Lev Rebet

under the title

The Comparative Method in the Science of Law (1947)

I). Content. The work encompasses the following chapters: a) General definition. b) History of comparison. c) Concept of comparison. d) Essence of comparison. e) Demarcation of comparison of law from sociology, ethnology, and philosophy. f) Types of comparison of law. g) Comparability. h) Ethnological comparison. i) Historical comparison. j) Dogmatic comparison. k) Comparative method against the background of cross influences of major orientations in the science of law. m) Literature.

In all the work encompasses 156 typewritten pages.

II) Mistakes and shortcomings. a) Despite the evident sincerity of the author to use correct Ukrainian terminology, the work contains a number of terminological and linguistic mistakes [here omitted].

б) When citing examples the development of the law of various peoples is taken into account, completely avoiding Ukraine.

Legal norms are not properly differentiated from moral norms (p. 2). As a material indicator of a legal norm there is cited the "coercion of public force" existing in such a broad concept identically in legal and moral relations.

Patriarchy and matriarchy are described too imprecisely (the mother is the "center of the family") – p. 19.

It is not shown in what precisely the influence of the philosophy of Hegel and his dialectical method on the work by Post is manifested (p. 19).

The definition of science is incorrect: first is the task of a full description of phenomena, and then the explanation thereof and determination of the material relations of these phenomena with other phenomena which condition them (p. 26).

The conclusion of the author which he draws on the basis of a definition of science presented by him that the comparison of law is not a science has no logical link with this definition.

The view of the author concerning the controversiality of the question of whether sociology is an auxiliary science for law, or the science of law is an auxiliary science for sociology is substantiated by nothing – p. 39.

The thesis of the non-comparability of the law of the USSR with Western European systems is untrue (p. 60).

The author does not precisely differentiate tribes from peoples and hence the are misunderstandings with respect to the "law" of tribes and the law of peoples.

The raising of the problem that it has still not been proved "whether the unique individual development of a separate human essence is possible" is erroneous - p. 93. Since the time of Aristotle this [...] question is scientifically resolved without mentioning [even] philosophy.

If one casts aside the laws of societal development of mankind, all of history would be merely a series of unconnected facts.

III) Good aspects of the work. The author soundly collected material and processed it diligently. He relies on this material very well and suitably according to the scientific method. The work would have been perfect if the author had engaged more deeply with the sociological point of view.

IV) General assessment: The result of the work should be evaluated as very good, and the author admitted on this basis to a strict doctoral examination.

Munich, 5 October 1947.

Second reviewer: M. Stakhiv.

# Index of Names

www.ingramcontent.com/pod-product-compliance
Lightning Source LLC
LaVergne TN
LVHW092117300926
849161LV00002B/158
*9781616196653*